Disney Connections & Collections

VOLUME ONE: MOVIES

James R. Mason, Ph.D

Theme Park Press
The Happiest Books on Earth
www.ThemeParkPress.com

Theme Park Press publishes its books in a variety of print and electronic formats. Some content that appears in one format may not appear in another.

Editor: Bob McLain

Layout: Artisanal Text

ISBN 978-1-68390-182-2

Printed in the United States of America

Theme Park Press | www.ThemeParkPress.com

Address queries to bob@themeparkpress.com

To Andrew Oakes: I've never had a friend like you.

Contents

Introduction

The world of Disney movies is huge. Beyond animation, Disney movies encompass natural history documentaries, sports comedies, super-hero franchises, the Star Wars saga and so much more. Disney movies provide inspiration, characters and cross-overs with television series, theatrical shorts, comic book stories, sequels and prequels, as well as spin-offs such as soundtrack albums, making-of books and DVDs packed with extra features. There's so much content and merchandise in the Disney universe that navigating it as a fan and collector can be a tricky business. And that's where *Disney Connections & Collections: Movies* comes in.

In the following pages you will discover how every Disney movie released to theatres and direct to home video connects to the wider Disney media universe. You'll also find out which movies and their merchandise are available to collect on a range of different media formats. Although the entertainment business, Disney included, is moving ever more rapidly to supporting streaming and non-physical formats, there is something particularly satisfying about being able to hold your favourite Disney movies in your hand. They are something precious that can be passed down through the generations, shared with friends and family, or sold on for a profit.

As a fan and collector of Disney movies and merchandise, it is some-times frustrating that Disney movies are often perceived by audiences as beginning and ending with animated features. The listings in this book illustrate quite clearly that Disney's animated back catalogue is the richest source of theme park rides, spin-off shorts, computer games, and comic book adaptations when compared with most Disney live-action features. But while Disney's animated roots and successes are undeniably a core part of the company's business, it seems a shame that many of the studio's live-action movies often go over-looked and underappreciated.

Disney Connections & Collections: Movies grew out of a personal interest that turned academic as part of a three year PhD research project that focused on Disney movies and their audiences. The research involved a comprehensive review of Disney movies in order to define the Disney movie genre. At the same time, over 3,500 audience members were questioned about their understanding of Disney movies, and they tended to understandably equate Disney movies almost exclusively with animation.

This book therefore acts not just as a guide to Disney movie spin-offs and merchandise, but also provides a historical overview of the ways in which Disney movies have changed since 1937. It does so by treating all Disney movies equally, without favouring animation over live-action, or censoring flops or problematic movies.

You will see how Disney grew from a small studio that produced an animated feature every year or two, to releasing *True-Life Adventures* alongside live-action adventure and comedy movies. Then, following the death of Walt Disney, the studio underwent a period of experimentation and a search for an identity, before producing a massive growth in output under Michael Eisner, including the emergence of the direct-to-video market. Continuing into the 21st century, Disney movies changed in new ways as Pixar, Marvel and Lucasfilm became important parts of the Disney movie family.

Where the Disney movie story will evolve in the future is a mystery, but as *Disney Connections & Collections: Movies* shows, Disney's movie history is ripe for exploration.

How to Use This Book

Disney Connections & Collections: Movies is not a book that is designed to be read cover-to-cover, although you are welcome to do so. Instead you can dip in to discover the rich, interconnected worlds of Disney movies and their many spin-offs, or look up specific titles to find out whether the soundtrack is available on CD or where you can read more about it.

Every Disney movie that has been released theatrically and direct-to-video/DVD/digital in the US is included, along with a number of original international releases. Included is every movie released with the Disney name attached to producer and/or distributor, including those of Marvel Studios, Pixar and Lucasfilm distributed in the US by Walt Disney Studios Motion Pictures (formerly Buena Vista). Not included are movies produced by Disney-owned Touchstone Pictures and Hollywood Pictures and distributed through Buena Vista, or Miramax Pictures and Dimension Films – these studios were kept at arm's length and did not carry the Disney name.

The entries are arranged chronologically by their earliest premiere or release date, whether in the US or internationally, from 1937 to 2019. Included with each entry is the tagline for the movie taken from a key original poster, as well as the names of the stars listed 'above the line' on the poster (more comprehensive credits can be found elsewhere). Details on release dates and running time follow.

CONNECTIONS lists all of the Disney movies and a selection of other media that have been spun-off from the movie or feature its characters. In this section, Collections > indicates where these spin-offs can be found on home media or in print.

COLLECTIONS details the availability of the movie on home media, as well as soundtracks and non-fiction books about the making of the movie (NB: only books of particular interest to adult readers and collectors are included). In some cases, a book with a wider focus than the single movie is included where it contains a significant chapter about the movie in question. In this section, spin-off movies marked with > can be cross-referenced to their own entry elsewhere in the book.

The format and layout of each entry is as follows:

Title (Year)

Tagline from an original movie poster.

- **AKA**: Alternative (English) titles
- **Source**: Details of the book/comic/short story/video game/true story that inspired the movie
- **Writers**: Credited writers on the movie
- **Director**: Credited directors on the movie
- **Stars**: Actors who appear 'above the line' on the movie poster
- **Premiere**: Date and location of premiere, or release date if direct-to-video (DTV)
- **US Release**: If movie premiered outside the US
- **Re-releases**: Years of theatrical re-release in the US
- **Length**: Including details of alternate cuts

Connections

- **Comic Strips**: Comic book adaptations; Good Housekeeping pages;
- **Newspaper Strips**: Treasury of Classic Tales (TCT), Silly Symphonies (SS), Disney Christmas Story (DCS), Disney Holiday Story (DHS)
- **Movies**: Sequels, prequels and remakes, released theatrically or direct-to-video (DTV)
- **Shorts**: Theatrical, propaganda, direct-to-video (DTV), and educational shorts
- **Stage**: Stage Play or Stage Musical adaptations, including Disney Theatrical Licensing shows
- **TV**: TV Series, Movies or Anthology episode spin-offs, with years of release and channel
- **Theme Parks**: Rides and attractions based on the film or characters at Disney theme parks, including years of operation and park location:
    - *Disneyland Resort*: Disneyland (DL), Disney California Adventure Park (DCA)
    - *Walt Disney World Resort* (WDW): Magic Kingdom (MK), Epcot (E), Disney-MGM Studios (MGM) / Disney's Hollywood Studios (HS), Disney's Animal Kingdom (AK)

- *Tokyo Disney Resort*: Tokyo Disneyland (TDL), Tokyo DisneySea (TDS)
- *Disneyland Paris*: Disneyland Park (DP), Walt Disney Studios Park (WDS)
- *Hong Kong Disneyland Resort* (HKD), Shanghai Disney Resort (SD)

■ **Video Games**: Amiga, Amstrad CPC (ACPC), Apple II, Aquarius, Atari 8-bit (A8), Atari 2600 (A2600), Atari ST (AST), Commodore 64 (C64), Game Boy (GB), Game Boy Advance (GBA), Game Boy Color (GBC), GameCube (GC), Game Gear (GG), Intellivision, Mac, Mega Drive/Genesis (MD/G), Nintendo DS (DS), Nintendo 3DS (3DS), Nintendo Entertainment System (NES), Nintendo Switch (NS), PC, PlayStation (PS), PlayStation 2 (PS2), PlayStation 3 (PS3), PlayStation 4 (PS4), PlayStation Vita (PSV), PSP, Sega Master System (SMS), Super Nintendo Entertainment System (SNES), Xbox, Xbox One (X1), Xbox 360 (X360), Xbox 360 Games Store (X360S), Wii, Wii U (WU), ZX Spectrum (ZXS)

Collections

All Collections releases relate to the US only. However, if the media was only released outside the US in a particular format, then the relevant country will be listed.

- ■ **Video**: VHS releases and editions
- ■ **Laserdisc**: Laserdisc releases and editions
- ■ **DVD*/Blu-ray**: DVD/Blu-ray releases and editions (*DVD-only releases)
- ■ **Digital**: Availability via Amazon, iTunes, Vudu (accurate at press time; check justwatch.com for up-to-date listings)
- ■ **Soundtrack**: LP and CD releases and re-releases (and digital only releases)
- ■ **Books**: Titles, authors and years of publication for non-fiction books relating to the film, including releases from Disney Editions, Hyperion, and Theme Park Press, etc.

The information contained in this book has been compiled from official Disney sources as well as other reference books, websites and media consulted by the author (see Further Reading for detail). If you are aware of any glaring omissions or inaccuracies, please do let the author know by emailing JamesDoesDisney@outlook.com

PART ONE

Movies: 1937–1949

Academy Award Review of Walt Disney Cartoons (1937)

MUSIC—LAUGHTER—FUN...as only Walt Disney can combine them into magical entertainment!

AKA:

Walt Disney's Academy Award Revue

Source:

- *Flowers and Trees* (1932), *Three Little Pigs* (1933), *The Tortoise and the Hare* (1935), *Three Orphan Kittens* (1935), *The Country Cousin* (1936)
- 1966 version includes: *The Old Mill* (1937), *Ferdinand the Bull* (1938), *The Ugly Duckling* (1939), *Lend a Paw* (1941)

Premiere:

May 19, 1937

Re-release:

1966 (extended version)

Length:

41 min (1937), 74 min (1966 version)

COLLECTIONS

Laserdisc:

1985 (Japan only; both versions)

Snow White and the Seven Dwarfs (1937)

HIS FIRST FULL- LENGTH FEATURE PRODUCTION

Source:

Grimm's Fairy Tales (1812) The Brothers Grimm

Writers:

Ted Sears, Richard Creedon, Otto Englander, Dick Richard, Earl Hurd, Merrill De Maris, Dorothy Ann Blank, Webb Smith

Director:

David Hand (supervising director)

Premiere:

Dec 21, 1937, Hollywood

Re-releases:

1944, 1952, 1958, 1967, 1975, 1983, 1987, 1993 (restored version)

Length:

83 min

CONNECTIONS

Comic Strips:

- *Snow White and the Seven Dwarfs* (Sunday Strips, Dec 12 1937 – Apr 24 1938) [Collection > *Walt Disney's Silly Symphonies Vol 2* (2016)]
- *Thumper Meets the Seven Dwarfs* (Four Color Comics #19, 1943)
- *Donald Duck and the Seven Dwarfs* (Four Color Comics #43, Apr 1944)
- *Snow White and the Seven Dwarfs* & *The Seven Dwarfs and Dumbo* (Four Color Comics #49, Jul 1944) [Collection > *Disney Comics: The Classics Collection* (2006)]
- *The Seven Dwarfs and the Witch-Queen* (TCT, Mar 2, 1958 – Apr 27, 1958) [Collection > *Walt Disney's Treasure of Classic Tales Vol 2* (2017)]
- *Snow White's Christmas Surprise* (DCS, Nov 28 – Dec 24 1966)*
- *The Quest for Christmas* (DCS, Dec 1 – 24 1969)*
- *Snow White's Sinister Christmas Gift* (DCS, Nov 30 – Dec 24 1987)* [*Collection > *Disney's Christmas Classics* (2017)]

Shorts:

- *Seven Wise Dwarfs* (1941) Propaganda [Collection > WD Treasures: *Walt Disney On the Front Lines* DVD (2004)]

- *The Winged Scourge* (1943) Educational [Collection > WD Treasures: *Walt Disney On the Front Lines* DVD (2004)]
- Snow White: A Lesson in Cooperation (1978) Educational

Stage Musical:

- *Snow White and the Seven Dwarfs* (1979–1980); broadcast as *Snow White Live* on HBO (1980) and Disney Channel (1987)

TV Series:

- *The 7D* (2014-2016) Disney XD, 44 episodes

Theme Parks:

- Snow White's Adventures (DL 1955–1982), (MK 1971–1994), (TDL 1983+)
- Snow White Grotto (DL 1961+), (TDL 1983+), (HKD 2005+)
- Snow White's Scary Adventures (DL 1983+), (MK, 1994–2012)
- Blanche-Neige et les Sept Nains (DP 1992+)
- Snow White: An Enchanting New Musical (DL 2004–2006)
- Seven Dwarfs Mine Train (MK 2014+)

Video Games:

- *Walt Disney's Snow White and the Seven Dwarfs* (2001) GBC
- *Snow White and the Seven Dwarfs* (2002) Atari
- *Disney Princess* (2003) GBA

COLLECTIONS

Video:

1994 Walt Disney Masterpiece, 2001

Laserdisc:

1994 Walt Disney Masterpiece, 1994 Deluxe CAV Edition

DVD*/Blu-ray:

2001 Platinum Edition*, 2009 Diamond Edition + Collector's Book Set + Ltd Edition Collector's Set, 2012 The Royal Wedding Collection, 2016 Signature Collection

Digital:

Amazon, iTunes, Vudu

Soundtrack:

1938, 1949, 1957, 1960, 1962, 1967 Camarata Conducts, 2016 (LP), 1987, 1988, 1993, 1998, 2001 (CD)

Books:

- *Walt Disney's Snow White and the Seven Dwarfs & the Making of the Classic Film* (1987) Richard Hollis & Brian Sibley
- *Snow White and the Seven Dwarfs, an Art in the Making* (1994) Martin Krause & Linda Witowski
- *Blanche Neige* (2000) Pierre Lambert
- *The Fairest One of All: The Making of Walt Disney's Snow White and the Seven Dwarfs* (2012) JB Kaufman
- *Snow White and the Seven Dwarfs: The Art and Creation of Walt Disney's Classic Animated Film* (2012) JB Kaufman
- *The Walt Disney Film Archives: The Animated Movies 1921-1968* (2016). Ed. Daniel Kothenschulte
- *Snow White's People: An Oral History of the Disney Film Snow White and the Seven Dwarfs* (Volume 1) (2017) David Johnson, Ed. Didier Ghez
- *Snow White's People: An Oral History of the Disney Film Snow White and the Seven Dwarfs* (Volume 2) (2018) David Johnson, Ed. Didier Ghez

Pinocchio (1940)

Full length FEATURE production.

Source:

The Adventures of Pinocchio (1883) Carlo Collodi

Writers:

Ted Sears, Otto Englander, Webb Smith, William Cottrell, Joseph Sabo, Erdman Penner, Aurelius Battaglia, Bill Peet

Directors:

Hamilton Luske, Ben Sharpsteen (supervising directors)

Premiere:

Feb 7, 1940, New York

Re-releases:

1945, 1954, 1962, 1971, 1978, 1984, 1992 (restored version)

Length:

87 min

CONNECTIONS

Comic Strips:

- *The Wonderful Adventures of Pinocchio* (Four Color Comics #92, Jan 1946)
- *Pinocchio's Dilemma* (Four Color Comics #517, Nov 1953)
- *Pinocchio* (SS, Dec 24, 1939 – Apr 7, 1940) [Collection > *Walt Disney's Silly Symphonies Vol 3* (2017)]
- *Pinocchio's Christmas Story* (DCS, Nov 27 – Dec 23, 1961) [Collection > *Disney's Christmas Classics* (2017)]
- *Pinocchio* (Sunday Strips, Sep 3, 1978 – Nov 26, 1978)
- *Pinocchio & Jiminy Crickett: A Coat Tale* (TCT, Sep 30 – Dec 30, 1984)

Shorts:

- *Figaro and Cleo* (1943)
- *Bath Day* (1946)
- *Figaro and Frankie* (1947) [Collection > WD Treasures: The Complete Pluto, Volume Two (2006)]
- *Pinocchio: A Lesson in Honesty* (1978) Educational

Stage Musicals:

- *My Son Pinocchio: Geppetto's Musical Tale* (2006, Kansas City, MO) aka *Disney's Geppetto & Son*; based on *Geppetto* TV movie
- *My Son Pinocchio JR.* (?) Disney Theatrical Licensing
- *Pinocchio* (2017+, London) National Theatre production

TV Movie:

Geppetto (May 7, 2000) on *The Wonderful World of Disney*, ABC [Collection > Video (2000), CD Soundtrack (2000), DVD (2009)]

Theme Parks:

- Pinocchio's Daring Journey (TDL 1983+), (DL 1983+)
- Les Voyages de Pinocchio (DP 1992+)

Video Games:

Pinocchio (1996) SNES, GB, MD/G

COLLECTIONS

Video:

1985, 1993, 1999, 2000 Gold Classic Collection

Laserdisc:

1987, 1993

DVD*/Blu-ray:

1999 Limited Issue*, 2000 Gold Classic Collection*, 2009 70th Anniversary Platinum Edition, 2017 Signature Collection

Digital:

Amazon, iTunes, Vudu

Soundtrack:

1940, 1951, 1956, 1957, 1960, 1963, 1970, 1980 (LP), 1990, 1992, 2006, 2015 Legacy Collection (CD)

Books:

- *Pinocchio* (1995/1997) Pierre Lambert
- *Pinocchio: The Making of the Disney Epic* (2015) J.B. Kaufman
- *The Walt Disney Film Archives: The Animated Movies 1921-1968* (2016) Ed. Daniel Kothenschulte

Fantasia (1940)

Walt Disney's Technicolor FEATURE triumph with Stokowski.

Sections:

Toccata and Fugue in D Minor, The Nutcracker Suite, The Sorcerer's Apprentice, Rite of Spring, Pastoral, Dance of the Hours, Night on Bald Mountain, Ave Maria

Sources:

Bach, Tchaikovsky, Dukas, Stravinski, Beethoven, Ponchielli, Moussorgsky, Schubert (respectively)

Premiere:

Nov 13, 1940, New York

Re-releases:

1944, 1946, 1954, 1956, 1963, 1966, 1969, 1977, 1990 (Restored version) 1982, 1984 (Irwin Kostal soundtrack version)

Length:

125 min (roadshow version), 80 min (general release)

CONNECTIONS

Comic Strips:

- *The Sorcerer's Apprentice* (Four Color #13, Feb 1941)

- Fantasia 50th Anniversary (Mickey Mouse Adventures #9, Feb 1991)

Concert:

Disney Fantasia: Live in Concert (2013+) Touring production

Movies:

Fantasia/2000 (1999) Sequel featuring *The Sorcerer's Apprentice* (2010) remake

Shorts:

A World is Born (1955) 16mm

Theme Parks:

- Fantasmic! (DL 1992+), (HS 1998+), TDS (2011+)
- Fantasia Gardens (DL 1993-2006)
- Fantasia Gardens Miniature Golf and Garden Pavilion (WDW 1996+)

Video Games:

- *Sorcerer's Apprentice* (1983) A2600
- *Fantasia* (1991) MD/G
- *Fantasia: Music Evolved* (2014) X1, X360

COLLECTIONS

Video:

1991 Walt Disney Masterpiece

Laserdisc:

1991 Walt Disney Masterpiece + Special Edition

DVD*/Blu-ray:

2000 60th Anniversary Edition* + The Fantasia Anthology/Collector's Edition*, 2010 Special Edition + 2-Movie Collection

Digital:

Netflix

Soundtrack:

1957, 1982 Irwin Kostal version (LP), 1990, 1992, 1999, 2001, 2015 Legacy Collection (Includes Irwin Kostal version) (CD)

Books:

- *Walt Disney's Fantasia* (1940) Deems Taylor
- *Walt Disney's Fantasia* (1983) John Culhane

- *The Walt Disney Film Archives: The Animated Movies 1921-1968* (2016) Ed. Daniel Kothenschulte

The Reluctant Dragon (1941)

The BIG FEATURE SHOW WITH A THOUSAND SURPRISES!

Sections:

Old MacDonald Duck, How to Ride a Horse, Baby Weems, The Reluctant Dragon

Source:

"The Reluctant Dragon" in *Dream Days* (1898) Kenneth Grahame

Writers:

Ted Sears, Al Perkins, Larry Clemmons, Bill Cottrell, Harry Clork

Directors:

Alfred L. Werker (live action) and Hamilton Luske (animation)

Stars:

Robert Benchley

Premiere:

Jun 20, 1941

Length:

73 min

CONNECTIONS

Comic Strips:

The Reluctant Dragon, How to Ride a Horse, Baby Weems, Old MacDonald Duck (Four Color #13, Feb 1941)

Shorts:

- *Old MacDonald Duck* (1941) Edited from movie [Collection > WD Treasures: *The Chronological Donald Volume One* (2004)]
- *How to Ride a Horse* (1950) Edited from movie

COLLECTIONS

Video:

1987 *The Reluctant Dragon*, 1991, 1998

Laserdisc:

1988 *Mickey and the Beanstalk/The Reluctant Dragon* Mini Classics

DVD:

- 2002 WD Treasures: *Behind the Scenes at the Walt Disney Studios*
- 2007 Disney Movie Club Exclusive

Blu-ray:

2014 *The Adventures of Ichabod and Mr. Toad / Fun and Fancy Free* 2-Movie Collection

Digital:

Amazon, iTunes, Vudu

Book:

- *The Lost Notebook: Herman Schultheis & the Secrets of Walt Disney's Movie Magic* (2014) John Canemaker
- *The Walt Disney Film Archives: The Animated Movies 1921–1968* (2016) Ed. Daniel Kothenschulte

Dumbo (1941)

WALT DISNEY'S Full length FEATURE production.

Source:

Roll-A-Book story by Helen Aberson and Harold Pearl (unpublished)

Writers:

Joe Grant, Dick Huemer

Director:

Ben Sharpsteen (Supervising Director)

Premiere:

Oct 23, 1941, New York

Re-releases:

1946, 1949, 1959, 1972, 1976

Length:

64 min

CONNECTIONS

Comic Strips:

- *Dumbo of the Circus* (Four Color #7, Jul 1941) [Collection > *Disney Comics: The Classics Collection* (2006)]
- *The Seven Dwarfs and Dumbo* (Four Color Comics #49, Jul 1944) [Collection > *Disney Comics: The Classics Collection* (2006)]

- *Walt Disney's Dumbo in Sky Voyage* (Four Color Comics #234, Jul 1949)
- *The Flying Elephant* (Walt Disney's Silly Symphonies #4, Aug 1952)
- *Dumbo's Christmas Gift* (Walt Disney's Comics and Stories #148, Jan 1953)
- *Dumbo's Dilemma* (Four Color Comics #1204, Oct 1961)
- *Dumbo* (TCT, Jul 4 – Sep 26, 1965)
- *Dumbo and the Christmas Mystery* (DCS, Nov 27 – Dec 23, 1967) [Collection > *Disney's Christmas Classics* (2017)]
- *Aristokittens with Dumbo* (Aristokittens #2, Jan 1972)
- *Santa's Crucial Christmas* (DCS, Dec 2 – 24, 1974) [Collection > *Disney's Christmas Classics* (2017)]
- *Dumbo, the Substitute Stork* (TCT, Jan 1 to Mar 25 1984)

Movies:
Dumbo (2019) Live-action remake

Shorts:
Dumbo: A Lesson in Being Prepared (1981) Educational

TV:
Dumbo's Circus (1985-1989) Disney Channel, 120 episodes

Theme Parks:
- Casey Jr. Circus Train (DL 1955+), Le Petit Train du Cirque (DP 1994+)
- Dumbo Flying Elephants (DL 1955+), (MK 1971+), (TDL 1983+), (HKD 2005+), (SD 2016+)
- Casey Jr. Splash 'n' Soak Station (MK 2012+)

COLLECTIONS

Video:
1981, 1985, 1991, 1994 Masterpiece Collection, 2001

Laserdisc:
1982, 1991, 1995 Masterpiece Collection

DVD*/Blu-ray:
2001 60th Anniversary Edition*, 2006 Big Top Edition*, 2011 70th Anniversary Edition + Premium Collector's Edition, 2016 75th Anniversary Edition, Disney Movie Club Exclusive

Digital:

Amazon, iTunes, Vudu

Soundtrack:

1957, 1959, 1963 (LP), 1997, 2001 (CD)

Books:

The Walt Disney Film Archives: The Animated Movies 1921-1968 (2016)
Ed. Daniel Kothenschulte

Bambi (1942)

Enchanting Entertainment for Everyone!

Source:

Bambi, a Life in the Woods (1923) Felix Salten

Writer:

Larry Morey

Director:

David Hand (supervising director)

Premiere:

Aug 8, 1942, London

US Release:

Aug 13, 1942

Re-releases:

1946, 1956, 1963, 1969, 1977, 1982, 1988

Length:

70 min

CONNECTIONS

Comic Strips:

- *Walt Disney's Bambi* (Good Housekeeping, Sep–Nov 1942) [Collection > *Walt Disney's Mickey and the Gang: Classic Stories in Verse* (2005) David Gerstein]
- *Bambi* (Four Color Comics #12, 1942) [Collection > *Disney Comics: The Classics Collection* (2006) *Bambi's Children* (Four Color Comics #30, Oct 1943)]
- *Bambi* (Four Color Comics #186, Apr 1948)
- *Bambi's Christmas Adventure* (DCS, Nov 29 – Dec 24, 1965)*

- *A Castle for Christmas* (DCS, Dec 3 – 24, 1973)* [*Collection > *Disney's Christmas Classics* (2017)]

Movies:

Bambi II (2006) Midquel

Shorts:

Bambi: A Lesson in Perseverance (1978) Educational

COLLECTIONS

Video:

1989, 1997 Walt Disney Masterpiece

Laserdisc:

1990, 1997 55th Anniversary Limited Edition; Walt Disney Masterpiece

DVD*/Blu-ray:

2005 Platinum Edition*, 2011 Diamond Edition + Premium Collector's Edition, 2017 Anniversary Edition/Signature Collection + 2-Movie Collection/Disney Movie Club Exclusive

Digital:

Amazon, iTunes, Vudu

Soundtrack:

1957, 1960, 1963, 1982, 2015 (LP), 1997, 2001, 2005 (CD)

Books:

- *Bambi, the Story and the Film* (1990) Frank Thomas & Ollie Johnston
- *Walt Disney's Bambi: The Sketchbook Series* (1997)
- *The Walt Disney Film Archives: The Animated Movies 1921-1968* (2016) Ed. Daniel Kothenschulte
- *Bambi* (2017) Pierre Lambert

Saludos Amigos (1942)

WALT DISNEY Goes South American IN HIS GAYEST MUSICAL TECHNICOLOR FEATURE

Sections:

Lake Titicaca, Pedro, Aquarela do Brasil, El Gaucho Goofy

Source:

1941 visit to South America by Walt and several Disney artists

Writers:

Homer Brightman, Ralph Wright, Roy Williams, Harry Reeves, Dick Huemer, Joe Grant

Director:

Bill Roberts, Jack Kinney, Hamilton Luske, Wilfred Jackson

Premiere:

Aug 24, 1942, Rio de Janeiro

US Release:

Feb 6, 1943, Boston

Re-releases:

1949

Length:

42 min (edited version censors Goofy smoking in *El Gaucho Goofy*)

CONNECTIONS

Comic Strips:

- *El Gaucho Goofy* (Good Housekeeping, Jun 1942)
- *Lake Titicaca* (Good Housekeeping, Dec 1942)
- *José Carioca* (Good Housekeeping, Jan 1943)
- *Pedro* (Good Housekeeping, Mar 1943) [Collection > *Walt Disney's Mickey and the Gang: Classic Stories in Verse* (2005) David Gerstein]
- José Carioca (Daily Newspaper Series Oct 11, 1942 – Oct 1, 1944)
- *Pedro* (Walt Disney's Silly Symphonies #1, 1952)

Movies:

Walt & El Grupo (2008) Documentary

Shorts:

- *South of the Border with Disney* (1942) Documentary [Collection > *Saludos Amigos* DVD (2000, 2008)]
- *Lake Titicaca* (1955) edited from movie
- *Pedro* (1955) edited from movie
- *Aquarela do Brasil* (1955) edited from movie
- *El Gaucho Goofy* (1955) edited from movie

COLLECTIONS

Video:

2000 Gold Classic Collection (Edited)

Laserdisc:

1995 *The Three Caballeros/Saludos Amigos* Exclusive Archive Collection

DVD:

- 2000 Gold Classic Collection (Edited), 2008 Classic Caballeros Collection (edited)
- 2010 *Walt & El Grupo* (unedited version of *Saludos Amigos* as bonus feature)

Blu-ray:

2018 Disney Movie Club Exclusive/2-Movie Collection/75th Anniversary Edition

Digital:

iTunes, Vudu

Soundtrack:

1944 (LP), 2007 (iTunes)

Books:

- *South of the Border with Disney: Walt Disney and the Good Neighbor Program 1941–1948* (2009) J.B. Kaufman
- *The Walt Disney Film Archives: The Animated Movies 1921–1968* (2016) Ed. Daniel Kothenschulte

Victory Through Air Power (1943)

THERE'S A THRILL IN THE AIR!

Source:

Victory Through Air Power (1942) Major Alexander P. de Seversky

Writers:

T. Hee, Erdmann Penner, William Cottrell, Jim Bodrero, George Stallings

Directors:

H.C Potter (live action), James Algar, Clyde Geronimi, Jack Kinney (animation)

Premiere:

Jul 17, 1943

Length:

65 min

CONNECTIONS

Comic Strips:

Victory Through Air Power (Good Housekeeping, Jul 1943) [Collection > *Walt Disney's Mickey and the Gang: Classic Stories in Verse* (2005) David Gerstein]

Shorts:

History of Aviation (1952) Educational, 16mm

COLLECTIONS

DVD:

2004, Walt Disney Treasures: *Walt Disney on the Front Lines*

Books:

- *Donald Duck Joins Up* (1976) Richard Shale
- *Disney During World War II: How the Walt Disney Studio Contributed to Victory in the Second World War* (2014) John Baxter
- *Service With Character: The Disney Studios and World War II* (2014) David Lesjak
- *The Walt Disney Film Archives: The Animated Movies 1921–1968* (2016) Ed. Daniel Kothenschulte

The Three Caballeros (1944)

A CARTOON FIESTA of FUN and FANTASY!

Sections:

The Cold-Blooded Penguin, The Flying Gauchito, Baia, La Piñata

Source:

1940s visits to South America by Walt and several Disney artists

Writers:

Homer Brightman, Ernest Terrazas, Ted Sears, Bill Peet, Ralph Wright, Elmer Plummer, Roy Williams, William Cottrell, Del Connell, James Bodrero

Director:

Norman Ferguson

Stars:

Donald Duck, José Carioca, Panchito

Premiere:

Dec 21, 1944, Mexico City

US Release:

Feb 3, 1945, New York

Re-releases:

1977 (Abridged)

Length:

71 min (original), 41 min (abridged)

CONNECTIONS

Comic Strips:

- *The Cold-Blooded Penguin* (Good Housekeeping, Apr 1943) [Collection > *Walt Disney's Mickey and the Gang: Classic Stories in Verse* (2005) David Gerstein]
- Panchito (Daily Newspaper Series Oct 8, 1944 – Oct 7, 1945)
- *The Three Caballeros* (Four Color Comics #71, 1945)
- *The Three Caballeros Ride Again* (Walt Disney's Comic and Stories #635-637, Aug-Oct 2003)

Movies:

Walt & El Grupo (2008) Documentary

Shorts:

- *The Flying Gauchito* (1955) Edited from movie
- *The Cold-Blooded Penguin* (1971) Edited from movie, 16mm
- *Feliz Navidad* (1974) Edited from movie, 16mm

Theme Parks:

Gran Fiesta Tour Starring The Three Caballeros (E 2007+)

COLLECTIONS

Video:

1982, 1987, 1994 Masterpiece Collection, 2000 Gold Classic Collection

Laserdisc:

1994, 1988, 1995 *The Three Caballeros/Saludos Amigos* Exclusive Archive Collection

DVD:

2000 Gold Classic Collection, 2008 Classic Caballeros Collection

Blu-ray:

2018 Disney Movie Club Exclusive/2-Movie Collection/75th Anniversary Edition

Digital:

Amazon, iTunes, Vudu

Soundtrack:

1944 (LP), 2007 *Saludos Amigos* (iTunes)

Books:

- *South of the Border with Disney: Walt Disney and the Good Neighbor Program 1941-1948* (2009) J.B. Kaufman
- *The Walt Disney Film Archives: The Animated Movies 1921-1968* (2016) Ed. Daniel Kothenschulte

Make Mine Music (1946)

Walt Disney's HAPPY COMEDY MUSICAL

Sections:

The Martins and the Coys, Blue Bayou, All the Cats Join In, Without You, Casey at the Bat, Two Silhouettes, Peter and the Wolf, After You've Gone, Johnny Fedora and Alice Bluebonnet, The Whale Who Wanted to Sing at the Met

Sources:

- "Casey at the Bat: A Ballad of the Republic Sung in the Year 1888" (1888) Ernest Thayer
- "Peter and the Wolf" (1936) Sergei Prokofiev

Writers:

Homer Brightman, Dick Huemer, Dick Kinney, John Walbridge, Tom Oreb, Dick Shaw, Eric Gurney, Sylvia Holland, T. Hee, Ed Penner, Dick Kelsey, Jim Bobrero, Roy Williams, Cap Palmer, Jesse Marsh, Erwin Graham

Directors:

Jack Kinney, Robert Cormack, Clyde Geronimi, Hamilton Luske, Joshua Meador

Premiere:

Apr 20, 1946, New York

Length:

75 min (original), 67 min (edited)

CONNECTIONS
Comic Strips:
Peter and the Wolf (TCT, Jun 6 – Jul 25, 1954) [Collection > *Walt Disney's Treasury of Classic Tales Vol 1* (2016)]

Movies:
Music Land (1955) compilation

Shorts:
- *The Martins and the Coys* (1954) edited from movie
- *Two for the Record* (1954) edited from movie
- *Casey at the Bat* (1954) edited from movie
- *Casey Bats Again* (1954) sequel [Collection > *Melody Time* DVD (2000)]
- *Johnny Fedora and Alice Bluebonnet* (1954) edited from movie
- *Willie the Operatic Whale* (1954) edited from movie [Collection > Video (1991) Mini Classics]
- *Peter and the Wolf* (1955) edited from movie [Collection > Video (1991) Mini Classics]
- *Festival of Folk Heroes* (1971) edited from movie, 16mm

COLLECTIONS
Video/DVD:
2000 Gold Classic Collection (edited)

DVD:
2013 (UK, original)

Books:
The Walt Disney Film Archives: The Animated Movies 1921-1968 (2016) Ed. Daniel Kothenschulte

Song of the South (1946)
THE ZIP-A-DEE-DOO-DAH! SHOW!

Source:
Uncle Remus (1881) Joel Chandler Harris

Writers:
Dalton S. Reymond, Morton Grant, Maurice Rapf, Bill Peet, Ralph Wright, Vernon Stallings

Directors:

Harve Foster (live action), Wilfred Jackson (animation)

Premiere:

Nov 12, 1946, Atlanta

Re-releases:

1956, 1972, 1980, 1986

Length:

94 min

CONNECTIONS

Comic Strips:

- *Uncle Remus and His Tales of Br'er Rabbit* [(Sunday Newspaper Series, Oct 14, 1945 – Dec 31, 1972)]
- *Uncle Remus and His Tales of Brer Rabbit* (Four Color Comics #129, Dec 1946)
- *Brer Rabbit Does It Again* (Four Color Comics #208, Jan 1949)
- *Song of the South featuring Brer Rabbit* (Four Color Comics #693, Apr 1956)
- *Brer Rabbit and Bailed Buddies* (Walt Disney's Picnic Party #8, 1957)
- *Brer Rabbit at Catfish Cove* (Donald and Mickey in Disneyland #1, 1958)
- *Song of the South* (TCT, Aug 3 – Nov 16, 1986)

Theme Parks:

Splash Mountain (DL 1989+), (MK 1992+), (TDL 1992+)

COLLECTIONS

Video:

1991 (UK)

Laserdisc:

1985, 1990 (Japan)

Soundtrack:

1947, 1949, 1955, 1956, 1958, 1963, 1975 (LP)

Books:

- *Disney's Most Notorious Film: Race, Convergence, and the Hidden Histories of Song of the South* (2012) Jason Sperb

- *Who's Afraid of the Song of the South? And Other Forbidden Disney Stories* (2012) Jim Korkis
- *The Walt Disney Film Archives: The Animated Movies 1921-1968* (2016) Ed. Daniel Kothenschulte

Fun and Fancy Free (1947)

FULL-LENGTH MUSICAL CARTOON FEATURE.

Sections:

Bongo, Mickey and the Beanstalk

Sources:

- "Little Bear Bongo" (1930) Sinclair Lewis
- "Jack and the Beanstalk (1890) Joseph Jacobs

Writers:

Homer Brightman, Harry Reeves, Ted Sears, Lance Nolley, Eldon Dedini, Tom Oreb

Directors:

William Morgan (Live-action), Jack Kinney, Bill Roberts, Hamilton Luske (Animation)

Stars:

Edgar Bergen, Dinah Shore

Premiere:

Sep 27, 1947

Length:

73 min

CONNECTIONS

Comic Strips:

- *Mickey and the Beanstalk* (Four Color Comics #157, Jul 1947)
- *Bongo and Lumpjaw* (Four Color Comics #706, Jun 1956 & #886, Mar 1958)
- *B is For Bongo* (Walt Disney's Comics and Stories #261, Jun 1962)

Shorts:

Bongo (1971) Edited from movie

COLLECTIONS

Video:
1982, 1988 Mini Classics, 1989 Mini Classics, 1997 Masterpiece Collection

Laserdisc:
1988 *Mickey and the Beanstalk/The Reluctant Dragon* Mini Classics, 1991 *Ben & Me/Bongo* Mini Classics, 1998 Masterpiece Collection/50th Anniversary Ltd Edition

DVD*/Blu-ray:
2000 Gold Classic Collection*, 2014 *The Adventures of Ichabod and Mr. Toad / Fun and Fancy Free* 2-Movie Collection

Digital:
Amazon, iTunes, Vudu

Soundtrack:
1947, 1967 (LP)

Books:
The Walt Disney Film Archives: The Animated Movies 1921–1968 (2016) Ed. Daniel Kothenschulte

Melody Time (1948)

FOR YOUR ALL-TIME GOOD TIME! Walt Disney's Great NEW TECHNICOLOR Musical Comedy

Sections:
Once Upon a Wintertime, Bumble Boogie, Johnny Appleseed, Little Toot, Trees, Blame It on the Samba, Pecos Bill

Sources:
- Life of John Chapman aka Johnny Appleseed (1774–1845)
- "Little Toot" (1939) Hardie Gramatky
- "Trees" (1913) Joyce Kilmer
- Pecos Bill stories (first published 1917) Edward O'Reilly

Writers:
Winston Hibler, Erdman Penner, Harry Reeves, Homer Brightman, Ken Anderson, Ted Sears, Joe Rinaldi, Bill Cottrell, Art Scott, Jesse Marsh, Bob Moore, John Walbridge

Directors:
Clyde Geronimi, Wilfred Jackson, Jack Kinney, Hamilton Luske

Premiere:
May 27, 1948

Length:
75 min

CONNECTIONS

Movies:
- *Music Land* (1955) compilation
- *Tall Tale* (1995) live-action

Shorts:
- *Once Upon a Wintertime* (1954) edited from movie
- *Contrasts in Rhythm* (1954) edited from movie
- *Little Toot* (1954) edited from movie
- *Johnny Appleseed* (1955) edited from movie aka *Legend of Johnny Appleseed* (16mm)
- *Blame It on the Samba* (1955) aka *Legend of Johnny Appleseed* (16mm)
- *Pecos Bill* (1955) aka *Legend of Johnny Appleseed* (16mm) [Collection > *American Legends* DVD/Amazon/iTunes (2002)]
- *Festival of Folk Heroes* (1971) aka *Legend of Johnny Appleseed* (16mm), 16mm

Theme Parks:
Pecos Bill Café / Pecos Bill Tall Tale Inn & Café (MK 1971+), (TDL 1983+)

COLLECTIONS

Video:
1998 Masterpiece Collection/50th Anniversary (*Pecos Bill* edited for smoking)

DVD:
2000 Gold Classic Collection (*Pecos Bill* edited for smoking)

Soundtracks:
1972 Disneyland Double Feature (with *The Littlest Outlaw*) (LP)

Books:
The Walt Disney Film Archives: The Animated Movies 1921-1968 (2016) Ed. Daniel Kothenschulte

So Dear to My Heart (1949)

Music! Laughter! Heartwarming Drama! A once-in-your-lifetime experience!

Source:

Midnight and Jeremiah (1943) Sterling North

Writers:

John Tucker Battle, Maurice Rapf, Ted Sears

Director:

Harold D. Schuster (live-action), Hamilton Luske (animation)

Stars:

Burl Ives, Beulah Bondi, Harry Carey

Premiere:

Jan 19, 1949

Re-releases:

1964

Length:

82 min

COLLECTIONS

Video:

1986, 1992

Laserdisc:

1992

DVD:

2008 Disney Movie Club Exclusive

Digital:

Amazon, iTunes, Vudu

Soundtrack:

1949 (LP)

Books:

- *The Revised Vault of Walt* (2012) Jim Korkis
- *The Walt Disney Film Archives: The Animated Movies 1921-1968* (2016) Ed. Daniel Kothenschulte

The Adventures of Ichabod and Mr. Toad (1949)

Hear BING sing

Sections:
The Wind in the Willows, The Legend of Sleepy Hollow

Source:
- *The Wind in the Willows* (1908) Kenneth Grahame
- "The Legend of Sleepy Hollow" (1820) Washington Irving

Writers:
Erdman Penner, Winston Hibler, Joe Rinaldi, Ted Sears, Homer Brightman, Harry Reeves

Directors:
James Algar, Clyde Geronimi, Jack Kinney

Stars:
Bing Crosby, Basil Rathbone (Narrators)

Premiere:
Oct 5, 1949

Length:
68 min

CONNECTIONS

Comic Strips:
- *The Adventures of Mr. Toad* (TCT, Jul 3 – Sep 25, 1983)
- *A Christmas Present for Mr. Toad* (DCS, Dec 3 – 22, 1984) [Collection > *Disney's Christmas Classics* (2017)]

Movies:
Mr. Toad's Wild Ride (1998, Video) Live-action

Shorts:
- *The Legend of Sleepy Hollow* (1958) edited from movie
- *The Madcap Adventures of Mr. Toad* (1975) edited from movie
- *The Adventures of J. Thaddeus Toad* (1980) edited from movie, educational

Theme Parks:
Mr. Toad's Wild Ride (DL 1955+), (MK 1971-1998)

COLLECTIONS

Video:

1982, 1988 Mini Classics, 1990 Mini Classics, 2000 Gold Classic Collection

Laserdisc:

1992

DVD:

2000 Gold Classic Collection, 2014 Special Edition

Blu-ray:

2014 Special Edition + *The Adventures of Ichabod and Mr. Toad / Fun and Fancy Free* 2-Movie Collection

Digital:

Amazon, iTunes, Vudu

Soundtrack:

1949, 1949 (LP)

Books:

The Walt Disney Film Archives: The Animated Movies 1921-1968 (2016) Ed. Daniel Kothenschulte

PART TWO

Movies: 1950–1959

Cinderella (1950)

For All the World to LOVE! A LOVE STORY WITH MUSIC Greatest since SNOW WHITE

Source:

"Cinderella" in *Histoires ou contes du temps passé* (1697) Charles Perrault

Writers:

Bill Peet, Erdman Penner, Ted Sears, Winston Hibler, Homer Brightman, Harry Reeves, Ken Anderson, Joe Rinaldi

Directors:

Clyde Geronimi, Wilfred Jackson, Hamilton Luske

Premiere:

Feb 15, 1950, New York

Re-releases:

1957, 1965, 1973, 1981, 1987

Length:

74 min

CONNECTIONS

Comic Strips:

- *Cinderella* (TCT, Mar 5 – Jun 18, 1950) [Collection > *Walt Disney's Treasury of Classic Tales Vol 1* (2016)]
- *Gus & Jaq* (TCT, Feb 3 – Mar 31, 1957) [Collection > *Walt Disney's Treasury of Classic Tales Vol 2* (2017)]
- *The Captured Castle* (Walt Disney's Vacation in Disneyland, 1958)
- *Cinderella's Christmas Party* (DSC, Nov 23 – Dec 24, 1964) [Collection > *Disney's Christmas Classics* (2017)]
- *Cinderella* (TCT, Apr 1 – Jun 24, 1973)

- *Cinderella's Christmas Crisis* (DCS, Nov 30 – Dec 24, 1981) [Collection > *Disney's Christmas Classics* (2017)]
- *Cinderella: Bibbidi-Bobbodi-Who?* (TCT, Jul 1 – Sep 23, 1984)

Movies:

- *Cinderella II: Dreams Come True* (DTV, 2002) sequel
- *Cinderella III: A Twist in Time* (DTV, 2007) alternate version
- *Cinderella* (2015) live-action remake

Shorts:

Cinderella: A Lesson in Compromise (1981) educational

Stage Musical:

Disney's Cinderella KIDS (?) Disney Theatrical Licensing

TV Movie:

Cinderella (1997) Based on *Rodgers & Hammerstein's Cinderella*

Theme Parks:

- Cinderella Castle (DL 1971+), (TDL 1983+)
- Cinderella's Golden Carrousel (MK 1971–2010) aka Prince Charming Regal Carrousel (MK 2010+)
- Castle Carrousel (TDL 1983+)
- Cinderella Carousel (HKD 2005+)
- Cinderella Castle Mystery Tour (TDL 1986–2006)

Video Games:

- *Disney Princess* (2003) GBA
- *Disney Princess: My Fairytale Adventure* (2012) Wii, 3DS, PC, Mac

COLLECTIONS

Video:

1988, 1995 Masterpiece Collection

Laserdisc:

1988, 1995 Masterpiece Collection

DVD*/Blu-ray:

2005 Platinum Edition* + Collector's Edition Gift Set*, 2012 Diamond Edition + 3-Movie Jewlery Box Collection

Soundtrack:

- 1957, 1958, 1960, 1963, 1981, 2015 (LP)

- 1995, 1997, 2001, 2005 Special Edition, 2010 Songs and Story, 2012 Collector's Edition, 2015 The Legacy Collection (includes The Lord Chords) (CD)

Books:

- *Cinderella* (2007) Mary Blair
- *A Wish Your Heart Makes: From the Grimm Brothers' Aschenputtel to Disney's Cinderella* (2015) Charles Solomon
- *The Walt Disney Film Archives: The Animated Movies 1921-1968* (2016) Ed. Daniel Kothenschulte

Treasure Island (1950)

PIRATES' PUNDER a young cabin boy, a roguish buccaneer...match wits in a swashbuckling adventure!

Source:

Treasure Island (1883) Robert Louis Stevenson

Writers:

Lawrence Edward Watkin

Director:

Byron Haskin

Stars:

Robert Newton, Bobby Driscoll, Basil Sydney

Premiere:

Jun 22, 1950, London

US Release:

Jul 19, 1950

Re-release:

1975 (edited for violence)

Length:

96 min (original), 87 min (edited)

CONNECTIONS

Comic Strips:

Treasure Island (Four Color Comics #624, Apr 1955)

Movies:

- *Long John Silver* (1954) 20th Century Fox release featuring Robert Newton [Collection > *Long John Silver's Return to Treasure Island* DVD (2011)]
- *Muppet Treasure Island* (1996) adapts same story
- *Treasure Planet* (2002) adapts same story

TV Series:

- *The Adventures of Long John Silver* (1956) Australian series featuring Robert Newton
- *Return to Treasure Island* (1986) Disney Channel, 10 episodes [Collection > UK Network DVD (2008)]

COLLECTIONS

Video:

1981, 1986 Edited, 1992 Studio Film Collection, 1997 Fantastic Adventures Series

Laserdisc:

1983, 1992 Studio Film Collection

DVD:

2003

Blu-ray:

2015 Disney Movie Club Exclusive / 65th Anniversary Edition

Digital:

Amazon, iTunes, Vudu

Soundtrack:

- 1950, 1970 (LP)
- 2005 *The Film Music of Clifton Parker* UK (CD) Recordings by BBC Concert Orchestra

Books:

- *Byron Haskin* (1984) Joe Adamson
- *The Disney Live-Action Productions/Walt Disney and Live Action* (1994/2016) John G. West

Alice in Wonderland (1951)

The all-cartoon Musical Wonderfilm!

Source:

Alice's Adventures in Wonderland (1865) & *Through the Looking-Glass, and What Alice Found There* (1871) Lewis Carroll

Writers:

Winston Hibler, Ted Sears, Bill Peet, Erdman Penner, Joe Rinaldi, Milt Banta, Bill Cottrell, Dick Kelsey, Joe Grant, Dick Huemer, Del Connell, Tom Oreb, John Walbridge

Director:

Clyde Geronimi, Wilfred Jackson, Hamilton Luske

Premiere:

Jul 26, 1951, London

US Release:

Jul 28, 1951, New York

Re-releases:

1974, 1981

Length:

75 min

CONNECTIONS

Comic Strips:

- *Alice in Wonderland* (Four Color Comics #331, May 1951) [Collection > *Disney Comics: The Classics Collection* (2006)]
- *Unbirthday Party with Alice in Wonderland* (Four Color Comics #341, Jul 1951)
- *Alice in Wonderland* (TCT, Sep 2 – Dec 16, 1951) [Collection > *Walt Disney's Treasury of Classic Tales Vol 1* (2016)]
- *Alice in Wonderland* (TCT, Feb 3 – Apr 28, 1974)

Movies:

- *Alice in Wonderland* (2010) live-action remake
- *Alice Through the Looking Glass* (2016) live-action remake

Shorts:

Alice in Wonderland: A Lesson in Appreciating Differences (1978) Educational

Stage Musical:

Alice in Wonderland JR. (?) Disney Theatrical Licensing

TV Special:

One Hour in Wonderland (1950) NBC, first Disney TV production [Collection > *Alice in Wonderland* Laserdisc (1995) DVD, Blu-ray]

TV Series:

Disney's Adventures in Wonderland (1992-1995) Disney Channel, 100 episodes

Theme Parks:

- Mad Tea Party (DL 1955+), (MK 1971+)
- Alice in Wonderland (DL 1958+)
- Alice's Tea Party (TDL 1986+)
- Alice's Curious Labyrinth (DP 1992+)
- Mad Hatter's Tea Cups (DP 1992+)
- Mad Hatter Tea Cups (HKD 2005+)
- Alice in Wonderland Maze (SD 2016+)

Video Games:

Walt Disney's Alice in Wonderland (2000) GBC

COLLECTIONS

Video:

1981, 1986, 1991, 1994

Laserdisc:

1982, 1993, 1995 Archive Collection

DVD*/Blu-ray:

2000 Gold Classic Collection*, 2004 The Masterpiece Edition*, 2010 Special Un-Anniversary Edition*, 2011 60th Anniversary Edition, 2016 Disney Movie Club Exclusive / 65th Anniversary Edition

Digital:

Amazon, iTunes, Vudu

Soundtrack:

- 1957, 1958, 1959, 1962, 2015, 2016 (LP)
- 1997, 2001 (CD)

Books:

- *Alice's Adventures in Wonderland* (1986) Ed. Brian Sibley

- *Alice in Wonderland* (2008) Mary Blair
- *The Walt Disney Film Archives: The Animated Movies 1921-1968* (2016) Ed. Daniel Kothenschulte
- *Walt Disney's Alice in Wonderland: An Illustrated Journey Through Time* (2016) Mark Salisbury

The Story of Robin Hood and His Merrie Men (1952)

AN ALL LIVE-ACTION PICTURE

AKA:

The Story of Robin Hood

Source:

Legend of Robin Hood

Writers:

Lawrence Edward Watkin

Director:

Ken Annakin

Stars:

Richard Todd, Joan Rice

Premiere:

Mar 13, 1952, London

US Release:

Jun 26, 1952

Length:

84 min

CONNECTIONS

Comic Strips:

- *Robin Hood* (Four Color Comics #413, Aug 1952)
- *The Story of Robin Hood* (TCT, Jul 13 – Dec 28 1952) [Collection > *Walt Disney's Treasury of Classic Tales Vol 1* (2016)]

Movies:

Robin Hood (1973) based on same legend

Shorts:

The Riddle of Robin Hood (1952) promotional

COLLECTIONS

Video:

1987, 1992 Studio Film Collection

Laserdisc:

1992 Studio Film Collection

DVD:

2009 Disney Movie Club Exclusive

Digital:

Vudu

Soundtrack:

1952, 1963 (LP)

Books:

- *The Disney Live-Action Productions/Walt Disney and Live Action* (1994/2016) John G. West
- *So You Wanna Be a Director?* (2001) Ken Annakin

Peter Pan (1953)

It will live in your heart forever!

Source:

Peter and Wendy (1904) J.M. Barrie

Writers:

Ted Sears, Erdman Penner, Bill Peet, Winston Hibler, Joe Rinaldi, Milt Banta, Ralph Wright, Bill Cottrell

Director:

Clyde Geronimi, Wilfred Jackson, Hamilton Luske

Premiere:

Feb 5, 1953

Re-releases:

1958, 1969, 1976, 1982, 1989

Length:

77 min

CONNECTIONS
Comic Strips:
- *Peter Pan* (Four Color Comics #442, Dec 1952) [Collection > *Disney Comics: The Classics Collection* (2006)]
- *Peter Pan* (TCT, Jan 4 – Jun 14, 1953) [Collection > *Walt Disney's Treasury of Classic Tales Vol 1* (2016)]
- *Peter Pan's Christmas Story* (DCS, Nov 28 – Dec 24, 1960)*
- *Santa Claus in Never Land* (DCS, Nov 25 – Dec 24, 1968)*
- *Captain Hook's Christmas Caper* (DCS, Nov 29 – Dec 24, 1976)*
- *No Puppets for Christmas* (DCS, Dec 5 – 24, 1977)*
- *Christmas Comes to Never Land* (DCS, Nov 28 – Dec 24, 1983) *Collection > *Disney's Christmas Classics* (2017)]

Movies:
- *Return to Never Land* (2002) sequel
- *Tinker Bell* (DTV, 2008) spin-off that launched a franchise

Stage Play:
Peter and the Starcatcher (2009+)

Stage Musical:
Peter Pan JR. (?) Disney Theatrical Licensing

TV Special:
The Peter Pan Story (1952)

TV Series:
Jake and the Never Land Pirates (2011-2016) Disney Junior, 115 episodes

Theme Parks:
Peter Pan's Flight (DL 1955+), (MK 1971+), (TDL 1983+), (DP 1992+), (SD 2016+)

Video Games:
Disney's Peter Pan – The Legend of Never Land (2005) PS2

COLLECTIONS
Video:
1990, 2002 Special Edition

Laserdisc:
1990, 1998 Masterpiece Edition / 45th Anniversary / Limited Edition

DVD:

1999 Limited Issue, 2002 Special Edition, 2007 Platinum Edition,

DVD/Blu-ray:

2013 Diamond Edition

Soundtrack:

- 1958, 1961, 1962, 1972 EP, 1982, 2015 (LP)
- 1998, 2013 Songs and Story (CD)
- 2013 The Lost Chords (Digital)

Books:

- *Walt Disney's Peter Pan: The Sketchbook Series* (1998) Limited edition of 2,500
- *Peter Pan* (2009) Mary Blair
- *The Walt Disney Film Archives: The Animated Movies 1921-1968* (2016) Ed. Daniel Kothenschulte

RKO Shorts Compilations (1953)

Series of themed features comprised of theatrical shorts and released by RKO.

Compilations:

- *Mickey's Birthday Party* [Connections: *Mickey's Birthday Party* (1942), *The Pointer* (1939), *The Nifty Nineties* (1941), *Tiger Trouble* (1945), *Mr. Mouse Takes a Trip* (1940), *The Whalers* (1938)]
- *Walt Disney's All-Cartoon Festival*
- *Walt Disney's Christmas Jollities*
- *Walt Disney's Drive-In Frivolities*
- *Walt Disney's Easter Parade*
- *Walt Disney's Election Day Gaieties*
- *Walt Disney's Fall Varities*
- *Walt Disney's 4th of July Firecrackers*
- *Walt Disney's Halloween Hilarities*
- *Walt Disney's New Year's Jamboree*
- *Walt Disney's Spring Frolics*
- *Walt Disney's Summer Jubilee*
- *Walt Disney's Thanksgiving Day Mirthquakes*
- *Walt Disney's Winter Hilarities*

The Sword and the Rose (1953)

New Excitement to Romance!

AKA:

When Knighthood Was in Flower (1956) Title on *Disneyland* TV anthology

Source:

When Knighthood Was in Flower (1898) Charles Major

Writers:

Lawrence Edward Watkin

Director:

Ken Annakin

Stars:

Richard Todd, Glynis Johns

Premiere:

Jul 23, 1953

Length:

92 min

CONNECTIONS

Comic Strips:

- *The Sword and the Rose* (TCT, Jun 21 – Oct 25, 1953) [Collection > *Walt Disney's Treasury of Classic Tales Vol 1* (2016)]
- *The Sword and the Rose* (Four Color Comics #505, Oct 1953)

COLLECTIONS

Video:

1985, 1993 Studio Film Collection

Laserdisc:

1993 Studio Film Collection

DVD:

2010 Disney Movie Club Exclusive

Digital:

Vudu

Soundtrack:

2005 *The Film Music of Clifton Parker* UK (CD)

Books:

- *The Disney Live-Action Productions/Walt Disney and Live Action* (1994/2016) John G. West
- *So You Wanna Be a Director?* (2001) Ken Annakin

Rob Roy: The Highland Rogue (1953)

Every minute Flames with furious action!

Source:

Life of Rob Roy MacGregor (1671–1734)

Writers:

Lawrence Edward Watkin

Director:

Harold French

Stars:

Richard Todd, Glynis Johns

Premiere:

Oct 26, 1953, London

US Release:

Feb 3, 1954

Length:

81 min

CONNECTIONS

Comic Strips:

- *Rob Roy, the Highland Rogue* (TCT, Jan 3rd – May 30th 1954) [Collection > *Walt Disney's Treasury of Classic Tales Vol 1* (2016)]
- *Rob Roy* (Four Color Comics #544, Mar 1954)

COLLECTIONS

Video:

1985

DVD:

2007 Disney Movie Club Exclusive

Digital:

Google Play

The Living Desert (1953)

First FEATURE-LENGTH TRUE-LIFE ADVENTURE! SAVAGELY REAL! EXCITINGLY DIFFERENT! FABULOUSLY BEAUTIFUL!

Writers:

James Algar, Winston Hibler, Ted Sears

Director:

James Algar

Premiere:

Nov 10, 1953

Length:

69 min

CONNECTIONS

Comic Strips:

The Living Desert (with Jiminy Cricket) (TCT, Nov 7 – Dec 26, 1971)

Movies:

- *The Best of Walt Disney's True-Life Adventures* (1975) Compilation

Shorts:

- *Animals at Home in the Desert* (1974) educational, 16mm
- *Predators of the Desert* (1974) educational, 16mm
- *What is a Desert?* (1974) educational, 16mm

COLLECTIONS

Video:

1986

Laserdisc:

1985 (Japan)

DVD:

2006 *Walt Disney Legacy Collection Vol 2: Lands of Exploration*

Digital:

Vudu

Soundtrack:

1964, 1970 *The Living Desert and The Vanishing Prairie* (LP)

Books:

True-Life Adventures: A History of Walt Disney's Nature Documentaries (2017) Christian Moran

The Vanishing Prairie (1954)

Walt Disney's Stirring NEW True-Life Adventure Feature!

Writers:

James Algar, Winston Hibler, Ted Sears

Director:

James Algar

Premiere:

Aug 16, 1954, New York

Length:

71 min

CONNECTIONS

Movies:

The Best of Walt Disney's True-Life Adventures (1975) compilation

Shorts:

- *Large Animals that Once Roamed the Plains* (1962) educational, 16mm
- *Pioneer Trails, Indian Lore and Bird Life of the Plains* (1962) educational, 16mm
- *Small Animals of the Plains* (1962) educational, 16mm
- *The Buffalo: Majestic Symbol of the Plains* (1962) educational, 16mm

COLLECTIONS

Video:

1985

DVD:

2006 *Walt Disney Legacy Collection Vol 2: Lands of Exploration*

Digital:

Vudu

Soundtrack:

1954, 1964 & 1970 *The Living Desert and The Vanishing Prairie* (LP)

Books:

True-Life Adventures: A History of Walt Disney's Nature Documentaries (2017) Christian Moran

20,000 Leagues Under the Sea (1954)

The adventure written a hundred years before its time becomes a motion picture to be remembered forever!

Source:

Twenty Thousand Leagues Under the Sea (1870) Jules Verne

Writers:

Earl Felton

Director:

Richard Fleischer

Stars:

Kirk Douglas, James Mason, Paul Lukas, Peter Lorre

Premiere:

Dec 23, 1954

Re-releases:

1963, 1971

Length:

127 min

CONNECTIONS

Comic Strips:

- *20,000 Leagues Under the Sea* (TCT, Aug 1 – Dec 26, 1954) [Collection > *Walt Disney's Treasury of Classic Tales Vol 1* (2016)]
- *20,000 Leagues Under the Sea* (Four Color Comics #614, Feb 1955)

TV Anthology:

"Operation Undersea" (1954) documentary on *Disneyland*

Theme Parks:

- 20,000 Leagues Under the Sea Exhibit (DL 1955-1966)
- 20,000 Leagues Under the Sea (MK 1971-1994), (TDS 2001+)
- Les Mystères du Nautilus (DP 1994+)

COLLECTIONS

Video:

1980, 1985, 1992, 1994 Family Film Collection

Laserdisc:

1983, 1993 Archive Collection

DVD:

2003 Special Edition

Digital:

Amazon, iTunes, Vudu

Soundtrack:

1954, 1963 (LP), 2011 Intrada (CD/iTunes)

Books:

The Disney Live-Action Productions/Walt Disney and Live Action (1994/2016) John G. West

Davy Crockett: King of the Wild Frontier (1955)

NOW... on the MOTION PICTURE SCREEN!

Source:

"Davy Crockett – Indian Fighter'," "Davy Crockett Goes to Congress," "Davy Crockett at the Alamo" (1955) edited from episodes of *Disneyland* TV anthology series

Writers:

Tom Blackburn

Director:

Norman Foster

Stars:

Fess Parker, Buddy Ebsen

Premiere:

May 25, 1955

Length:

93 min

CONNECTIONS

Comic Strips:

- *The Legends of Davy Crockett* (TCT, Jul 17, 1955 – Jan 8, 1956) [Collection > *Walt Disney's Treasury of Classic Tales Vol 2* (2017)]
- *Davy Crockett Indian Fighter* (Four Color Comics #631, May 1955)
- *Davy Crockett at the Alamo* (Four Color Comics #639, Jul 1955)
- *Walt Disney's Davy Crockett: King of the Wild Frontier* (Sep 1955)

Movies:

Davy Crockett and the River Pirates (1956) midquel

TV Episodes:

- "Davy Crockett—Indian Fighter" (1955)
- "Davy Crockett Goes to Congress" (1955)
- "Davy Crockett at the Alamo" (1955)
- "Davy Crockett's Keelboat Race" (1955)
- "Davy Crockett and the River Pirates" (1955) [Collection > WD Treasures: *Davy Crockett* (2004)]
- "Davy Crockett: Rainbow in the Thunder" (1988)
- "Davy Crockett: A Natural Man" (1988)
- "Davy Crockett: Guardian Spirit" (1989)
- "Davy Crockett: A Letter to Polly" (1989)
- "Davy Crockett: Warrior's Farewell" (1989)

Theme Parks:

- Davy Crockett Museum (DL 1955–1956)
- Davy Crockett Explorer Canoes (DL 1956+), (MK 1971–1994)

COLLECTIONS

Video:

1980, 1985, 1993 Studio Film Collection, 1997 Great American Legends Series

DVD:

2004 2-Movie Set

Blu-ray:

2015 Disney Movie Club Exclusive / 2-Movie Collection / 60th Anniversary Edition

Digital:

Amazon, iTunes, Vudu

Soundtrack:

1956, 1971, 1977 (LP), 2004 *Riders in the Sky Present...* (CD)

Books:

- *The Disney Live-Action Productions/Walt Disney and Live Action* (1994/2016) John G. West
- *The Davy Crockett Craze* (1996) Paul F. Anderson

The Littlest Outlaw (1955)

WATCH OUT! FOR THE BOY...WHO STOLE THE GENERAL'S HORSE THE MATADOR'S CHEERS...THE BANDITS' THUNDER AND THE HEARTS OF EVERYONE!

Writers:

Bill Walsh, Larry Lansburgh (Story)

Director:

Roberto Gavaldón

Premiere:

Dec 22, 1955

Length:

73 min

CONNECTIONS

Comic Strips:

- *The Littlest Outlaw* (Four Color Comics #609, Dec 1954)
- *The Littlest Outlaw* (TCT, Jan 15 – Mar 25, 1956) [Collection > *Walt Disney's Treasury of Classic Tales Vol 2* (2017)]

COLLECTIONS

Video:

1987

DVD:

2011 Disney Movie Club Exclusive

Digital:

Vudu

Soundtrack:

1955, 1963, 1972 Disneyland Double Feature (with *Pecos Bill*) (LP)

Lady and the Tramp (1955)

and NOW...his Happiest Motion Picture! with the Happiest songs of all!

Source:

"Happy Dan, the Whistling Dog" (c.1937) Ward Greene

Writers:

Erdman Penner, Joe Rinaldi, Ralph Wright, Don DaGradi

Directors:

Clyde Geronimi, Wilfred Jackson, Hamilton Luske

Premiere:

Jun 16, 1955, Chicago

Re-releases:

1962, 1971, 1980, 1986, 2013

Length:

76 min

CONNECTIONS

Comic Strips:

- *Lady and the Tramp* (TCT, Jan 2 – Jul 10, 1955) [Collection > *Walt Disney's Treasury of Classic Tales Vol 1* (2016)]
- *Lady and the Tramp with Jock* (Four Color Comics #629, May 1955)
- *Lady and the Tramp Album* (Four Color Comics #634, Jun 1955)
- *Scamp* (Newspaper Daily + Sunday Series, Oct 31, 1955 – Jun 19, 1988)
- *Scamp* (Four Color Comics #703, #777, #806, #833, #1204, 1956-1961)
- *Scamp* (Walt Disney's Comics & Stories #204-254, #275-279, #303, #305, 1957-1966)
- *Walt Disney's Scamp* (#5-15, 1958)
- *Tramp's Cat-astrophe* (TCT, Nov 23, 1986 – Feb 15, 1987)

Movies:

- *Lady and the Tramp II: Scamp's Adventure* (DTV, 2001)
- *Lady and the Tramp* (TBC) live-action remake

Shorts:

Lady and the Tramp: A Lesson in Sharing Attention (1978) Educational

COLLECTIONS

Video:

1987, 1998 Masterpiece Collection

Laserdisc:

1987, 1998 Masterpiece Collection

DVD*/Blu-ray:

- 1999 Limited Issue*, 2006 50th Anniversary Platinum Edition*, 2012 Diamond Edition
- 2018 The Signature Collection

Soundtrack:

- 1957, 1962, 1969, 1980, 2015 (LP)
- 1997, 2001, 2006, 2015 The Legacy Collection (CD)

Books:

- *Walt Disney's Lady and the Tramp: The Sketchbook Series* (1998)
- *The Vault of Walt: Volume 3* (2014) Jim Korkis
- *The Walt Disney Film Archives: The Animated Movies 1921-1968* (2016) Ed. Daniel Kothenschulte

Music Land (1955)

The BIG Parade of MIRTH and MELODY!

Sections:

Trees, All the Cats Join In, After You've Gone, Once Upon a Wintertime, Pecos Bill, Johnny Fedora and Alice Bluebonnet, Bumble Boogie, Casey at the Bat, Blame It on the Samba

Source:

Sections compiled from *Make Mine Music* (1946), *Melody Time* (1948)

Premiere:

Oct 5, 1955

Length:

75 min

The African Lion (1955)

HERE COMES ENTERTAINMENT! Walt Disney's Most EXCITING True-Life Adventure FEATURE!

Unstaged! Unrehearsed! Unbelievable!

AKA:

"His Majesty, King of the Beasts" (1958) abridged TV broadcast on *Walt Disney Presents*

Writers:

James Algar, Winston Hibler, Ted Sears, Jack Moffitt

Director:

James Algar

Premiere:

Sep 14, 1955

Length:

75 min

CONNECTIONS

Comic Strips:

The African Lion: A True-Life Adventure Feature (Four Color Comics #665, Nov 1955)

Movies:

The Best of Walt Disney's True-Life Adventures (1975) Compilation

Shorts:

- *The African Lion and His Realm* (1969) educational, 16mm
- *Elephants and Hippos in Africa* (1969) educational, 16mm
- *Birds, Baboons, and Other Animals – Their Struggle for Survival* (1969) educational, 16mm

TV Anthology:

"Cameras in Africa" (1954) Documentary on *Disneyland* [Collection > *Walt Disney Legacy Collection Vol 3* DVD (2006)]

COLLECTIONS

Laserdisc:

1985 (Japan)

DVD:

2006 *Walt Disney Legacy Collection Vol 3: Creatures of the Wild*

Digital:

Vudu

Books:

True-Life Adventures: A History of Walt Disney's Nature Documentaries (2017) Christian Moran

The Great Locomotive Chase (1956)

A REMARKABLE TRUE SPY STORY...NOW A GREAT MOTION PICTURE!

AKA:

"Andrew' Raiders" (1961) 2-part TV broadcast on *Walt Disney Presents*

Source:

Great Locomotive Chase of April 22, 1862

Writers:

Lawrence Edward Watkin

Director:

Francis Lyon

Stars:

Fess Parker, Jeff Hunter

Premiere:

Jun 8, 1956

Length:

87 min

CONNECTIONS

Comic Strips:

- *The Great Locomotive Chase* (TCT, Apr 1 –Jul 29, 1956) [Collection > *Walt Disney's Treasury of Classic Tales Vol 2* (2017)]
- *The Great Locomotive Chase* (Four Color Comics #712, Jul 1956)

TV Anthology:

"Behind the Scenes with Fess Parker" (1956) documentary on *Disneyland*

COLLECTIONS

Video:

1983

DVD:

2000 Anchor Bay, 2004

Digital:

Amazon, Vudu

Books:

All Aboard: The Wonderful World of Disney Trains (2015) Dana Amendola

Davy Crockett and the River Pirates (1956)

EXCITING NEW ADVENTURES…as two frontier giants, Davy Crockett and Mike Fink, challenge the river raiders!

Source:

"Davy Crockett's Keelboat Race," "Davy Crockett and the River Pirates" (1956) edited from episodes of *Disneyland* TV anthology series

Writers:

Tom Blackburn, Norman Foster

Director:

Norman Foster

Stars:

Fess Parker, Buddy Ebsen, Jeff York

Premiere:

Jul 18, 1956

Length:

81 min

CONNECTIONS

Comic Strips:

- *The Great Keelboat Race* (Four Color Comics #664, Nov 1955)
- *The River Pirates* (Four Color Comics #671, Dec 1955)

Movies:

Davy Crockett: King of the Wild Frontier (1955)

COLLECTIONS

Video:

1981, 1985, 1994

Laserdisc:

1982

DVD:

2004 2-Movie Set

Blu-ray:

2015 Disney Movie Club Exclusive / 2-Movie Collection / 60th Anniversary Edition

Digital:

Amazon, iTunes, Vudu

Books:

The Davy Crockett Craze (1996) Paul F. Anderson

Secrets of Life (1956)

NEVER BEAFORE...has a Motion Picture so Entertainingly Revealed Nature's Most Intimate Secrets...A Wondrous World of Sheer Drama...Stark Conflict...Delightful Humor...and Startling Beauty! THE MOST AMAZING AND MIRACULOUS TRUE-LIFE ADVENTURE FEATURE!

Writers:

James Algar

Director:

James Algar

Premiere:

Nov 6, 1956

Length:

70 min

CONNECTIONS

Comic Strips:

Secrets of Life: A True-Life Adventure (Four Color Comics #749, Nov 1956)

Movies:

The Best of Walt Disney's True-Life Adventures (1975) Compilation

Shorts:

- *Secrets of the Ant and Insect World* (1960) educational
- *Secrets of the Bee World* (1960) educational
- *Secrets of the Plant World* (1960) educational
- *Secrets of the Underwater World* (1960) educational

TV Anthology:

'Searching for Nature's Mysteries" (1956) Documentary on *Disneyland* [Collection > *Walt Disney Legacy Collection Vol 4* DVD (2006)]

COLLECTIONS

Video:

1985

Laserdisc:

1985 (Japan)

DVD:

- 2006 *Walt Disney Legacy Collection Vol 4: Nature's Mysteries*,
- 2012 Disney Movie Club Exclusive

Digital:

iTunes, Vudu

Soundtrack:

1956 (LP), 2004 (CD-on-Demand), 2007 (iTunes Exclusive)

Books:

True-Life Adventures: A History of Walt Disney's Nature Documentaries (2017) Christian Moran

Westward Ho, the Wagons! (1956)

WALT DISNEY TELLS THE REAL STORY OF THE FIGHTING FAMILIES WHO WON THE WEST!

Source:

Children of the Covered Wagon (1934) Mary Jane Carr

Writers:

Tom Blackburn

Director:

William Beaudine

Stars:

Fess Parker, Kathleen Crowley, Jeff York

Premiere:

Dec 20, 1956

Length:

90 min

CONNECTIONS

Comic Strips:

- *Westward Ho The Wagons* (Four Color Comics #738, Oct 1956)
- *Westward Ho, the Wagons!* (TCT, Oct 7, 1956 – Jan 27, 1957) [Collection > *Walt Disney's Treasury of Classic Tales Vol 2* (2017)]

TV Anthology:

"Along the Oregon Trail" (1956) Documentary on *Disneyland*

COLLECTIONS

Video:

1986

DVD:

2011 Disney Movie Club Exclusive

Digital:

Google Play

Soundtrack:

1956, 1957 EP (LP) ? (iTunes)

Johnny Tremain (1957)

Run...Johnny...Run! Run – AS ADVENTURE'S GREATEST HOUR EXPLODES WITH GLORY AND EXCITEMENT!

Source:

Johnny Tremain (1944) Esther Forbes

Writers:

Tom Blackburn

Director:

Robert Stevenson

Premiere:

Jun 19, 1957

Length:

80 min

CONNECTIONS

Comic Strips:

- *Johnny Tremain* (TCT, Apr 7 – Jun 30, 1957) [Collection > *Walt Disney's Treasury of Classic Tales Vol 2* (2017)]
- *Paul Revere's Ride with Johnny Tremain* (Four Color Comics #822, Aug 1957)
- *Old Ironsides with Johnny Tremain* (Four Color Comics #874, Jan 1958)

Shorts:

- *The Boston Tea Party* (1966) educational, 16mm
- *The Shot Heard 'Round the World* (1966) educational, 16mm

TV Anthology:

"The Liberty Story" (1957) Documentary on *Disneyland* [Collection > *Johnny Tremain* DVD (2005)]

COLLECTIONS

Video:

1983, 2003 Great American Legends Series

Laserdisc:

1997 Studio Film Collection

DVD:

2005

Digital:

iTunes, Vudu

Soundtrack:

1957 (LP)

Books:

The Disney Live-Action Productions/Walt Disney and Live Action (1994/2016) John G. West

Perri (1957)

A Fabulous First...IN MOTION PICTURE STORY-TELLING!!! First true-life Fantasy

Source:

Perri: The Youth of a Squirrel (1938) Felix Salten

Writers:

Ralph Wright, Winston Hibler

Directors:

N. Paul Kenworthy Jr., Ralph Wright

Premiere:

Aug 28, 1957

Length:

75 min

CONNECTIONS

Comic Strips:

- *Perri* (TCT, Jul 7 – Nov 24, 1957) [Collection > *Walt Disney's Treasury of Classic Tales Vol 2* (2017)]
- *Perri: A True-Life Fantasy* (Four Color Comics #847, Jun 1957)

TV Anthology:

"Adventure in Wildwood Heart" (1957) Documentary on *Disneyland* [Collection > *Walt Disney Legacy Collection Vol 4* DVD (2006)]

COLLECTIONS

DVD:

2006 *Walt Disney Legacy Collection Vol 4: Nature's Mysteries*

Digital:

Amazon, iTunes, Vudu

Soundtrack:

Perri: A Story with Songs Told by Jimmie Dodd - 1957 and 1967 (LP) 2010 (Digital)

Books:

True-Life Adventures: A History of Walt Disney's Nature Documentaries (2017) Christian Moran

Old Yeller (1957)

WALT DISNEY'S MOST DRAMATIC MOTION PICTURE!

Source:

Old Yeller (1956) Fred Gipson

Writers:

Fred Gipson, William Tunberg

Director:

Robert Stevenson

Stars:

Dorothy McGuire, Fess Parker

Premiere:

Dec 25, 1957

Re-releases:

1965, 1974

Length:

83 min

CONNECTIONS

Comic Strips:

- *Old Yeller* (TCT, Dec 1, 1957 – Feb 23, 1958) [Collection > *Walt Disney's Treasury of Classic Tales Vol 2* (2017)]
- *Old Yeller* (Four Color Comics #869, Jan 1958)

Movies:

Savage Sam (1963) Sequel

Shorts:

Love and Duty: Which Comes First? (1975) Educational

TV Anthology:

"The Best Doggoned Dog in the World" (1957) documentary on *Disneyland* [Collection > *Old Yeller* Laserdisc (1997), DVD (2002, 2005)]

COLLECTIONS

Video:

1981, 1992 Family Film Collection, 1997 40th Anniversary Limited Edition, 2002 Vault Disney Collection

Laserdisc:

1983, 1992 Family Film Collection, 1997 40th Anniversary Limited Edition

DVD:

2002 Vault Disney Collection, 2005 2-Movie Collection

Blu-ray:

2015 Disney Movie Club Exclusive

Digital:

Amazon, iTunes, Vudu

Soundtrack:

1964 *The Legend of Lobo* (Plus the Complete Story of Old Yeller) (LP)

Books:

The Disney Live-Action Productions/Walt Disney and Live Action (1994/2016) John G. West

The Light in the Forest (1958)

Two Refreshing New Stars in a DIFFERENT Motion Picture!

Source:

The Light in the Forest (1953) Conrad Richter

Writers:

Lawrence Edward Watkin

Director:

Herschel Daugherty

Stars:

Fess Parker, Wendell Corey, Joanne Dru, James MacArthur, Carol Lynley

Premiere:

Jul 8, 1958, Harrisburg, PA

Length:

93 min

CONNECTIONS

Comic Strips:

- *The Light in the Forest* (Four Color Comics #891, Mar 1958)

- *The Light in the Forest* (TCT, May 4 – Jul 27 1958) [Collection > *Walt Disney's Treasury of Classic Tales Vol 2* (2017)]

Shorts:

Prejudice: Hatred or Ignorance? (1976) educational

COLLECTIONS

Video:

1986, 1997 Great American Legends Series

Laserdisc:

1997 Studio Film Collection

Books:

The Disney Live-Action Productions/Walt Disney and Live Action (1994 / 2016) John G. West

White Wilderness (1958)

FROM THE TOP OF THE WORLD! A FABULOUS NEW ADVENTURE IN EXCITING ENTERTAINMENT

Writers:

James Algar

Director:

James Algar

Premiere:

Aug 12, 1958

Re-releases:

1972

Length:

72 min

CONNECTIONS

Comic Strips:

White Wilderness (Four Color Comics #943, Oct 1958)

Movies:

The Best of Walt Disney's True-Life Adventures (1975) Compilation

Shorts:

- *The Arctic Region and Its Polar Bears* (1964) educational, 16mm

- *Large Animals of the Arctic* (1964) educational, 16mm
- *The Lemmings and Arctic Bird Life* (1964) educational, 16mm

COLLECTIONS

Video:
1985

Laserdisc:
1985 (Japan)

DVD:
2006 *Walt Disney Legacy Collection Vol 1: Wonders of the World*

Digital:
iTunes, Vudu

Books:

- *Arctic Wild: The Remarkable True Story of One Couple's Adventures Living Among Wolves* (1996) Lois Crisler
- *True-Life Adventures: A History of Walt Disney's Nature Documentaries* (2017) Christian Moran

The Sign of Zorro (1958)

flashing swords… high adventure!

Source:

- Edited from following episodes of *Zorro*: 1.1 "Presenting Senor Zorro," 1.7 "Monastario Sets a Trap," 1.11 "Double Trouble for Zorro," 1.12 "The Luckiest Swordsman Alive," 1.13 "The Fall of Monastario." Includes scenes from 1.6 "Zorro Saves a Friend," 1.8 "Zorro's Ride Into Terror," and 1.9 "A Fair Trial."
- Character of Zorro created by Johnston McCulley in 1919.

Writers:
Norman Foster, Lowell S. Hawley, Bob Wehling, John Meredyth Lucas

Directors:
Lewis R. Foster, Norman Foster

Stars:
Guy Williams

Premiere:
Nov 18, 1958, Japan

US Release:

Jun 11, 1960

Re-release:

Jun 9, 1978 (edited)

Length:

90 min

CONNECTIONS

Comic Strips:

Walt Disney's Zorro (Four Color Comics #882, 920, 933, 960, 976, 1003, 1037 Feb 1958 – Sep/Nov 1959) [Collection > *The Classic Alex Toth Zorro* (1998)]

Movies:

The Sign of Zorro (1959)

TV Series:

- *Zorro* (1957-1959) ABC, 78 episodes [Collection > *WD Treasures: Zorro The Complete First/Second Season* (2009)]
- "El Bandido" and "Adios, El Cuchillo" (1960), "The Postponed Wedding" and "Auld Acquaintance" (1961) Specials on *Walt Disney Presents*. [Collection > *WD Treasures: Zorro The Complete Second Season* (2009)]
- *Zorro and Son* (1983) CBS, 5 episodes

COLLECTIONS

Video:

1982

Books:

- *The Disney Live-Action Productions/Walt Disney and Live Action* (1994/2016) John G. West
- *The Zorro Television Companion* (2005) Gerry Dooley

Tonka (1958)

The Untold Story behind the West's Strangest Legend!

AKA:

- "Comanche" (1962) 2-part TV broadcast on *Walt Disney's Wonderful World of Color*

- "A Horse Called Comanche" (1977–1978) serialization on *The New Mickey Mouse Club*

Source:

Comanche: The Story of America's Most Heroic Horse (1951) David Appel

Writers:

Lewis R. Foster, Lillie Hayward

Director:

Lewis R. Foster

Stars:

Sal Mineo, Jerome Courtland, Philip Carey, Rafael Campos

Premiere:

Dec 25, 1958

Length:

96 min

CONNECTIONS

Comic Strips:

Tonka (Four Color Comics #966, Jan 1959)

COLLECTIONS

Video:

1986

Laserdisc:

1998 (Japan)

DVD:

2009 Disney Movie Club Exlusive

Digital:

iTunes, Vudu

Sleeping Beauty (1959)

WONDROUS TO SEE...GLORIOUS TO HEAR...A magnificent new motion picture!

Source:

"The Sleeping Beauty" in *Histoires ou contes du temps passé* (1697) Charles Perrault

Writers:

Erdman Penner

Director:

Clyde Geronimi

Premiere:

Jan 29, 1959, Los Angeles

Re-releases:

1970, 1979, 1986

Length:

75 min

CONNECTIONS

Comic Strips:

- *Sleeping Beauty* (TCT, Aug 3 – Dec 28, 1958) [Collection > *Walt Disney's Treasury of Classic Tales Vol 2* (2017)]
- *Sleeping Beauty's Fairy Godmothers* (Four Color Comics #984, Apr 1959)
- *Sleeping Beauty and the Prince* (Four Color Comics #973, May 1959)
- *Sleeping Beauty's Christmas Story* (DCS, Nov 26 – Dec 24, 1962)*
- *Santa's Christmas Crisis* (DCS, Nov 30 – Dec 24, 1970)* [*Collection > *Disney's Christmas Classics* (2017)]
- *The Search for Sleeping Beauty* (TCT, Feb 2 – Apr 27, 1986)

Movies:

- *Maleficent* (2014) live-action remake
- *Disney Princess Enchanted Tales: Follow Your Dreams* (DTV 2007) [Section: "Keys to the Kingdom"]

Stage:

Sleeping Beauty KIDS (?) Disney Theatrical Licensing

Theme Parks:

- Sleeping Beauty Castle (DL 1955+), (HKD 2005+)
- Le Château de la Belle au Bois Dormant (DP 1992+)

Video Games:

Disney Princess (2003) GBA

COLLECTIONS

Video:

1986, 1997 Masterpiece Collection / Limited Edition

Laserdisc:

1997 Masterpiece Collection / Limited Edition

DVD*/Blu-ray:

2003 Special Edition*, 2008 50th Anniversary Platinum Edition, 2014 Diamond Edition

Soundtrack:

- 1958, 1959, 1962, 1970, 2015 (LP)
- 1997, 2001, 2008 50th Anniversary Edition, 2008 *Sleeping Beauty and Friends*, 2012 Songs and Story, 2014 The Legacy Collection (CD)

Books:

- *Walt Disney's Sleeping Beauty: The Sketchbook Series* (1997)
- *La Belle au Bois Dormant* (2013) Pierre Lambert
- *Once Upon a Dream: From Perrault's Sleeping Beauty to Disney's Maleficent* (2014) Charles Solomon
- *The Walt Disney Film Archives: The Animated Movies 1921-1968* (2016) Ed. Daniel Kothenschulte

The Shaggy Dog (1959)

a new kind of HORROR movie... HORRIBLY FUNNY!

Source:

The Hound of Florence (1923) Felix Salten

Writers:

Bill Walsh, Lillie Hayward

Director:

Charles Barton

Stars:

Fred MacMurray, Jean Hagen

Premiere:

Mar 19, 1959

Length:

101 min

CONNECTIONS

Comic Strips:

- *Walt Disney's Shaggy Dog* (Four Color Comics #985, May 1959)
- *The Shaggy Dog* (TCT, Jan 4 – Apr 26, 1959) [Collection > *Walt Disney's Treasury of Classic Tales Vol 2* (2017)]

Movies:

- *The Shaggy D.A.* (1976) sequel
- *The Shaggy Dog* (2006) remake

TV Movies:

- *The Return of the Shaggy Dog* (1987) ABC, *The Disney Sunday Movie*, sequel
- *The Shaggy Dog* (1994) ABC, remake

COLLECTIONS

Video:

1981, 1993, 1997 (colorized)

Laserdisc:

1983, 1993 Studio Film Collection (colorized)

DVD:

- 2006 Wild & Woolly Edition (original & colorized)
- 2009 Double Feature (original & colorized)
- 2012 Disney 4-Movie Collection: Dogs 1 (original & colorized)

Digital:

Amazon, Vudu

Soundtrack:

1959, 1960 (LP)

Books:

- *The Disney Live-Action Productions/Walt Disney and Live Action* (1994/2016) John G. West
- *The Vault of Walt: Volume 2* (2013) Jim Korkis

Darby O'Gill and the Little People (1959)

A touch of O'Blarney... a heap O'Magic and A LOAD OF LAUGHTER!

Source:

- *Darby O'Gill and the Good* People (1903)

- *Ashes of Old Wishes and Other Darby O'Gill Tales* (1926) H.T. Kavanagh

Writers:

Lawrence Edward Watkin

Director:

Robert Stevenson

Stars:

Albert Sharpe, Janet Munro, Sean Connery, Jimmy O'Dea

Premiere:

Jun 24, 1959, Dublin

US Release:

Jun 26, 1959, Los Angeles

Re-releases:

1969, 1977

Length:

90 min

CONNECTIONS

Comic Strips:

- *Darby O'Gill and the Little People* (TCT, May 3 – Aug 30, 1959) [Collection > *Walt Disney's Treasury of Classic Tales Vol 3* (2018)]
- *Darby O'Gill and the Little People* (Four Color Comics #1024, Aug 1959)

TV Anthology:

- "I Captured the King of the Leprechauns" (1959) documentary on *Walt Disney Presents* [Collection > *WD Treasures: Your Host, Walt Disney* DVD (2006)
- *Darby O'Gill and the Little People* DVD (2004, 2012)

COLLECTIONS

Video:

1981, 1992 Studio Film Collection

Laserdisc:

1983, 1993 Studio Film Collection

DVD:

2004, 2012 Disney 4-Movie Collection: Classics

Digital:

Amazon, iTunes, Vudu

Books:

- *The Disney Live-Action Productions/Walt Disney and Live Action* (1994/2016) John G. West
- *The Vault of Walt: Volume 3* (2014) Jim Korkis

Third Man on the Mountain (1959)

BREATHTAKING. Their strong young love gave him the courage to defy tradition and challenge the "KILLER" mountain!

AKA:

"Banner in the Sky" (1963) 2-part broadcast on *Walt Disney's Wonderful World of Color*

Source:

Banner in the Sky (1954) James Ramsey Ullman

Writers:

Eleanore Griffin

Director:

Ken Annakin

Stars:

Michael Rennie, James MacArthur, Janet Munro, James Donald, Herbert Lom, Laurence Naismith

Premiere:

Nov 10, 1959

Length:

107 min

CONNECTIONS

Comic Strips:

Third Man on the Mountain (TCT, Sep 6 – Dec 27, 1959) [Collection > *Walt Disney's Treasury of Classic Tales Vol 3* (2018)]

Short:

Ambition: What Price Fulfilment? (1976) Educational

TV Anthology:

"Perilous Assignment" (1959) documentary on *Walt Disney Presents*

COLLECTIONS

Video:

1986

Laserdisc:

1997 Studio Film Collection

DVD:

2004

Digital:

iTunes, Vudu

Books:

The Disney Live-Action Productions/Walt Disney and Live Action (1994/2016) John G. West

Zorro the Avenger (1959)

ADVENTURE'S GOLDEN AGE!

Source:

- Edited from following episodes of *Zorro*: 1.35 "The Tightening Noose," 1.36 "The Sergeant Regrets," 1.37 "The Eagle Leaves the Nest," 1.39 "Day of Decision." Includes scenes from 1.38 "Bernardo Faces Death" and 1.27 "The Eagle's Brood."
- Character of Zorro created by Johnston McCulley in 1919

Writers:

Lowell S. Hawley, Bob Wehling

Director:

Charles Barton

Stars:

Guy Williams

Premiere:

Sep 10, 1959, Japan

Length:

97 min

CONNECTIONS

Movies:

See *The Sign of Zorro* (1958) for more

Jungle Cat (1959)

LUNGING ONTO THE SCREEN OUT OF THE DARK, MYSTERIOUS DEPTHS OF THE AMAZON!

Writers:

James Algar

Director:

James Algar

Premiere:

Dec 16, 1959 / Aug 10, 1960 (general release)

Length:

70 min

CONNECTIONS

Comic Strips:

Jungle Cat (Four Color Comics #1136, Sep 1960)

Movies:

The Best of Walt Disney's True-Life Adventures (1975) compilation

Shorts:

- *Animals of the South American Jungle* (1974) educational, 16mm
- *Jungle Cat of the Amazon* (1974) educational, 16mm

COLLECTIONS

Video:

1986

Laserdisc:

1985 (Japan)

DVD:

2006 *Walt Disney Legacy Collection Vol 3: Creatures of the Wild*, 2012 Disney Movie Club Exclusive

Digital:

iTunes, Vudu

Books:

True-Life Adventures: A History of Walt Disney's Nature Documentaries (2017) Christian Moran

PART THREE

Movies: 1960–1969

Toby Tyler, or
Ten Weeks with a Circus (1960)

STRIKE UP THE BAND! HERE COMES THE HAPPIEST SHOW ON EARTH!

Source:

Toby Tyler; or, Ten Weeks with a Circus (1877) James Otis Kaler

Writers:

Lillie Hayward, Bill Walsh

Director:

Charles Barton

Stars:

Kevin Corcoran, Henry Calvin, Gene Sheldon, Bob Sweeney, Richard Eastham

Premiere:

Jan 21, 1960

Length:

95 min

CONNECTIONS

Comic Strips:

- *Toby Tyler* (TCT, Jan 3 – Mar 27, 1960) [Collection > *Walt Disney's Treasury of Classic Tales Vol 3* (2018)]
- *Toby Tyler* (Four Color Comics #1092, Mar 1960)

COLLECTIONS

Video:

1986

Laserdisc:

1997 Studio Film Collection

DVD:

2005

Digital:

Amazon, iTunes, Vudu

Soundtrack:

1960 Story of Toby Tyler in the Circus (LP)

Books:

- *The Disney Live-Action Productions/Walt Disney and Live Action* (1994/2016) John G. West
- *The Vault of Walt: Volume 2* (2013) Jim Korkis

Kidnapped (1960)

EXCITEMENT...DANGER...SUSPENSE as this classic adventure story sweeps across the screen!

Source:

Kidnapped (1886) Robert Louis Stevenson

Writers:

Robert Stevenson

Director:

Robert Stevenson

Stars:

Peter Finch, James MacArthur, Bernard Lee

Premiere:

Feb 24, 1960

Length:

97 min

CONNECTIONS

Comic Strips:

- *Kidnapped* (TCT, Apr 3 – Jun 26, 1960) [Collection > *Walt Disney's Treasury of Classic Tales Vol 3* (2018)]
- *Kidnapped* (Four Color Comics #1101, May 1960)

COLLECTIONS

Video:

1983, 1992 Studio Film Collection

Laserdisc:

1992 Studio Film Collection

DVD:

2006 Disney Movie Club Exclusive

Digital:

iTunes, Vudu

Pollyanna (1960)

Walt Disney BRINGS ONE OF THE WORLD'S GREATEST STORIES TO THE SCREEN! Meet The People...The Pleasure...The Entertainment...Of The Year! Here Is All The Love...Laughter...And Drama That Life Can Hold—All Poured Into One Unforgettable Motion Picture!

Source:

Pollyanna (1913) Eleanor H. Porter

Writers:

David Swift

Director:

David Swift

Stars:

Jane Wyman, Richard Egan, Karl Malden, Nancy Olson, Adolphe Menjou, Donald Crisp, Agnes Moorehead, Kevin Corcoran, Hayley Mills

Premiere:

May 19, 1960

Length:

134 min

CONNECTIONS

Comic Strips:

- *Pollyanna* (TCT, Jul 3 – Sep 25, 1960) [Collection > *Walt Disney's Treasury of Classic Tales Vol 3* (2018)]
- *Pollyanna* (Four Color Comics #1129, Aug 1962)

Shorts:

Optimist/Pessimist: Which Are You? (1975) Educational

TV Movies:

- *The Adventures of Pollanna* (1982) CBS, *Walt Disney*, remake
- *Polly* (1989) NBC, *The Magical World of Disney*, remake

COLLECTIONS

Video:

1982, 1993 Studio Film Collection

Laserdisc:

1983, 1993 Studio Film Collection

DVD:

2002 Vault Disney Collection

Blu-ray:

2015 Disney Movie Club Exclusive / 55th Anniversary Edition

Digital:

Amazon, iTunes, Vudu

Books:

The Disney Live-Action Productions/Walt Disney and Live Action (1994 / 2016) John G. West

Ten Who Dared (1960)

ONE TERRIFYING MILE STRAIGHT DOWN INTO A CANYON OF DESTRUCTION!

Source:

The Exploration of the Colorado River and Its Canyons (1895) John Wesley Powell

Writers:

Lawrence Edward Watkin

Director:

William Beaudine

Premiere:

Oct 18, 1960

Length:

92 min

CONNECTIONS

Comic Strips:

Ten Who Dared (Four Color Comics #1178, Dec 1960)

COLLECTIONS

Video:

1986

DVD:

2009 Disney Movie Club Exclusive

Digital:

iTunes, Vudu

Swiss Family Robinson (1960)

THE GREATEST ADVENTURE STORY OF THEM ALL!

Source:

The Swiss Family Robinson (1812) Johann David Wyss

Writers:

Lowell S. Hawley

Director:

Ken Annakin

Stars:

John Mills, Dorothy McGuire, James MacArthur, James Munro

Premiere:

Dec 10, 1960

Re-releases:

1969, 1972, 1975 1981

Length:

126 min

CONNECTIONS

Comic Strips:

- *Swiss Family Robinson* (TCT, Oct 2 – Dec 25, 1960) [Collection > *Walt Disney's Treasury of Classic Tales Vol 3* (2018)]
- *Swiss Family Robinson* (Four Color Comics #1156, Dec 1960)

TV Anthology:

"Escape to Paradise" (1960) Documentary on *Walt Disney Presents* [Collection > *Swiss Family Robinson* DVD (2002)]

TV Movies:

- *Beverly Hills Family Robinson* (1997) ABC, remake
- *The New Swiss Family Robinson* (1999) ABC, *The Wonderful World of Disney*, remake

Theme Parks:

- Swiss Family Treehouse (DL 1962–1999), (MK 1971+), (TDL 1993+)
- La Cabane des Robinson (DP 1992+)

COLLECTIONS

Video:

1982, 1997 Fantastic Adventures Series

Laserdisc:

1983, 1993 Archive Collection

DVD:

2002 Vault Disney Collection

Blu-ray:

2015 Disney Movie Club Exclusive / 55th Anniversary Edition

Digital:

Amazon, iTunes, Vudu

Soundtrack:

1960 (LP)

Books:

The Disney Live-Action Productions/Walt Disney and Live Action (1994/2016) John G. West

One Hundred and One Dalmatians (1961)

THE CANINE CAPER OF THE CENTURY. Crafty Cruella… chasing every spotted puppy in town. A great animated adventure story

AKA:

101 Dalmatians

Source:

The Hundred and One Dalmatians (1956) Dodie Smith

Writers:

Bill Peet

Director:

Clyde Geronimi, Hamilton Luske, Wolfgang Reitherman

Premiere:

Jan 25, 1961

Re-releases:

1969, 1979, 1985, 1991

Length:

79 min

CONNECTIONS

Comic Strips:

- *101 Dalmatians* (TCT, Jan 1 – Mar 26, 1961) [Collection > *Walt Disney's Treasury of Classic Tales Vol 3* (2018)]
- *101 Dalmatians* (Four Color Comics #1183, Mar 1961)
- *Cruella's Very Furry Christmas* (DCS, Dec 2 – 24, 1985) [Collection > *Disney's Christmas Classics* (2017)]

Movies:

- *101 Dalmatians* (1996) live-action remake
- *101 Dalmatians II: Patch's London Adventure* (DTV 2003)
- *Cruella* (2018) live-action remake

Shorts:

- *101 Dalmatians: A Lesson in Assertion* (1981) Educational
- *101 Dalmatians: The Further Adventures of Thunderbolt* (DTV 2015) [Collection > *One Hundred and One Dalmatians* Blu-ray (2015)]

Stage Musical:

101 Dalmatians KIDS (?) Disney Theatrical Licensing

TV Anthology:

"The Best Doggoned Dog in the World" (1961) Documentary on *Walt Disney Presents* [Collection > *101 Dalmatians* Blu-ray (2015)]

TV Series:

101 Dalmatians: The Series (1997-1998) ABC, 65 episodes

COLLECTIONS

Video:

1992, 1999 Masterpiece Collection

Laserdisc:

1999 Masterpiece Collection

DVD:

1999 Limited Issue, 2008 Platinum Edition

Blu-ray:

2015 Diamond Edition

Digital:

Vudu

Soundtrack:

1961 (LP) 1998, 2002, 2008 *101 Dalmatians and Friends* (CD)

Books:

The Walt Disney Film Archives: The Animated Movies 1921-1968 (2016) Ed. Daniel Kothenschulte

The Absent-Minded Professor (1961)

The funniest discover since laughter!! All about a scrambled egghead... a flying flivver and FLUBBER (the GOO that Flew)!

Source:

"A Situation of Gravity" in *Liberty* (1943) Samuel W. Taylor

Writers:

Bill Walsh

Director:

Robert Stevenson

Stars:

Fred MacMurray, Nancy Olson, Keenan Wynn, Tommy Kirk

Premiere:

Mar 16, 1961

Re-releases:

1967, 1974

Length:

92 min

CONNECTIONS

Comic Strips:

The Absent-Minded Professor (Four Color Comics #1199, Apr 1961)

Movies:

- *Son of Flubber* (1963) sequel
- *Flubber* (1997) remake

TV Movies:

The Absent-Minded Professor (1988) NBC, *The Magical World of Disney*, Remake

COLLECTIONS

Video:

1981, 1986 (Colorized), 1993

Laserdisc:

1983, 1993 Studio Film Collection, 1997 Studio Film Collection (Colorized)

DVD:

2003 Comedy Favourites Series, 2008 Double Feature

Blu-ray:

2016 Disney Movie Club Exclusive / 55th Anniversary Edition

Digital:

Amazon, iTunes, Vudu

Soundtrack:

1961 (LP)

Books:

The Disney Live-Action Productions/Walt Disney and Live Action (1994/2016) John G. West

The Parent Trap (1961)

It's strictly a Laugh Affair. DEDICATED TO THE PROPOSITION THAT TEENAGERS and PARENTS ARE CREATED EQUALLY HILARIOUS!

Source:

Lottie and Lisa (1949) Erich Kästner

Writers:

David Swift

Director:

David Swift

Stars:

Hayley Mills, Hayley Mills, Maureen O'Hara, Brian Keith

Premiere:

Jun 12, 1961

Re-releases:

1968

Length:

129 min

CONNECTIONS

Comic Strips:

- *The Parent Trap* (TCT, Jul 2 – Sep 24, 1961) [Collection > *Walt Disney's Treasury of Classic Tales Vol 3* (2018)]
- *The Parent Trap* (Four Color Comics #1210, Aug 1961)

Movies:

The Parent Trap (1998) Remake

TV Movies:

- *The Parent Trap II* (1986) Disney Channel Premiere Film, sequel
- *Parent Trap III* (1989) NBC, *The Magical World of Disney*, sequel
- *Parent Trap: Hawaiian Honeymoon* (1989) NBC, *The Magical World of Disney*, sequel

COLLECTIONS

Video:

1984, 1992, 1997 Hayley Mills Collection

Laserdisc:

1992 Studio Film Collection

DVD:

2002 Vault Disney Collection, 2005 2-Movie Collection

Blu-ray:

2018 Disney Movie Club Exclusive

Digital:

Amazon, iTunes, Vudu

Soundtrack:

1961 (LP) 2007 (Digital)

Books:

The Disney Live-Action Productions/Walt Disney and Live Action (1994 / 2016) John G. West

Nikki, Wild Dog of the North (1961)

THE WILD COUNTRY WAS ONLY FOR THE BRAVE... SURVIVAL ONLY FOR THE FITTEST... MAN OR BEAST!

Source:

Nomads of the North (1919) James Oliver Curwood

Writers:

Ralph Wright, Winston Hibler

Directors:

Jack Couffer, Don Haldane

Premiere:

Jul 12, 1961

Length:

73 min

CONNECTIONS

Comic Strips:

- *Nikki, Wild Dog of the North* (TCT, Apr 2 – Jun 25, 1961) [Collection > *Walt Disney's Treasury of Classic Tales Vol 3* (2018)]
- *Nikki, Wild Dog of the North* (Four Color Comics #1226, Sep 1961)

COLLECTIONS

Video:

1986

DVD:

2000 Anchor Bay

Digital:

iTunes, Vudu

Soundtrack:

1961 (LP)

Books:

True-Life Adventures: A History of Walt Disney's Nature Documentaries (2017) Christian Moran

Greyfriars Bobby (1961)

SUCH A TINY DOG TO CREATE SUCH A BIG FUSS! This is Bobby...the begrinned, bewitching little Sky Terrier who lived an astonishing adventure that sparked a city-wide uproar and wrought a heart-stealing miracle without equal!

AKA:

Greyfriars Bobby: The True Story of a Dog

Source:

Greyfriars Bobby (1912) Eleanor Atkinson

Writers:

Robert Westerby

Director:

Don Chaffey

Stars:

Donald Crisp, Laurence Naismith

Premiere:

Jul 17, 1961

Length:

91 min

CONNECTIONS

Comic Strips:

Greyfriars Bobby (Four Color Comics #1189, Nov 1961)

COLLECTIONS

Video:

1986

DVD:

2004

Digital:

Google Play

Soundtrack:

1961 (LP)

Babes in Toyland (1961)

Source:

Babes in Toyland Operetta (1903) Victor Herbert

Writers:

Ward Kimball, Joe Rinaldi, Lowell S. Hawley

Director:

Jack Donohue

Stars:

Ray Bolger, Tommy Sands, Annette, Ed Wynn

Premiere:

Dec 14, 1961

Length:

106 min

CONNECTIONS

Comic Strips:

- *Babes in Toyland* (TCT, Oct 1 – Dec 31, 1961) [Collection > *Walt Disney's Treasury of Classic Tales Vol 3* (2018)]
- *Babes in Toyland* (Four Color Comics #1282, Jan 1962)

TV Anthology:

"Backstage Party" (1961) Documentary on *Walt Disney's Wonderful World of Color* [Collection > *WD Treasures: Your Host, Walt Disney* DVD (2006)]

Theme Parks:

Babes in Toyland Exhibit (DL 1961-1963)

COLLECTIONS

Video:

1982

Laserdisc:

1992

DVD:

2002

Blu-ray:

2012

Digital:

Amazon, iTunes, Vudu

Soundtrack:

1961 (LP) 2013 (Digital)

Moon Pilot (1962)

A funny thing happened to me on the way to the moon...

Source:

Starfire (1960) Robert Buckner

Writers:

Maurice Tombragel

Director:

James Neilson

Stars:

Tom Tryon, Brian Keith, Edmund O'Brien, Dany Saval

Premiere:

Feb 9, 1962

Length:

98 min

CONNECTIONS

Comic Strips:

- *Moon Pilot* (TCT, Jan 7 – Mar 25, 1962) [Collection > *Walt Disney's Treasury of Classic Tales Vol 3* (2018)]
- *Moon Pilot* (Four Color Comics #1313, Mar 1962)

TV Anthology:

"'Spy in the Sky" (1962) documentary on *Walt Disney's Wonderful World of Color*

COLLECTIONS

Video:

1986

DVD:

2008 Disney Movie Club Exclusive

Digital:

Amazon, iTunes, Vudu

Soundtrack:

1962 (LP)

Books:

The Disney Live-Action Productions/Walt Disney and Live Action (1994 / 2016) John G. West

Bon Voyage! (1962)

LOOK OUT, PAREE

Source:

Bon Voyage (1957) Marrijane Hayes & Joseph Hayes

Writers:

Bill Walsh

Director:

James Neilson

Stars:

Fred MacMurray, Jane Wyman

Premiere:

May 17, 1962

Length:

132 min

CONNECTIONS

Comic Strips:

- *Bon Voyage* (TCT, Apr 1 1962 – Jun 24, 1962) [Collection > *Walt Disney's Treasury of Classic Tales Vol 3* (2018)]
- *Bon Voyage* (Dec 1962)

COLLECTIONS

Video:

1987

DVD:

2004

Digital:

Vudu

Books:

The Disney Live-Action Productions/Walt Disney and Live Action (1994 / 2016) John G. West

Big Red (1962)

IN ONE DECISIVE MOMENT...a courageous boy and a Big Red dog teach a brave man the meaning of devotion!

Source:

Big Red (1945) Jim Kjelgaard

Writers:

Louis Pelletier

Director:

Norman Tokar

Stars:

Walter Pidgeon, Gilles Payant

Premiere:

Jun 6, 1962

Length:

89 min

CONNECTIONS

Comic Strips:

- *Big Red* (TCT, Jul 1 – Sep 30, 1962) [Collection > *Walt Disney's Treasury of Classic Tales Vol 3* (2018)]
- *Big Red* (Nov 1962)

COLLECTIONS

Video:

1984

DVD:

2000 Anchor Bay, 2008 Disney Movie Club Exclusive

Digital:

Amazon, iTunes, Vudu

Soundtrack:

1962 (LP)

Books:

The Disney Live-Action Productions/Walt Disney and Live Action (1994 / 2016) John G. West

Almost Angels (1962)

Boys will by boys…even during the most important performance of their lives! Almost Angels…BUT ONLY WHEN THEY'RE SINGING!

AKA:

Born to Sing (UK)

Writers:

Vernon Harris, Robert A. Stemmle (Original story)

Director:

Steve Previn

Stars:

Peter Weck, Sean Scully, Vincent Winter

Premiere:

Sep 26, 1962

Length:

93 min

COLLECTIONS

Video:

1986

DVD:

2010 Disney Movie Club Exclusive

The Legend of Lobo (1962)

THE HUNTER… THE HUNTED! in one lifetime he was both.

Source:

"Lobo the King of Currumpaw" in *Wild Animals I Have Known* (1898) Ernest Thompson Seton

Writers:

Dwight Hauser, James Algar

Director:
James Algar, Jack Couffer

Premiere:
Nov 7, 1962

Length:
67 min

CONNECTIONS

Comic Strips:
- *The Legend of Lobo* (Mar 1963)
- *The Legend of Lobo* (TCT, Jul 2 – Sep 24, 1972)

COLLECTIONS

Video:
1985

DVD:
2008 Disney Movie Club Exclusive

Digital:
Vudu

Soundtrack:
1964 (LP)

Books:
True-Life Adventures: A History of Walt Disney's Nature Documentaries (2017) Christian Moran

In Search of the Castaways (1962)

An earthquake of Entertainment! An avalanche of Adventure!

Source:
In Search of the Castaways (1867–1868) Jules Verne

Writers:
Lowell S. Hawley

Director:
Robert Stevenson

Stars:
Maurice Chevalier, Hayley Mills, George Sanders, Wilfrid Hyde-White

Premiere:

Nov 14, 1962, London

US Release:

Dec 19, 1962

Re-releases:

1970, 1978

Length:

98 min

CONNECTIONS

Comic Strips:

- *In Search of the Castaways* (TCT, Oct 7 – Dec 30, 1962) [Collection > *Walt Disney's Treasury of Classic Tales Vol 3* (2018)]
- *Walt Disney Presents Jules Verne's In Search of the Castaways* (Mar 1963)

COLLECTIONS

Video:

1984, 1992 Studio Film Collection

Laserdisc:

1992 Studio Film Collection

DVD

2005

Digital:

iTunes, Vudu

Soundtrack:

1962, 1968 *Music from Three Walt Disney Motion Pictures* (LP)

Son of Flubber (1963)

The Professor's "OFF"... AGAIN!

Source:

Sequel to *The Absent-Minded Professor* (1961) inspired by "Danny Dunn" books (1956–1977) by Raymond Abrashkin & Jay Williams

Writers:

Bill Walsh, Don DaGradi, Samuel W. Taylor (story)

Director:

Robert Stevenson

Stars:

Fred MacMurray, Nancy Olson, Keenan Wynn

Premiere:

Jan 18, 1963

Length:

103 min

CONNECTIONS

Comic Strips:

- *Son of Flubber* (TCT, Jan 6 – Mar 31, 1963)
- *Son of Flubber* (Apr 1963)

COLLECTIONS

Video:

1984, 1997 (colorized)

Laserdisc:

1997 Studio Film Collection

DVD:

2004, 2008 Double Feature

Blu-ray:

2016 Disney Movie Club Exclusive

Digital:

Amazon, iTunes, Vudu

Soundtrack:

1963 (LP)

Books:

The Disney Live-Action Productions/Walt Disney and Live Action (1994 / 2016) John G. West

Miracle of the White Stallions (1963)

One chance at the impossible...they risked everything for a prize greater than victory!

AKA:

Flight of the White Stallions (1965) 2-part TV airing on *Walt Disney's Wonderful World of Color*

Source:

The White Stallions of Vienna (1963) Alois Podhajsky

Writers:

AJ Carothers

Director:

Arthur Hiller

Stars:

Robert Taylor, Lilli Palmer, Curt Jurgens

Premiere:

Mar 29, 1963

Length:

118 min

CONNECTIONS

Comic Strips:

- *Miracle of the White Stallions* (TCT, Apr 7 – Jun 30, 1963)
- *Miracle of the White Stallions* (Jun 1963)

COLLECTIONS

Video:

1987

DVD:

2004

Savage Sam (1963)

The fury of an untamed land!

Source:

Savage Sam (1962) Fred Gipson

Writers:

Fred Gipson, William Tunberg

Director:

Norman Tokar

Stars:

Brian Keith, Tommy Kirk, Marta Kristen, Kevin Corcoran

Premiere:

Jun 1, 1963

Length:

103 min

CONNECTIONS

Comic Strips:

- *Savage Sam* (TCT, Jul 7 – Sep 29, 1963)
- *Savage Sam* (Walt Disney's World of Adventure #3, Oct 1963)

COLLECTIONS

Video:

1986

DVD:

2003, 2005 2-Movie Collection

Digital:

iTunes, Vudu

Books:

The Disney Live-Action Productions/Walt Disney and Live Action (1994 / 2016) John G. West

Summer Magic (1963)

That WONDERFUL HAYLEY! a-flitterin' in a romantic whirl of her own!

Source:

Mother Carey's Chickens (1911) Kate Douglas Wiggin

Writers:

Sally Benson

Director:

James Neilson

Stars:

Hayley Mills, Burl Ives, Dorothy McGuire, Deborah Walley

Premiere:

Jul 7, 1963

Length:

109 min

CONNECTIONS

Comic Strips:

Summer Magic (Sep 1963)

COLLECTIONS

Video:

1985

DVD:

2005

Digital:

Amazon, iTunes, Vudu

Soundtrack:

1963, 1968 *Music from Three Walt Disney Motion Pictures* (LP) 2004 (Digital)

Books:

The Disney Live-Action Productions/Walt Disney and Live Action (1994 / 2016) John G. West

The Incredible Journey (1963)

Three against the wilderness...nothing could stop them—only instinct to guide then across 200 perilous miles of Canadian wilderness!

Source:

The Incredible Journey (1961) Sheila Burnford

Writers:

James Algar

Director:

Fletcher Markle

Stars:

Bodger, Tao, Luath

Premiere:

Oct 30, 1963

Re-releases:

1969

Length:

80 min

CONNECTIONS

Movies:

Homeward Bound: The Incredible Journey (1993)

COLLECTIONS

Video:

1984, 1994

Laserdisc:

1994

DVD:

2008 Disney Movie Club Exclusive, 2015

Digital:

Amazon, Vudu

Soundtrack:

1964 *Treasury of Dog Stories* (LP)

Books:

True-Life Adventures: A History of Walt Disney's Nature Documentaries (2017) Christian Moran

The Three Lives of Thomasina (1963)

"I am Thomasina! I have three of my nine lives to a little girl lost...a lonely man and a beautiful witch!"

Source:

Thomasina, the Cat Who Thought She Was a God (1957) Paul Gallico

Writers:

Robert Westerby

Director:

Don Chaffey

Stars:

Patrick McGoohan, Susan Hampshire

Premiere:

Dec 11, 1963, New York

Length:

97 min

CONNECTIONS

Comic Strips:

The Three Lives of Thomasina (TCT, Apr 5 – Jun 28, 1964)

COLLECTIONS

Video:

1985, 1993 Studio Film Collection

Laserdisc:

1992 Studio Film Collection

DVD:

2004

Books:

The Disney Live-Action Productions/Walt Disney and Live Action (1994 / 2016) John G. West

Dr. Syn, Alias the Scarecrow (1963)

SMUGGLER'S LOOT...By day, a country parson...by night, a phantom rider!

AKA:

The Scarecrow of Romney Marsh

Source:

- Edited from episodes of *Walt Disney's Wonderful World of Color* TV anthology series
- *Doctor Syn: A Tale of the Romney Marsh* (1915) William Buchanan, Russell Thorndike

Writers:

Robert Westerby

Director:

James Neilson

Stars:

Patrick McGoohan

Premiere:

Dec 22, 1963, UK

US Release:

Nov 21, 1975

Length:

98 min (UK version), 75 min (US edit)

CONNECTIONS

Comic Strips:

The Scarecrow of Romney Marsh (Apr 1964)

TV Anthology:

"The Scarecrow of Romney Marsh" Parts 1–3 (1964), NBC, *Walt Disney's Wonderful World of Color* [Collection > WD Treasures: Dr. Syn: The Scarecrow of Romney Marsh DVD]

COLLECTIONS

Video:

1986

DVD:

2008 *WD Treasures: Dr. Syn: The Scarecrow of Romney Marsh* (UK version)

Books:

The Disney Live-Action Productions/Walt Disney and Live Action (1994 / 2016) John G. West

The Sword in the Stone (1963)

WHIZ-BANG WHIZARD of WHIMSY! The Untold Legend of Young King Arthur and Merlin, the Madcap Magician!

Source:

The Sword in the Stone (1938) T.H. White

Writers:

Bill Peet

Director:

Wolfgang Reitherman

Premiere:

Dec 25, 1963

Re-releases:
1972, 1983

Length:
79 min

CONNECTIONS

Comic Strips:
- *The Sword in the Stone* (TCT, Oct 6 – Dec 29, 1963)
- *The Sword in the Stone* (Feb 1964)
- *The Magic Christmas Tree* (DCS, Dec 4 – 23, 1972)*
- *Madam Mim's Christmas Grudge* (DCS, Dec 3 – 24, 1979)*
- *The Mysterious Christmas Spell* (DCS, Nov 29 – Dec 24, 1982)*
  [*Collection > *Disney's Christmas Classics* (2017)]

Theme Parks:
- King Arthur Carrousel (DL 1955+)
- The Sword in the Stone Ceremony (DL 1983+), (MK 1994+)

COLLECTIONS

Video:
1986, 1994 Masterpiece Collection, 2001 Gold Classic Collection

Laserdisc:
1995 Masterpiece Collection

DVD*/Blu-ray:
2001 Gold Classic Collection*, 2008 45th Anniversary Special Edition*
+ Collector's Box*, 2013 50th Anniversary Edition

Digital:
Amazon, iTunes, Vudu

Soundtrack:
1964, 1972 (LP)

Books:
The Walt Disney Film Archives: The Animated Movies 1921-1968 (2016)
Ed. Daniel Kothenschulte

The Misadventures of Merlin Jones (1964)

The Professor's apprentice turns the town TOPSY-TURVY in the craziest unscientific experiment since FLUBBER!

Writers:

Alfred Lewis Levitt (Tom August), Helen Levitt (Helen August), Bill Walsh (Story)

Director:

Robert Stevenson

Stars:

Tommy Kirk, Annette, Leon Ames, Stuart Erwin

Premiere:

Jan 22, 1964

Re-releases:

1972

Length:

91 min

CONNECTIONS

Comic Strips:

The Misadventures of Merlin Jones (May 1964)

Movies:

The Monkey's Uncle (1965) Sequel

COLLECTIONS

Video:

1986

DVD:

2004

Digital:

Amazon, Vudu

Soundtrack:

1964 (LP)

A Tiger Walks (1964)

A young girl's faith… A town's raw courage… against a frightened tiger on the loose!

Source:

A Tiger Walks (1960) Ian Niall

Writers:

Lowell S. Hawley

Director:

Norman Tokar

Stars:

Brian Keith, Vera Miles

Premiere:

Mar 12, 1964

Length:

91 min

CONNECTIONS

Comic Strips:

- *A Tiger Walks* (TCT, Jan 5 – Mar 29, 1964)
- *A Tiger Walks* (Jun 1964)

COLLECTIONS

Video:

1986

DVD:

2006 Disney Movie Club Exclusive

Books:

The Disney Live-Action Productions/Walt Disney and Live Action (1994 / 2016) John G. West

The Moon-Spinners (1964)

HAYLEY…on a Carefree Holiday…suddenly plunged into the strange world of the Moon-Spinners WALT DISNEY'S surprise in suspense!

Source:

The Moon-Spinners (1962) Mary Stewart

Writers:

Michael Dyne

Director:

James Neilson

Stars:

Hayley Mills, Eli Wallach, Peter McEnery, Joan Greenwood, Irene Papas, Pola Negri

Premiere:

Jul 2, 1964

Length:

119 min

CONNECTIONS

Comic Strips:

- *The Moon-Spinners* (TCT, Jul 5 – Sep 27, 1964)
- *The Moon-Spinners* (Oct 1964)

COLLECTIONS

Video:

1985

Laserdisc:

1997 Studio Film Collection

DVD:

2003 Hayley Mills Collection

Digital:

Amazon, Vudu

Soundtrack:

1964 (LP)

Books:

The Disney Live-Action Productions/Walt Disney and Live Action (1994 / 2016) John G. West

Mary Poppins (1964)

The FAIREST of them all...The FUNNIEST of them all...

Source:

"Mary Poppins" series (1934–1988) P.L. Travers

Writers:

Bill Walsh, Don DaGradi

Director:

Robert Stevenson

Stars:

Julie Andrews, Dick Van Dyke, David Tomlinson, Glynis Johns

Premiere:

Aug 27, 1964, Los Angeles

Re-releases:

1973, 1980

Length:

139 min

CONNECTIONS

Comic Strips:

- *Mary Poppins* (TCT, Oct 4 – Dec 27, 1964)
- *Mary Poppins* (Jan 1965)

Movies:

- *Saving Mr. Banks* (2013) dramatizes the making of *Mary Poppins*
- *Mary Poppins Returns* (2018) sequel

Stage Musical:

Mary Poppins (2004+)

COLLECTIONS

Video:

1980, 1987, 1997 Limited Edition Masterpiece Collection

Laserdisc:

1983, 1992 Archive Collection, 1997 Limited Edition Masterpiece Collection

DVD*/Blu-ray:

1998 Masterpiece Collection*, 2000 Gold Classic Collection*, 2004 40th Anniversary Edition*, 2009 45th Anniversary Special Edition*, 50th Anniversary Edition

Digital:

Amazon, iTunes, Vudu

Soundtrack:

- 1964, 1966, 1973, 1981 (LP)
- 1989, 1991, 1997, 2001, 2004 Special Edition, 2014 The Legacy Collection (CD)

Books:

- *The Disney Live-Action Productions/Walt Disney and Live Action* (1994/2016) John G. West
- *Mary Poppins: Practically Perfect in Every Way* (2007) Brian Sibley
- *The Vault of Walt: Volume 2* (2013) Jim Korkis
- *The Walt Disney Film Archives: The Animated Movies 1921–1968* (2016) Ed. Daniel Kothenschulte

Emil and the Detectives (1964)

WANTED: THREE SKRINKS REWARD: A MILLION LAUGH$!!! laugh it up in lootsville!

AKA:

"The Three Skrinks" (1977–78) TV serialization on *The New Mickey Mouse Club*

Source:

Emil and the Detectives (1929) Erich Kästner

Writers:

AJ Carothers

Director:

Peter Tewksbury

Stars:

Walter Slezak, Bryan Russell, Roger Mobley, Cindy Cassell

Premiere:

Dec 18, 1964

Length:

99 min

CONNECTIONS

Comic Strips:

Emil and the Detectives (Feb 1965)

COLLECTIONS

Video:

1987

DVD:

2011 Disney Movie Club Exclusive

Digital:

iTunes, Vudu

Those Calloways (1965)

They dared to dream the impossible!…with a bear in the cellar, a crow in the kitchen and a lop-eared hound they're A FAMILY YOU'LL NEVER FORGET!

Source:

Swiftwater (1950) Paul Annixter

Writers:

Louis Pelletier

Director:

Norman Tokar

Stars:

Brian Keith, Vera Miles, Brandon de Wilde, Walter Brennan, Ed Wynn

Premiere:

Jan 28, 1965, Atlanta, Georgia

Length:

131 min

CONNECTIONS

Comic Strips:

Those Calloways (TCT, Jan 3 – Mar 28, 1965)

Shorts:

Responsibility: What Are Its Limits? (1975) educational

COLLECTIONS

Video:

1985

DVD:

2004

Digital:

iTunes, Vudu

Soundtrack:

2013 Intrada Special Collection (CD)

Books:

The Disney Live-Action Productions/Walt Disney and Live Action (1994 / 2016) John G. West

The Monkey's Uncle (1965)

Look, Dad—NO ENGINE! Merlin smashes the laugh barrier in his man-powered flying contraption!

Source:

Sequel to *The Misadventures of Merlin Jones* (1964)

Writers:

Alfred Lewis Levitt, Helen Levitt

Director:

Robert Stevenson

Stars:

Tommy Kirk, Annette, Leon Ames, Frank Faylen, Arthur O'Connell

Premiere:

Jun 23, 1965

Length:

90 min

CONNECTIONS

Comic Strips:

- *The Monkey's Uncle* (TCT, Apr 4 – Jun 27, 1965)
- *Merlin Jones as The Monkey's Uncle* (Oct 1965)

Movies:

The Misadventures of Merlin Jones (1964)

COLLECTIONS

Video:
1986

DVD:
2008 Disney Movie Club Exclusive

Digital:
Amazon, Vudu

That Darn Cat! (1965)

It takes a Siamese secret agent to unravel the PURR-fect CRIME!

Source:
Undercover Cat (1963) The Gordons (Gordon Gordon, Mildred Gordon)

Writers:
Bill Walsh, The Gordons (Gordon Gordon, Mildred Gordon)

Director:
Robert Stevenson

Stars:
Hayley Mills, Dean Jones, Dorothy Provine, Roddy McDowall, Neville Brand

Premiere:
Dec 2, 1965

Length:
116 min

CONNECTIONS

Comic Strips:
- *That Darn Cat!* (TCT, Oct 3 – Dec 26, 1965)
- *That Darn Cat* (Feb 1966)

Movies:
That Darn Cat (1997) remake

COLLECTIONS

Video:
1985, 1993 Family Film Collection

Laserdisc:

1993 Studio Film Collection

DVD:

2005, 2009 Double Feature

Soundtrack:

1965 (LP)

Books:

The Disney Live-Action Productions/Walt Disney and Live Action (1994 / 2016) John G. West

The Ugly Dachshund (1966)

IT'S A HAPPY HONEYMOON...until a Great Dane disguised as a Dachshund CRASHES THE PARTY!

Source:

The Ugly Dachshund (1938) G.B. Stern

Writers:

Albert Aley

Director:

Norman Tokar

Stars:

Dean Jones, Suzanne Pleshette, Charlie Ruggles

Premiere:

Feb 4, 1966

Length:

93 min

COLLECTIONS

Video:

1986

DVD:

2004, 2012 Disney 4-Movie Collection: Dogs 1

Digital:

Amazon, Vudu

Lt. Robin Crusoe, U.S.N. (1966)

THE OTHER CRUSOE NEVER HAD IT SO GOOD!

Source:

Robinson Crusoe (1719) Daniel Defoe

Writers:

Don DaGradi, Bill Walsh, Retlaw Yensid [Walt Disney] (Story)

Director:

Byron Paul

Stars:

Dick Van Dyke, Nancy Kwan, Akim Tamiroff

Premiere:

Jul 29, 1966

Re-releases:

1974

Length:

100 min

CONNECTIONS

Comic Strips:

- *Lt. Robin Crusoe, U.S.N.* (TCT, Apr 3 – Jun 26, 1966)
- *Lt. Robin Crusoe, U.S.N.* (Oct 1966)

COLLECTIONS

Video:

1986

DVD:

2005

Digital:

iTunes, Vudu

Books:

The Vault of Walt: Volume 2 (2013) Jim Korkis

Follow Me, Boys! (1966)

IT CAPTURES ALL...all the happiness and heartbreak of being America's #1 hometown hero.

Source:

God and My Country (1954) MacKinlay Kantor

Writers:

Louis Pelletier

Director:

Norman Tokar

Stars:

Fred MacMurray, Vera Miles

Premiere:

Aug 24, 1966

Re-releases:

1976 (Edited)

Length:

131 min (Original), 107 min (Edited)

CONNECTIONS

Comic Strips:

Follow Me, Boys! (TCT, Oct 2 – Nov 27, 1966)

Shorts:

Alcoholism: Who Gets Hurt? (1975) educational

COLLECTIONS

Video:

1984 (edited)

DVD:

2004

Digital:

Amazon, iTunes, Vudu

Soundtrack:

1966 (LP)

Books:

The Disney Live-Action Productions/Walt Disney and Live Action (1994 / 2016) John G. West

The Fighting Prince of Donegal (1966)

A brash young rebel inspires a fight for freedom!

Source:

Red Hugh: Prince of Donegal (1957) Robert T. Reilly

Writers:

Robert Westerby

Director:

Michael O'Herlihy

Stars:

Peter McEnery, Susan Hampshire, Tom Adams, Gordon Jackson

Premiere:

Oct 1, 1966

Length:

100 min

CONNECTIONS

Comic Strips:

- *The Fighting Prince of Donegal* (TCT, Jul 3 – Sep 25, 1966)
- *The Fighting Prince of Donegal* (Jan 1967)

COLLECTIONS

Video:

1986

DVD:

2007 Disney Movie Club Exclusive

Digital:

Vudu

Books:

The Disney Live-Action Productions/Walt Disney and Live Action (1994 / 2016) John G. West

The Adventures of Bullwhip Griffin (1967)

SEE the most BEAUTIFUL BELLES of the Barbary Coast! GOOD GRIEF, GRIFFIN! SEE villainous BANDITS hold up the HANGTOWN STAGE!

Source:
By the Great Horn Spoon! (1963) Sid Fleischman

Writers:
Lowell S. Hawley

Director:
James Neilson

Stars:
Roddy McDowall, Suzanne Pleshette, Karl Malden, Harry Guardino, Richard Haydn

Premiere:
Mar 3, 1967

Length:
110 min

CONNECTIONS

Comic Strips:
- *The Adventures of Bullwhip Griffin* (TCT, Feb 5 – Apr 30, 1967)
- *Bullwhip Griffin* (Jun 1967)

COLLECTIONS

Video:
1986

DVD:
2005

Digital:
iTunes, Vudu

Soundtrack:
1967 (LP)

The Happiest Millionaire (1967)

So big... So lively... So one-in-a-million...THE HAPPIEST MUSICAL OF THE YEAR!

Source:

- *My Philadelphia Father* (1955) Cordelia Drexel Biddle & Kyle Crichton (book)
- *The Happiest Millionaire* (1956) Kyle Crichton (play)

Writers:

AJ Carothers

Director:

Norman Tokar

Stars:

Fred MacMurray, Tommy Steele, Greer Garson, Geraldine Page

Premiere:

Jun 23, 1967, Hollywood

Length:

164 min (original roadshow version), 159 min (roadshow edit), 144 min (stereo release), 141 min (mono release), 172 min (restored roadshow version)

CONNECTIONS

Comic Strips:

- *The Happiest Millionaire* (TCT, Aug 6, – Oct 29, 1967)
- *The Happiest Millionaire* (Apr 1968)

COLLECTIONS

Video:

1984 (Stereo release)

DVD:

1999 Anchor Bay: Road Show Edition, 2004 Restored Roadshow Edition, 2012 Disney 4-Movie Collection: Classics (restored roadshow version)

Digital:

Amazon, iTunes, Vudu (restored roadshow version)

Soundtrack:

1967 (LP), 2002 (CD/Digital)

Books:

The Disney Live-Action Productions/Walt Disney and Live Action (1994 / 2016) John G. West

The Gnome-Mobile (1967)

A TALL TALE ABOUT LITTLE PEOPLE! They cut a timber tycoon down to size!

Source:

The Gnomobile (1936) Upton Sinclair

Writers:

Ellis Kadison

Director:

Robert Stevenson

Stars:

Walter Brennan

Premiere:

Jul 12, 1967

Length:

85 min

CONNECTIONS

Comic Strips:

- *The Gnome-Mobile* (TCT, May 7 – Jul 30, 1967)
- *The Gnome-Mobile* (Oct 1967)

COLLECTIONS

Video:

1985

DVD:

2004, 2012 Disney 4-Movie Collection: Classics

Digital:

Amazon, Vudu

Books:

The Disney Live-Action Productions/Walt Disney and Live Action (1994 / 2016) John G. West

Charlie, the Lonesome Cougar (1967)

The exciting adventures of a TEEN-AGE MOUNTAIN LION!

Source:

Jack Speirs, Winston Hibler (Story)

Writers:

Jack Speirs

Director:

Winston Hibler

Premiere:

Oct 18, 1967

Length:

75 min

COLLECTIONS

Video:

1985

DVD:

2004

Digital:

Amazon, iTunes, Vudu

The Jungle Book (1967)

The Jungle is JUMPIN'!

Source:

Mowgli stories in *The Jungle Book* (1894) Rudyard Kipling

Writers:

Larry Clemmons, Ralph Wright, Ken Anderson, Vance Gerry

Director:

Wolfgang Reitherman

Stars:

Phil Harris, Sebastian Cabot, Louis Prima, George Sanders, Sterling Holloway

Premiere:

Oct 18, 1967

Re-releases:

1978, 1984, 1990

Length:

78 min

CONNECTIONS

Comic Strips:

- *The Jungle Book* (Jan 1967)
- *The Jungle Book* (TCT, Nov 5, 1967 – Jan 28, 1968)

Movies:

- *The Jungle Book* (1994) live-action remake
- *The Jungle Book: Mowgli's Story* (DTV 1998) live-action sequel
- *The Jungle Book 2* (2003) sequel
- *The Jungle Book* (2018) CGI/live-action remake

Shorts:

The Jungle Book: A Lesson in Accepting Change (1981) educational

Stage Musical:

The Jungle Books KIDS (?) Disney Theatrical Licensing

TV Movie:

TaleSpin: Plunder and Lightning (1990) syndicated

TV Series:

- *TaleSpin* (1990-1991) Disney Channel, 65 episodes [Collection > *TaleSpin Volumes* Vol 1–3 DVD (2013-2015), Digital (2016)]
- *Jungle Cubs* (1996-1998) ABC, 21 episodes [Collection > *Jungle Cubs* Digital (2016)]

Video Games:

- *Walt Disney's The Jungle Book* (1993) GB, GBA, GG, MD/G, NES, PC, SMS, SNES
- *Walt Disney's The Jungle Book: Mowgli's Wild Adventure* (2000) GBC
- *Walt Disney's The Jungle Book: Rhythm n' Groove/Groove Party* (2000) PS, PS2

COLLECTIONS

Video:

1991, 1997 30th Anniversary Limited Edition / Masterpiece Collection

Laserdisc:

1992, 1997 30th Anniversary Limited Edition / Masterpiece Collection

DVD*/Blu-ray:

1999 Limited Issue*, 2007 40th Anniversary Platinum Edition*, 2014 Diamond Edition

Soundtrack:

- 1967, 1968 *More Jungle Book*, 1981, 2016 (LP)
- 1990, 1997, 2001, 2014 *Songs and Story* (CD)

Books:

- *Le Livre de la Jungle* (2009) Pierre Lambert
- *The Walt Disney Film Archives: The Animated Movies 1921–1968* (2016) Ed. Daniel Kothenschulte

Blackbeard's Ghost (1968)

Free wheeling... fun loving...HE'S OUT'A SIGHT! IT'S SUPER... NATURALLY!

Source:

Blackbeard's Ghost (1965) Ben Stahl

Writers:

Bill Walsh, Don DaGradi

Director:

Robert Stevenson

Stars:

Peter Ustinov, Dean Jones, Suzanne Pleshette

Premiere:

Feb 8, 1968

Re-releases:

1976

Length:

107 min

CONNECTIONS

Comic Strips:

- *Blackbeard's Ghost* (TCT, Feb 4 – Apr 28, 1968)
- *Blackbeard's Ghost* (Jun 1968)

COLLECTIONS

Video:
1982, 1990

Laserdisc:
1990

DVD:
2002

Blu-ray:
2016 Disney Movie Club Exclusive

Digital:
Amazon, iTunes, Vudu

Books:
The Vault of Walt: Volume 2 (2013) Jim Korkis

The One and Only, Genuine, Original Family Band (1968)

Get ready to hear! Get ready to cheer!

Source:
The Family Band (1961) Laura Bower Van Nuys

Writers:
Lowell S. Hawley

Director:
Michael O'Herlihy

Stars:
Walter Brennan, Buddy Ebsen, Janet Blair

Premiere:
Mar 21, 1968, New York

Length:
110 min

COLLECTIONS

Video:
1981, 1985

Laserdisc:
1982

DVD:
2004, 2012 Disney 4-Movie Collection: Classics

Digital:
Amazon, Vudu

Soundtrack:
1968 (LP)

Never a Dull Moment (1968)

They're having such a wonderful crime...

Source:
A Thrill a Minute with Jack Albany (1967) John Godney

Writers:
AJ Carothers

Director:
Jerry Paris

Stars:
Dick Van Dyke, Edward G. Robinson, Dorothy Provine

Premiere:
Jun 26, 1968

Re-releases:
1977

Length:
100 min

CONNECTIONS

Comic Strips:
Never a Dull Moment (TCT, May 5 – Jul 28, 1968)

COLLECTIONS

Video:
1985 (90 min)

DVD:
2004

Digital:

Amazon, iTunes, Vudu

The Horse in the Gray Flannel Suit (1968)

JOIN-IN the all-Disney FUN-IN!

Source:

The Year of the Horse (1955) Eric Hatch

Writers:

Louis Pelletier

Director:

Norman Tokar

Stars:

Dean Jones, Diane Baker

Premiere:

Dec 20, 1968, New York

Length:

113 min

CONNECTIONS

Comic Strips:

The Horse in the Gray Flannel Suit (TCT, Oct 6 – Dec 29, 1968)

COLLECTIONS

Video:

1986, 1997 Kurt Russell Collection

DVD:

2003 Kurt Russell Collection, 2012 Disney 4-Movie Collection: Kurt Russell

The Love Bug (1968)

It's a Love-in for Herbie…the incredible little car who shifts for himself!

Source:

Car, Boy, Girl (1961) Gordon Buford

Writers:

Bill Walsh, Don DaGradi

Director:

Robert Stevenson

Stars:

Dean Jones, Michele Lee, David Tomlinson, Buddy Hackett

Premiere:

Dec 24, 1968 (Limited)

Re-releases:

1979

Length:

108 min

CONNECTIONS

Comic Strips:

- *The Love Bug* (TCT, Mar 2 – May 25, 1969)
- *The Love Bug* (Jun 1969)

Movies:

- *Herbie Rides Again* (1974) sequel
- *Herbie Goes to Monte Carlo* (1977) sequel
- *Herbie Goes Bananas* (1980) sequel
- *Herbie: Fully Loaded* (2005) sequel

TV Series:

Herbie, the Love Bug (1982) CBS, 5 episodes, sequel

TV Movie:

The Love Bug (1997) ABC, *The Wonderful World of Disney*, sequel

Video Games:

Disney's Herbie: Rescue Rally (2007) DS

COLLECTIONS

Video:

1980, 1992 Studio Film Collection

Laserdisc:

1982, 1992 Studio Film Collection

DVD:

2003 Special Edition, 2004 Herbie, the Love Bug Collection, 2012 Disney 4-Movie Collection: Herbie

Blu-ray:
2014 45th Anniversary Edition / Disney Movie Club Exclusive

Digital:
Amazon, Vudu

Soundtrack:
1969 *The Story of the Love Bug* (LP)

Books:
The Vault of Walt: Volume 6 (2017) Jim Korkis

Smith! (1969)

The trouble with Smith was Indians... the trouble with Indians was not enough Smiths! SMITH! ...his name is common but his kind is rare

Source:
Breaking Smith's Quarter Horse (1969) Paul St. Pierre

Writers:
Louis Pelletier

Director:
Michael O'Herlihy

Stars:
Glenn Ford

Premiere:
Mar 21, 1969

Length:
102 min

CONNECTIONS

Comic Strips:
Smith! (TCT, Jan 5 – Feb 23, 1969)

COLLECTIONS

Video:
1987

DVD:
2009 Disney Movie Club Exclusive

Digital:

Amazon, iTunes, Vudu

Rascal (1969)

Some things are IRRESISTIBLE...a ring-tailed rapscallion...a freckle-faced boy... and a summer warm with laughter!

Source:

Rascal (1963) Sterling North

Writers:

Harold Swanton

Director:

Norman Tokar

Stars:

Steve Forrest, Bill Mumy

Premiere:

Jun 11, 1969

Length:

85 min

COLLECTIONS

Video/DVD:

2002, 2012 Disney 4-Movie Collection: Dogs 2

Digital:

Amazon, Vudu

The Computer Wore Tennis Shoes (1969)

Programmed for laughs!

Writers:

Joseph L. McEveety

Director:

Robert Butler

Stars:

Kurt Russell, Cesar Romero, Joe Flynn

Premiere:

Dec 31, 1969

Length:

91 min

CONNECTIONS

Comic Strips:

The Computer Wore Tennis Shoes (TCT, Dec 7, 1969 – Feb 22, 1970)

Movies:

- *Now You See Him, Now You Don't* (1972) sequel
- *The Strongest Man in the World* (1975) sequel

TV Movie:

The Computer Wore Tennis Shoes (1995) ABC, remake

COLLECTIONS

Video:

1985

DVD:

2003 Kurt Russell Collection, 2010 Double Feature, 2012 Disney 4-Movie Collection: Kurt Russell

Blu-ray:

2014 45th Anniversary Edition / Disney Movie Club Exclusive

Digital:

Amazon, Vudu

Soundtrack:

1969 (LP)

PART FOUR

Movies: 1970–1979

King of the Grizzlies (1970)

HALF A TON AND TEN FEET TALL!

Source:

The Biography of a Grizzly (1900) Ernest Thompson Seton

Writers:

Jack Speirs (screenplay), Rod Peterson, Norman Wright (adaptation)

Director:

Ron Kelly

Premiere:

Feb 11, 1970

Length:

93 min

CONNECTIONS

Comic Strips:

King of the Grizzlies (TCT, Mar 1 – May 31, 1970)

COLLECTIONS

Video:

1986, 2002

DVD:

2002

Digital:

Amazon, iTunes, Vudu

The Boatniks (1970)

MAN THE LAFFBOATS! Here come those marina madcaps who go down to the sea in ships – EVERY BLESSED WEEKEND

Writers:

Arthur Julian, Marty Roth

Director:

Norman Tokar

Stars:

Robert Morse, Stefanie Powers, Phil Silvers

Premiere:

Jul 1, 1970

Length:

100 min

CONNECTIONS

Comic Strips:

- *The Boatniks* (TCT, Jun 7 – Aug 31, 1970)
- *The Boatniks* (Walt Disney Showcase #1, Oct 1970)

COLLECTIONS

Video:

1984

DVD:

2005

Blu-ray:

2016 45th Anniversary Edition / Disney Movie Club Exclusive

Digital:

Vudu

The Wild Country (1970)

THE NEWCOMERS...green as the mountain country, they stood together to claim a dream!

Source:

Little Britches (1950) Ralph Moody

Writers:

Calvin Clements Jr., Paul Savage

Director:

Robert Totten

Stars:

Steve Forrest, Vera Miles, Jack Elam, Ronny Howard

Premiere:

Dec 15, 1970

Length:

100 min

COLLECTIONS

Video:

1986

DVD:

2009 Disney Movie Club Exclusive

Digital:

Amazon, Vudu

The Aristocats (1970)

Meet the cats who know where it's at... for fun, music and adventure!

Source:

Unproduced *Walt Disney's Wonderful World of Color* story (1962) Tom McGowan, Tom Rowe

Writers:

Larry Clemmons, Vance Gerry, Ken Anderson, Frank Thomas, Eric Cleworth, Julius Svendsen, Ralph Wright

Director:

Wolfgang Reitherman

Premiere:

Dec 11, 1970, Los Angeles

Re-releases:

1980, 1987

Length:

78 min

CONNECTIONS
Comic Strips:
- *The Aristocats* (TCT, Sep 6 – Dec 27, 1970)
- *The Aristocats* (Mar 1971)
- *The Aristokittens Meet Jiminy Cricket* (#1, Oct 1971)
- *The Aristokittens* (#2–9, Jan 1972 – Oct 1975)

COLLECTIONS
Video:
1996 Masterpiece Collection, 2000 Gold Classic Collection

Laserdisc:
1996 Masterpiece Collection

DVD*/Blu-ray:
2000 Gold Classic Collection*, 2012 Special Edition + Disney Movie Club Exclusive

Digital:
Amazon, Vudu

Soundtrack:
1970 (LP), 1996, 2015 The Legacy Collection (CD)

Books:
The Revised Vault of Walt (2012) Jim Korkis

The Barefoot Executive (1971)
Look who's GONE BANANAS!

Writers:
Joseph L. McEveety (screenplay), Lila Garrett, Bernie Kahn, Stewart C. BIllett (story)

Director:
Robert Butler

Stars:
Kurt Russell, Joe Flynn, Harry Morgan, Wally Cox

Premiere:
Mar 17, 1971

Length:
96 min

CONNECTIONS

Comic Strips:

The Barefoot Executive (TCT, Jan 3 – Mar 28, 1971)

TV Movie:

The Barefoot Executive (1995) ABC, remake

COLLECTIONS

Video:

1985, 1997Kurt Russell Collection

DVD:

2004

Digital:

Amazon, Vudu

Soundtrack:

1971 (LP)

Scandalous John (1971)

McCanless—the one cowpoke crazy enough to fight the windmills of change!

Source:

Don Quixote (1605/1615) Miguel de Cervantes

Writers:

Bill Walsh, Don DaGradi

Director:

Robert Butler

Stars:

Brian Keith, Alfonso Arau

Premiere:

Jun 22, 1971 (limited)

Length:

114 min

COLLECTIONS

Video:

1986

DVD:

2009 Disney Movie Club Exclusive

Digital:

Amazon, iTunes, Vudu

Soundtrack:

1971 (LP)

The Million Dollar Duck (1971)

What an EGGstravaganza!...all about a drop-out duck who lays a 24 karat omelette in the tax assessor's lap!

AKA:

The $1,000,000 Duck

Writers:

Ted Key (story), Roswell Rogers

Director:

Vincent McEveety

Stars:

Dean Jones, Sandy Duncan, Joe Flynn, Tony Roberts, James Gregory

Premiere:

Jun 30, 1971

Length:

92 min

CONNECTIONS

Comic Strips:

- *The Million Dollar Duck* (TCT, Apr 4 – Jun 27, 1971)
- *$1,000,000 Duck* (Walt Disney Showcase #5, Oct 1971)

COLLECTIONS

Video:

1986

DVD:

2005

Digital:

Amazon, Vudu

Bedknobs and Broomsticks (1971)

You'll bewitched...you'll bedazzled! A most magical adventure...BEYOND ANYTHING BEFORE!

Source:

The Magic Bedknob (1943) & *Bonfires and Broomsticks* (1945) Mary Norton

Writers:

Bill Walsh, Don DaGradi (screenplay), Ralph Wright, Ted Berman (animation story)

Director:

Robert Stevenson

Stars:

Angela Lansbury, David Tomlinson

Premiere:

Oct 7, 1971, UK

US Release:

Nov 11, 1971, New York

Re-releases:

1979

Length:

117 min (original), 98 min (1979 cut), 139 min (restored version)

CONNECTIONS

Comic Strips:

- *Bedknobs and Broomsticks* (TCT, Jul 4 – Oct 31, 1971)
- *Bedknobs and Broomsticks* (Walt Disney Showcase #6, Jan 1972)

COLLECTIONS

Video:

1980 (1979 cut), 1985 (original), 1989 (original)

Laserdisc:

1983 (original), 1997 25th Anniversary Special Edition (restored version)

DVD*/Blu-ray:

- 2001 30th Anniversary Edition* (restored version)

- 2009 Enchanted Musical Edition* (restored version), 2014 Special Edition (original)

Digital:

Amazon, iTunes, Vudu (original)

Soundtrack:

1971 (LP), 2002 (CD)

The Biscuit Eater (1972)

TWO SMALL PARTNERS...they risked EVERYTHING for a loveable no count hound!

Source:

- Remake of Paramount's *The Biscuit Eater* (1940)
- "The Eater" (1939) James H. Street

Writers:

Lawrence Edward Watkin

Director:

Vincent McEveety

Stars:

Earl Holliman, Pat Crowley, Lew Ayres, Godfrey Cambridge

Premiere:

Mar 22, 1972

Length:

90 min

COLLECTIONS

DVD:

2002

Digital:

Amazon, Vudu

Napoleon and Samantha (1972)

Two runaways and a guardian lion lost in the wilderness...AN INCREDIBLE ADVENTURE!

Writers:

Stewart Raffill

Director:

Bernard McEveety

Stars:

Michael Douglas, Will Geer, Johnny Whitaker, Jodie Foster

Premiere:

Jul 5, 1972

Length:

91 min

CONNECTIONS

Comic Strips:

- *Napoleon and Samantha* (TCT, Jan 2 – Mar 26, 1972)
- *Napoleon and Samantha* (Walt Disney Showcase #10, Sep 1972)

Shorts:

Death: How Can You Live with It? (1976) Educational

COLLECTIONS

Video:

1986

DVD:

2004

Digital:

Amazon, Vudu

Soundtrack:

1972 (LP)

Now You See Him, Now You Don't (1972)

He's going...going...gone!

Source:

Sequel to *The Computer Wore Tennis Shoes* (1969)

Writers:

Joseph L. McEveety (screenplay), Robert L. King (story)

Director:

Robert Butler

Stars:

Kurt Russell, Cesar Romero, Joe Flynn, Jim Backus, William Windom

Premiere:

Jul 7, 1972, Edmonton, Canada

US Release:

Jul 12, 1972

Length:

88 min

CONNECTIONS

Comic Strips:

Now You See Him, Now You Don't (TCT, Apr 2 – Jun 25, 1972)

COLLECTIONS

Video:

1985

DVD:

2004, 2012 Disney 4-Movie Collection: Kurt Russell

Digital:

Amazon, iTunes, Vudu

Run, Cougar, Run (1972)

Free as the wind...But nowhere to run!

Source:

The Mountain Lion (1969) Robert William Murphy

Writers:

Louis Pelletier

Director:

Jerome Courtland

Stars:

Stuart Whitman

Premiere:

Oct 18, 1972

Length:

87 min

Snowball Express (1972)

SCHUSS-BOOM-OUCH!..it's fractured trees and flying skis!!

Source:

Chateau Bon Vivant (1967) Frankie & Johnny O'Rear

Writers:

Don Tait, Jim Parker, Arnold Margolin

Director:

Norman Tokar

Stars:

Dean Jones, Nancy Olson, Harry Morgan, Keenan Wynn

Premiere:

Dec 20, 1972, Bismark, North Dakota

Length:

93 min

CONNECTIONS

Comic Strips:

Snowball Express (TCT, Oct 1 – Dec 31, 1972)

COLLECTIONS

Video:

1982

DVD:

2003

Digital:

Amazon, iTunes, Vudu

The World's Greatest Athlete (1973)

From the JUNGLE to the GYM… HE'S THE GREATEST!

Writers:

Gerald Gardner, Dee Caruso

Director:

Robert Scheerer

Stars:

Tim Conway, Jan-Michael Vincent, John Amos, Roscoe Lee Browne

Premiere:

Feb 4, 1973, New York

Length:

93 min

CONNECTIONS

Comic Strips:

- *The World's Greatest Athlete* (TCT, Jan 7 – Mar 25, 1973)
- *The World's Greatest Athlete* (Walt Disney Showcase #14, Apr 1973)

COLLECTIONS

Video:

1986

DVD:

2005

Digital:

Amazon, Vudu

Charley and the Angel (1973)

SUPER (natural) COMEDY!

Source:

The Golden Evenings of Summer (1971) Will Stanton

Writers:

Roswell Rogers

Director:

Vincent McEveety

Stars:

Fred MacMurray, Cloris Leachman

Premiere:

Mar 23, 1973

Length:

93 min

COLLECTIONS

Video:

1986

DVD:

2011 Disney Movie Club Exclusive

Digital:

Amazon, iTunes, Vudu

One Little Indian (1973)

A boy turned Indian, a trooper turned deserter and ROSIE, a camel turned IMPOSSIBLE!

Writers:

Harry Spalding

Director:

Bernard McEveety

Stars:

James Garner, Vera Miles

Premiere:

Jun 20, 1973

Length:

91 min

CONNECTIONS

Comic Strips:

One Little Indian (TCT, Jul 1 – Sep 30, 1973)

COLLECTIONS

Video:

1986

DVD:

2003 Anchor Bay, 2004

Digital:

Amazon, iTunes, Vudu

Soundtrack:

2009 Intrada Special Collection, 2017 (CD)

Robin Hood (1973)

Join the MERRIEST MENagerie in the world's best-loved legend. The way it REALLY happened…

Source:

Legend of Robin Hood

Writers:

Larry Clemmons (story), Ken Anderson, Vance Gerry, Frank Thomas, Eric Cleworth, Julius Svendsen, David Michener

Premiere:

Nov 8, 1973

Re-releases:

1982

Length:

83 min

CONNECTIONS

Comic Strips:

- *Robin Hood* (TCT, Oct 7, 1973 – Jan 27, 1974)
- *King of the Forest* & *The Enchanted Sword** (Robin Hood, Dec 1973)
- *The Mystery of Sherwood Forest** & *The Lucky Hat** (Robin Hood: The Mystery of Sherwood Forest, Dec 1973)
- *In King Richard's Service** & *The Golden Arrow** (Robin Hood In King Richard's Service, Dec 1973)
- *The Wizard's Ring** & *The King's Ransom** (Robin Hood and the Wizard's Ring, Dec 1973) *Reprinted in The Adventures of Robin Hood #1-7, Mar 1974 – Jan 1975
- *Ring Out Glad Bell* (The Adventures of Robin Hood #4, Aug 1974)
- *Mirrors and Other Magic Things* (The Adventures of Robin Hood #5, Sep 1974)
- *The Imp of Doom* (The Adventures of Robin Hood #6, Nov 1974)
- *Robin Hood and the Baron of Bottomly* (The Adventures of Robin Hood #7, Jan 1975)
- *The Day Christmas Was Banned* (DCS, Dec 4 – 24, 1978) [Collection > *Disney's Christmas Classics* (2017)]
- *Robin Hood in: Rich John, Poor John* (TCT, Apr 1 – Jun 24, 1984)

Movies:

The Story of Robin Hood and His Merrie Men (1952) based on same legend

COLLECTIONS

Video:

1984, 1991, 1994 Masterpiece Collection

Laserdisc:

1991

DVD*/Blu-ray:

- 2000 Gold Classic Collection*
- 2006 Most Wanted Edition*
- 2013 40th Anniversary Edition

Digital:

Amazon, Vudu

Soundtrack:

1973 (LP), 2017 The Legacy Collection (CD)

Superdad (1973)

Young love is making waves…and Dad's about to get beached!

Writers:

Harlan Ware (story), Joseph L. McEveety

Director:

Vincent McEveety

Stars:

Bob Crane, Barbara Rush, Kurt Russell, Joe Flynn, Kathleen Cody

Premiere:

Dec 14, 1973, Los Angeles

Length:

96 min

COLLECTIONS

Video:

1985

DVD:

2008 Disney Movie Club Exclusive

Digital:

iTunes, Vudu

Herbie Rides Again (1974)

The Love Bug is back...doing his things! Herbie's DARING, Herbie's PLAYFUL, Herbie's ROMANTIC, Herbie's ATHLETIC, Herbie's DEFIANT

Source:

First sequel to *The Love Bug* (1968)

Writers:

Gordon Buford (story), Bill Walsh (screenplay)

Director:

Robert Stevenson

Stars:

Helen Hayes, Ken Berry, Stefanie Powers, John McIntire, Keenan Wynn

Premiere:

Feb 12, 1974, London

US Release:

Jun 6, 1974

Length:

88 min

CONNECTIONS

Comic Strips:

- *Herbie Rides Again* (TCT, May 5 – Jul 28, 1974)
- *Herbie Rides Again* (Walt Disney Showcase #24, Aug 1974)

COLLECTIONS

Video:

1982, 1993 Studio Film Collection

Laserdisc:

1983, 1993 Studio Film Collection

DVD:

- 2004 + Herbie, the Love Bug Collection, 2009 Double Feature,
- 2012 Disney 4-Movie Collection: Herbie

Blu-ray:

2014 Disney Movie Club Exclusive / 40th Anniversary Edition

Digital:

Amazon, iTunes, Vudu

The Bears and I (1974)

To find himself, he lost himself in adventurous high country!

Source:

The Bears and I (1971) Robert Franklin Leslie

Writers:

John Whedon (screenplay), Jack Speirs (narration)

Director:

Bernard McEveety

Stars:

Patrick Wayne

Premiere:

Jul 31, 1974

Length:

89 min

CONNECTIONS

Comic Strips:

The Bears and I (TCT, Aug 4 – Sep 29, 1974)

COLLECTIONS

DVD:

1999 Anchor Bay

Digital:

Amazon

The Castaway Cowboy (1974)

BIG ISLAND AVENTURES! He tamed the wild cattle...and the WILD natives of old Hawaii

Writers:

Richard M. Bluel, Hugh Benson (story), Don Tait (story/screenplay)

Director:

Vincent McEveety

Stars:

James Garner, Vera Miles, Robert Culp

Premiere:

Aug 7, 1974

Length:

91 min

COLLECTIONS

Video:

1984

DVD:

2000 Anchor Bay, 2009 Disney Movie Club Exclusive

Digital:

Amazon, Vudu

The Island at the Top of the World (1974)

ADVENTURE BEYOND IMAGINATION

Source:

The Lost Ones (1961) Ian Cameron

Writers:

John Whedon

Director:

Robert Stevenson

Stars:

David Hartman, Donald Sinden, Jacques Marin, Mako, David Gwillim, Agneta Eckemyr

Premiere:

Dec 16, 1974, London

US Release:

Dec 20, 1974

Length:

94 min

CONNECTIONS

Comic Strips:

The Island at the Top of the World (TCT, Oct 6, 1974 – Jan 26, 1975)

COLLECTIONS

Video:

1983, 1994 Studio Film Collection

Laserdisc:

1994 Studio Film Collection

DVD:

1999 Anchor Bay, 2002 Anchor Bay, 2004 30th Anniversary Edition

Digital:

Vudu

Soundtrack:

1974 (LP), 2012 Intrada Special Collection (CD)

The Strongest Man in the World (1975)

THE BIGGEST DUMBBELL ON CAMPUS...and the secret formula got it off the ground!

Source:

Second sequel to *The Computer Wore Tennis Shoes* (1969)

Writers:

Joseph L. McEveety, Herman Groves

Director:

Vincent McEveety

Stars:

Kurt Russell, Joe Flynn, Eve Arden, Cesar Romero, Phil Silvers

Premiere:

Feb 6, 1975

Length:

92 min

COLLECTIONS

Video:

1998

DVD:

2004, 2010 Double Feature, 2012 Disney 4-Movie Collection: Kurt Russell

Blu-ray:

2016 Disney Movie Club Exclusive / 40th Anniversary Edition

Digital:

Amazon, Vudu

Escape to Witch Mountain (1975)

Caught in a world where they don't belong...they have one chance to escape!

Source:

Escape to Witch Mountain (1968) Alexander Key

Writers:

Robert M. Young

Director:

John Hough

Stars:

Eddie Albert, Ray Milland, Donald Pleasance

Premiere:

Mar 21, 1975

Length:

97 min

CONNECTIONS

Comic Strips:

- *Escape to Witch Mountain* (TCT, Feb 3 – Apr 27, 1975)
- *Escape to Witch Mountain* (Walt Disney Showcase #29, Jun 1975)

Movies:

- *Return from Witch Mountain* (1978) sequel
- *Race to Witch Mountain* (2009) remake

TV Movies:

- *Beyond Witch Mountain* (1982) CBS, *Walt Disney*, TV pilot/sequel [Collection > DVD (2012 Disney Generations Collection)]
- *Escape to Witch Mountain* (1995) Disney Channel Premiere Film, remake

COLLECTIONS

Video:

1980, 1985, 1993 Studio Film Collection

Laserdisc:

1981, 1982, 1993 Studio Film Collection

DVD:

2003 Special Edition, 2009 Family Classics

Blu-ray:

2015 Disney Movie Club Exclusive / 40th Anniversary Edition

Digital:

Amazon, iTunes, Vudu

Soundtrack:

1975 (LP), 2015 Intrada Special Collection (CD)

The Apple Dumpling Gang (1975)

First they blew into town…then they BLEW IT UP! It's a 24-Karat caper…and that's NO BULLion!

Source:

The Apple Dumpling Gang (1971) Jack Bickham

Writers:

Don Tait

Director:

Norman Tokar

Stars:

Bill Bixby, Susan Clark, Don Knotts, Tin Conway, David Wayne, Slim Pickens

Premiere:

Jul 4, 1975

Length:

100 min

CONNECTIONS

Comic Strips:

The Apple Dumpling Gang (TCT, May 4 – Jun 29, 1975)

Movies:

The Apple Dumpling Gang Rides Again (1979) sequel

TV Movie:

Tales of The Apple Dumpling Gang (1982) CBS, *Walt Disney*, TV pilot/remake

TV Series:

Gun Shy (1983) CBS, 6 episodes

COLLECTIONS

Video:

1980, 1985, 1992 Studio Film Collection

Laserdisc:

1992 Studio Film Collection

DVD:

- 2003 Special Edition, 2008 2-Movie Collection,
- 2012 Disney 4-Movie Collection: Don Knotts

Blu-ray:

2014 Disney Movie Club Exclusive / 40th Anniversary Edition

Digital:

Amazon, iTunes, Vudu

One of Our Dinosaurs is Missing (1975)

A FUNKY FOSSIL FROLIC! THIS SIX-TON BAG OF BONES IS THE TARGET OF A WORLD-WIDE SEARCH

Source:

The Great Dinosaur Robbery (1970) David Forrest

Writers:

Bill Walsh

Director:

Robert Stevenson

Stars:

Peter Ustinov, Helen Hayes

Premiere:

Jul 9, 1975

Length:

94 min

CONNECTIONS

Comic Strips:

One of Our Dinosaurs Is Missing (TCT, Jul 6 – Sep 28, 1975)

COLLECTIONS

Video:

1986

DVD:

2004 (UK)

Digital:

Amazon, iTunes, Vudu

The Best of Walt Disney's True-Life Adventures (1975)

POWERFUL! PRIMITVE! UNTAMED! For the first time see all the drama, humor, warmth & excitement from 8 Academy Award Winners!

Source:

Compilation of clips from True-Life Adventure series: *Seal Island* (1948), *Beaver Valley* (1950), *Nature's Half Acre* (1951), *The Olympic Elk* (1952), *Water Birds* (1952), *Bear Country* (1953), *Prowlers of the Everglades* (1953), *The Living Desert* (1953), *The Vanishing Prairie* (1954), *The African Lion* (1955), *Secrets of Life* (1956), *White Wilderness* (1958), *Jungle Cat* (1960)

Writers:

James Algar, Winston Hibler, Ted Sears

Director:

James Algar

Premiere:

Oct 8, 1975

Length:

89 min

COLLECTIONS

Digital:

Amazon, iTunes, Vudu

Ride a Wild Pony (1975)

ALL HE ASKED WAS TO RUN FREE...

Source:

A Sporting Proposition (1973) James Aldridge

Writers:

Rosemary Anne Sisson

Director:

Don Chaffey

Stars:

Michael Craig, John Meillon

Premiere:

Nov 2, 1975, Australia

US Release:

Dec 25, 1975, Los Angeles

Length:

91 min

CONNECTIONS

Shorts:

Being Right: Can You Still Lose? (1976) educational

COLLECTIONS

Video:

1987, 1995

DVD:

2007 Disney Movie Club Exclusive, 2009

Digital:

Amazon, iTunes, Vudu

No Deposit, No Return (1976)

THE BIG HEIST! A pair of jokers make double trouble in a hullaba-lulu of a caper

Writers:

Joseph L. McEveety (story), Arthur Alsberg, Don Nelson (screenplay)

Director:

Norman Tokar

Stars:

David Niven, Darren McGavin, Don Knotts, Herschel Bernardi, Barbara Feldon

Premiere:

Feb 5, 1976

Length:

112 min

CONNECTIONS

Comic Strips:

No Deposit, No Return (TCT, Dec 7, 1975 – Feb 29, 1976)

COLLECTIONS

Video:

1986

DVD:

2004

Digital:

Amazon, iTunes, Vudu

The Littlest Horse Thieves (1976)

DARING – DETERMINED – they took the whole town… by surprise!

AKA:

Escape from the Dark (UK)

Writers:

Rosemary Anne Sisson (screenplay), Burt Kennedy (story)

Director:

Charles Jarrott

Stars:

Alastair Sim, Peter Barkworth, Maurice Colbourne, Susan Tibbs, Geraldine McEwan

Premiere:

May 26, 1976, UK

US Release:

Mar 11, 1977

Length:

104 min

COLLECTIONS

Video:

1986

DVD:

2003 Anchor Bay, 2009 Disney Movie Club Exclusive

Digital:

Amazon, Vudu

Soundtrack:

1976 (LP, UK), 2013 (CD, Spain)

Treasure of Matecumbe (1976)

Source:

A Journey to Matecumbe (1961) Robert Lewis Taylor

Writers:

Don Tait

Director:

Vincent McEveety

Stars:

Robert Foxworth, Joan Hackett, Peter Ustinov, Vic Morrow

Premiere:

Jul 1, 1976

Length:

116 min

CONNECTIONS

Comic Strips:

Treasure of Matecumbe (TCT, Jun 6 – Aug 29, 1976)

COLLECTIONS

Video:

1986

DVD:

2007 Disney Movie Club Exclusive, 2008

Digital:

iTunes, Vudu

Gus (1976)

It's the league's leading laugh scorer!

Writers:

Ted Key (story), Arthur Alsberg, Don Nelson

Director:

Vincent McEveety

Stars:

Edward Asner, Don Knotts, Gary Grimes, Tim Conway

Premiere:

Jul 7, 1976

Length:

96 min

CONNECTIONS

Comic Strips:

Gus (TCT, Mar 7 – May 30, 1976)

COLLECTIONS

Video:

1981, 1985

Laserdisc:

1983

DVD:

2003 Don Knotts Collection, 2012 Disney 4-Movie Collection: Don Knotts

Digital:

iTunes, Vudu

Freaky Friday (1976)

Daughter and mother become each other…A GREAT NEW COMEDY SWITCH from WALT DISNEY PRODUCTIONS

Source:

Freaky Friday (1972) Mary Rodgers

Writers:

Mary Rodgers

Director:

Gary Nelson

Stars:

Barbara Harris, Jodie Foster, John Astin

Premiere:

Dec 17, 1976, Los Angeles

Length:

98 min

CONNECTIONS

Comic Strips:

Freaky Friday (TCT, Dec 5, 1976 – Feb 27, 1977)

Movies:

Freaky Friday (2003) Remake

Stage Musical:

Freaky Friday (2016+)

TV Movie:

Freaky Friday (1995) ABC, Remake

COLLECTIONS

Video:

1982, 1992 Studio Film Collection

Laserdisc:

1992 Studio Film Collection

DVD:

2004

Blu-ray:

2018 Disney Movie Club Exclusive

Digital:

Amazon, iTunes, Vudu

Soundtrack:

1976 (LP)

The Shaggy D.A. (1976)

A REAL SHAGGY DOG STORY. THE ONLY CANDIDATE WITH A LAW DEGREE AND A PEDIGREE!

Source:

- Sequel to *The Shaggy Dog* (1959)
- *The Hound of Florence* (1923) Felix Salten

Writers:

Don Tait

Director:

Robert Stevenson

Stars:

Dean Jones, Tim Conway, Suzanne Pleshette, Keenan Wynn, Dick van Patten, Jo Anne Worley

Premiere:

Dec 17, 1976

Length:

92 min

CONNECTIONS

Comic Strips:

The Shaggy D.A. (TCT, Sep 5 – Nov 28, 1976)

COLLECTIONS

Video:

1985

Laserdisc:

1997 Studio Film Collection

DVD:

- 2006 Canine Candidate Edition, 2009 Double Feature,
- 2012 Disney 4-Movie Collection: Dogs 1

Digital:

Amazon, Vudu

The Many Adventures of Winnie the Pooh (1977)

HIP HIP POOHRAY!

Source:

Winnie the Pooh (1966) and *The House at Pooh Corner* (1928) A.A. Milne, compiled from theatrical shorts: *Winnie the Pooh and the Honey Tree* (1966), *Winnie the Pooh and the Blustery Day* (1968), *Winnie the Pooh and Tigger Too* (1974)

Writers:

Larry Clemmons, Ralph Wright, Vance Gerry, Xavier Atencio, Ken Anderson, Julius Svendsen, Ted Berman, Eric Cleworth

Directors:

John Lounsbery, Wolfgang Reitherman

Premiere:

Mar 11, 1977

Length:

74 min

CONNECTIONS

Comic Strips:

- *Winnie the Pooh and the Honey Tree* (TCT, Jan 2 – Mar 26, 1966)
- *Winnie the Pooh and the Blustery Day* (TCT, Aug 4 – Sep 29, 1968)
- *Winnie the Pooh and Tigger Too* (TCT, Oct 5 – Nov 30, 1975)
- Winnie the Pooh (#1–33, Jan 1977 – Jul 1984)

Movies:

- *Pooh's Grand Adventure: The Search for Christopher Robin* (DTV 1997) sequel
- *The Tigger Movie* (2000) spin-off
- *The Book of Pooh: Stories from the Heart* (DTV 2001) TV spin-off
- *Winnie the Pooh: A Very Merry Pooh Year* (DTV 2002) compilation/spin-off
- *Piglet's Big Movie* (2003) spin-off
- *Springtime with Roo* (DTV 2004) spin-off
- *Pooh's Heffalump Movie* (2005) spin-off
- *Pooh's Heffalump Halloween Movie* (DTV 2005) compilation/spin-off
- *My Friends Tigger & Pooh: Super Sleuth Christmas Movie* (DTV 2007) TV spin-off
- *My Friends Tigger & Pooh: Tigger & Pooh and a Musical Too* (DTV 2009) TV spin-off
- *My Friends Tigger & Pooh: Super Duper Super Sleuths* (DTV 2010) TV spin-off
- *Winnie the Pooh* (2011) sequel
- *Christopher Robin* (2018) live-action spin-off

Shorts:

- *Winnie the Pooh Discovers the Seasons* (1981) educational
- *Winnie the Pooh and a Day for Eeyore* (1983) sequel
- *Pooh's Great School Bus Adventure* (1986) educational
- *Winnie the Pooh's ABC of Me* (1990) educational
- *Think It Through with Winnie the Pooh* (1989) 2 x educational, *Responsible Persons* and *One and Only You*

TV Series:

- *Welcome to Pooh Corner* (1983-1986) Disney Channel, 120 episodes
- *The New Adventures of Winnie the Pooh* (1988-1991), Disney Channel/ABC, 50 episodes
- *The Book of Pooh* (2001-2003) Disney Channel, 23 episodes
- *My Friends Tigger & Pooh* (2007-2010) Disney Channel, 60 episodes

TV Specials:

- *Winnie the Pooh and Christmas Too* (1991) ABC [Collection > *Winnie the Pooh: A Very Merry Pooh Year* DVD (2002)] Blu-ray (2013 Gift of Friendship Edition)
- *Boo To You Too! Winnie the Pooh* (1996) CBS [Collection > Edited into *Pooh's Heffalump Halloween Movie* DVD (2005)]
- *A Winnie the Pooh Thanksgiving* (1998) ABC [Collection > *Winnie the Pooh: Seasons of Giving* DVD (2003)]
- *Winnie the Pooh: A Valentine for You* (1999) ABC [Collection > *Un-Valentine's Day/A Valentine for You* DVD (2004, 2010)]

Theme Parks:

- Winnie the Pooh and Friends, too! (DP 1998-2011)
- The Many Adventures of Winnie the Pooh [(MK 1999+), (DL 2003+), (HKD 2005+), (SD 2016+)]
- Pooh's Hunny Hunt (TDL 2000+)
- Pooh's Playful Spot (MK 2005-2010)
- Hunny Pot Spin (SD 2016+)

Video Games:

- *Winnie the Pooh in the Hundred Acre Wood* (1984) Amiga, Apple II, AST, C64, PC
- *Winnie the Pooh and Tigger Too* (1999) Mac, PC
- *Disney's Pooh and Tigger's Hunny Safari* (2001) GBC
- *Pooh's Party Game: In Search of the Treasure* (2001) PS, PC, PS3, PSP
- *Disney's Winnie the Pooh's Rumbly Tumbly Adventure* (2005) PS2, GBA, GC

COLLECTIONS

Video:

1981, 1996 Masterpiece Collection, 2002

Laserdisc:

1982, 1996 Masterpiece Collection

DVD*/Blu-ray:

2002 25th Anniversary Edition*, 2007 The Friendship Edition*, 2013

Digital:

Amazon, Vudu

Soundtrack:

1989, 1999, 2005 *The Best of Pooh & Heffalumps, Too* (CD)

Books:

- *The Art of Winnie the Pooh: Disney Artists Celebrate the Silly Old Bear* (2006)
- *Winnie the Pooh: A Celebration of the Silly Old Bear* (2011) Christopher Finch

The Rescuers (1977)

Two tiny agents vs. the world's wickedest woman IN A DAZZLING ANIMATED ADVENTURE!

Source:

The Rescuers (1959) and *Miss Bianca* (1962) Margery Sharp

Writers:

Larry Clemmons, Ken Anderson, Frank Thomas, Vance Gerry, David Michener, Ted Berman, Fred Lucky, Burny Mattinson, Dick Sebast

Director:

John Lounsbery, Wolfgang Reitherman, Art Stevens

Premiere:

Jun 19, 1977, Washington D.C.

Re-releases:

1983, 1989

Length:

78 min

CONNECTIONS

Comic Strips:

- *The Rescuers* (TCT, Mar 6 – May 29, 1977)
- *The Rescuers* (Walt Disney Showcase #40, Sep 1977)
- *The Return of the Rescuers* (TCT, Oct 2 – Dec 25, 1983)

Movies:

The Rescuers Down Under (1990) Sequel

COLLECTIONS

Video:

1992, 1999 Masterpiece Collection

Laserdisc:

1992, 1999 Masterpiece Collection

DVD*Blu-ray:

2003*, 2012 2-Movie Collection / 35th Anniversary Edition

Digital:

Amazon, Vudu

Soundtrack:

1977 (LP)

Herbie Goes to Monte Carlo (1977)

The Love Bug turns the great race into a HERBIE-DERBY!

Source:

Second sequel to *The Love Bug* (1968)

Writers:

Arthur Alsberg, Don Nelson

Director:

Vincent McEveety

Stars:

Dean Jones, Don Knotts, Julie Sommars

Premiere:

Jun 24, 1977

Length:

105 min

CONNECTIONS

Comic Strips:

- *Herbie Goes to Monte Carlo* (TCT, Jun 5 – Aug 28, 1977)
- *Herbie Goes to Monte Carlo* (Walt Disney Showcase #41, Oct 1977)

COLLECTIONS

Video:

1984, 1992, 1994, 1997 Studio Film Collection

Laserdisc:

1997 Studio Film Collection

DVD:

2004 + Herbie, the Love Bug Collection, 2009 Double Feature, 2012 Disney 4-Movie Collection: Herbie DVD

Blu-ray:

2015 Disney Movie Club Exclusive

Digital:

Amazon, iTunes, Vudu

Pete's Dragon (1977)

Brazzle Dazzle Brilliance!

Source:

"Pete's Dragon" short story (unpublished) Seton I. Miller, S.S. Field

Writers:

Malcolm Marmorstein

Director:

Don Chaffey

Stars:

Helen Reddy, Jim Dale, Mickey Rooney, Red Buttons, Shelley Winters

Premiere:

Nov 3, 1977

Re-releases:

1984

Length:

135 min (road show), 121 min (1977 edit), 106 min (1984 edit), 128 min (1985 edit)

CONNECTIONS

Comic Strips:

- *Pete's Dragon* (TCT, Sep 4 – Nov 27, 1977)
- *Pete's Dragon* (Walt Disney Showcase #43, Apr 1978)

Movies:

Pete's Dragon (2016) remake

COLLECTIONS

Video:

1980 (1977 edit), 1985 (1985 edit), 1991 (1985 edit), 1994 Masterpiece Collection (1985 edit)

Laserdisc:

1982 (Edit), 1991 (Edit)

DVD*/Blu-ray:

2001 Gold Collection* (1985 Edit), 2009 High-Flying Edition* (1985 Edit), 2012 35th Anniversary Edition (1985 Edit), 2013 UK release (1984 edit)

Digital:

Amazon, iTunes, Vudu

Soundtrack:

1977 (LP), 2002 (CD)

Books:

- *The Art of Disney's Dragons* (2016) Tom Bancroft
- *The Vault of Walt: Volume 5* (2016) Jim Korkis

Candleshoe (1977)

Laced with larceny...loaded with laughter! For 10% of the action and a red Ferrari, she'd can her own grandmother.

Source:

Christmas at Candleshoe (1953) Michael Innes

Writers:

David Swift, Rosemary Anne Sisson

Director:

Norman Tokar

Stars:

David Niven, Helen Hayes, Jodie Foster, Leo McKern

Premiere:

Dec 16, 1977, Los Angeles

Length:

101 min

CONNECTIONS

Comic Strips:
Candleshoe (TCT, Dec 4 1977 – Feb 26, 1978)

COLLECTIONS

Video:
1981, 1985, 1992 Studio Film Collection

Laserdisc:
1992 Studio Film Collection

DVD:
1999 Anchor Bay, 2004

Digital:
Amazon, iTunes, Vudu

Soundtrack:
2015 Intrada Special Collection (CD)

Return from Witch Mountain (1978)

Sinister forces from this world against two young space travelers from another

Source:
Sequel to *Escape to Witch Mountain* (1975)

Writers:
Malcolm Marmorstein

Director:
John Hough

Stars:
Bette Davis, Christopher Lee, Kim Richards, Ike Eisenmann

Premiere:
Mar 10, 1978

Length:
95 min

CONNECTIONS

Comic Strips:
Return from Witch Mountain (Walt Disney Showcase #44, May 1978)

COLLECTIONS

Video:
1983, 1986

DVD:
2003 Special Edition, 2009 Family Classics

Blu-ray:
2015 Disney Movie Club Exclusive

Digital:
Amazon, iTunes, Vudu

The Cat from Outer Space (1978)

MYSTERIOUS VISITOR WITH UNKNOWN POWERS ON OUR PLANET FOR SUPPLIES…A SIX-PACK OF TUNA?

Writers:
Ted Key

Director:
Norman Tokar

Stars:
Ken Berry, Sandy Duncan, Harry Horgan, Roddy McDowall, McLean Stevenson

Premiere:
Jun 30, 1978

Length:
104 min

CONNECTIONS

Comic Strips:
- *The Cat from Outer Space* (TCT, Mar 5 – May 28, 1978)
- *The Cat from Outer Space* (Walt Disney Showcase #46, Sep 1978)

COLLECTIONS

Video:
1981

DVD:
2002 Anchor Bay, 2004

Digital:

Amazon, Vudu

Hot Lead and Cold Feet (1978)

A BLAZING SAGA OF HOT LEAD & COLD FEET

Writers:

Rod Piffath (story), Joseph L. McEveety, Arthur Alsberg, Don Nelson (screenplay)

Director:

Robert Butler

Stars:

Jim Dale, Karen Valentine, Don Knotts, Jack Elam, Darren McGavin

Premiere:

Jul 5, 1978

Length:

90 min

CONNECTIONS

Comic Strips:

Hot Lead and Cold Feet (TCT, Jun 4 – Aug 27, 1978)

COLLECTIONS

Video:

1980, 1985

DVD:

2004, 2012 Disney 4-Movie Collection: Don Knotts

Digital:

Amazon, iTunes, Vudu

The North Avenue Irregulars (1979)

Gangbusters! What these ladies do to the mob is highly irregular!

AKA:

Hill's Angels (UK)

Source:

The North Avenue Irregulars (1968) Rev. Albert Fay Hill

Writers:

Don Tait

Director:

Bruce Bilson

Premiere:

Feb 9, 1979

Length:

100 min

CONNECTIONS

Comic Strips:

- *The North Avenue Irregulars* (TCT, Dec 3 1978 – Feb 25, 1979)
- *North Avenue Irregulars* (Walt Disney Showcase #49, Mar 1979)

COLLECTIONS

Video:

1980, 1985, 1999 Anchor Bay

DVD:

1999 Anchor Bay, 2004

Digital:

Vudu

The Apple Dumpling Gang Rides Again (1979)

It took 10 years to win the West, they lost it in a week!

Source:

Sequel to *The Apple Dumpling Gang* (1975)

Writers: Don Tait

Director: Vincent McEveety

Stars:

Tim Conway, Don Knotts, Tim Matheson, Kenneth Mars, Harry Morgan

Premiere:

Jun 27, 1979

Length:

89 min

CONNECTIONS

Comic Strips:

The Apple Dumpling Gang Rides Again (TCT, Mar 4th – May 27th 1979)

COLLECTIONS

Video:

1981, 1985

DVD:

2003 Don Knotts Collection, 2008 2-Movie Collection, 2012 Disney 4-Movie Collection: Don Knotts

Digital:

Amazon, iTunes, Vudu

Unidentified Flying Oddball (1979)

CHAOS IN THE COSMOS!

AKA:

- *The Spaceman and King Arthur* (UK)
- *The Spaceman in King Arthur's Court* (1982) 2-part TV broadcast on *Walt Disney*

Source:

A Connecticut Yankee in King Arthur's Court (1889) Mark Twain

Writers:

Don Tait

Director:

Russ Mayberry

Stars:

Dennis Dugan, Jim Dale, Ron Moody, Kenneth More, John Le Mesurier, Rodney Bewes, Sheila White

Premiere:

Jul 10, 1979, UK

US Release:

Jul 26, 1979

Length:

93 min

CONNECTIONS
Comic Strips:
- *Unidentified Flying Oddball* (TCT, Jun 3 – Aug 26, 1979)
- *Unidentified Flying Oddball* (Walt Disney Showcase #52, Sep 1979)

Movies:
A Kid in King Arthur's Court (1995) adapts same story

TV Movie:
A Knight in Camelot (1998) ABC *The Wonderful World of Disney*, adapts same story

COLLECTIONS
Video:
1986, 1999 Anchor Bay

DVD:
1999 Anchor Bay, 2004

Digital:
Amazon, iTunes, Vudu

Soundtrack:
2016 Intrada Special Collection (CD)

The Black Hole (1979)
A JOURNEY THAT BEGINS WHERE EVERYTHING ENDS

Writers:
Bob Barbash, Richard H. Landau (story), Jed Rosebrook, Gerry Day (screenplay)

Director:
Gary Nelson

Stars:
Maximilian Schell, Anthony Perkins, Robert Foster, Joseph Bottoms, Yvette Mimieux, Ernest Borgnine

Premiere:
Dec 18, 1979, London

US Release:
Dec 20, 1979

Length:

98 min

CONNECTIONS

Comic Strips:

- *The Black Hole* (TCT, Sep 2, 1979 – Feb 24, 1980)
- *The Black Hole* (Walt Disney Showcase #54, Jan 1980)

COLLECTIONS

Video:

1980, 1983, 1999 Anchor Bay / Anniversary Edition

Laserdisc:

1982

DVD:

2002 Anchor Bay, 2004

Digital:

Amazon, Vudu

Soundtrack:

1979 (LP), 2007 (iTunes), 2011 Intrada (CD)

PART FIVE

Movies: 1980–1989

Midnight Madness (1980)

The most fun you'll ever have… in the dark!

Writers:
David Wechter, Michael Nankin

Directors:
David Wechter, Michael Nankin

Stars:
David Naughton, Debra Clinger, Eddie Deezen, Brad Wilson, Maggie Roswell, Stephen Furst

Premiere:
Feb 8, 1980

Length:
112 min

COLLECTIONS

Video:
1985

DVD:
2001 Anchor Bay, 2004

Digital:
Amazon, iTunes, Vudu

The Watcher in the Woods (1980)

A MASTERPIECE OF SUSPENSE!

Source:
The Watcher in the Woods (1976) Florence Engel Randall

Writers:

Brian Clemens, Rosemary Anne Sisson, Harry Spalding

Director:

John Hough

Stars:

Bette Davis, Caroll Baker, David McCallum, Lynn-Holly Johnson, Kyle Richards, Ian Bannen, Richard Pasco

Premiere:

Apr 16, 1980, New York

Re-releases:

Oct 7, 1981 (Revised ending)

Length:

84 min

CONNECTIONS

Comic Strips:

The Watcher in the Woods (TCT, Mar 2 – May 25, 1980)

COLLECTIONS

Video:

1982

Laserdisc:

1992

DVD:

2002 Anchor Bay, 2004

Herbie Goes Bananas (1980)

YES, WE HAVE A BANANZA!

Source:

Third sequel to *The Love Bug* (1968)

Writers:

Don Tait

Director:

Vincent McEveety

Stars:

Cloris Leachman, Charles Martin Smith, John Vernon, Stephen W. Burns, Elyssa Davalos, Joaquin Garay III, Harvey Korman

Premiere:

Jun 25, 1980

Re-releases:

1981

Length:

100 min

COLLECTIONS

Video:

1985

Laserdisc:

1997 Studio Film Collection

DVD:

2004 + Herbie, the Love Bug Collection, 2012 Disney 4-Movie Collection: Herbie

Blu-ray:

2015 Disney Movie Club Exclusive / 35th Anniversary Edition

Digital:

Amazon, iTunes, Vudu

The Last Flight of Noah's Ark (1980)

Lost. 2,000 miles at sea in a 10-year-old bomber.

Source:

"The Gremlin's Castle" (1978) Ernest K. Gann

Writers:

Steven W. Carabatsos, Sandy Glass, George Arthur Bloom

Director:

Charles Jarrott

Stars:

Elliott Gould, Geneviève Bujold, Ricky Schroder, Vincent Gardenia

Premiere:

Jun 25, 1980

Length:

98 min

CONNECTIONS

Comic Strips:

The Last Flight of Noah's Ark (TCT, Jun 1 – Aug 24, 1980)

COLLECTIONS

Video:

1983

DVD:

2004

Blu-ray:

2017 Disney Movie Club Exclusive / 35th Anniversary Edition

Digital:

Amazon, Vudu

Soundtrack:

2012 Intrada Special Collection (CD)

Popeye (1980)

HAVES A HAPPY HOLIDAY WIT ME AN' OLIVE!

(Note: Disney/Paramount co-production)

Source:

Popeye comic strip (1929+) created by E.C. Segar

Writers:

Jules Feiffer

Director:

Robert Altman

Stars:

Robin Williams, Shelley Duvall

Premiere:

Dec 12, 1980, distributed by Paramount (US), Disney (International)

Length:

113 min

COLLECTIONS

Laserdisc:

1992 Paramount Pictures

DVD:

- Paramount: 2003, 2008 I Love the 80s, 2013 (US)
- Disney: 2006 (UK)

Digital:

Vudu

Soundtrack:

1980, 2016 Limited Edition (LP), 2017 Deluxe Edition (CD)

The Devil and Max Devlin (1981)

A new high in being low down their main goal is swiping soul

Writers:

Jimmy Sangster (story), Mary Rodgers (story/screenplay)

Director:

Steven Hilliard Stern

Stars:

Elliott Gould, Bill Cosby, Susan Anspach, Adam Rich, Julie Budd

Premiere:

Mar 6, 1981

Length:

95 min

CONNECTIONS

Comic Strips:

The Devil and Max Devlin (TCT, Aug 31 – Nov 23 1980)

COLLECTIONS

Video:

1981, 1998 Anchor Bay

DVD:

2000 Anchor Bay, 2006

Digital:

Vudu

Amy (1981)

She taught them to speak. They taught her to love.

Writers:

Noreen Stone

Director:

Vincent McEveety

Stars:

Jenny Agutter, Barry Newman, Kathleen Nolan, Chris Robinson, Lou Fant, Margaret O'Brien, Nanette Fabray

Premiere:

Mar 20, 1981

Length:

100 min

CONNECTIONS

Shorts:

Amy-on-the-Lips (1982) educational

COLLECTIONS

Video:

1981, 1985

DVD:

2011 Generations Collection

Digital:

iTunes, Vudu

Dragonslayer (1981)

In the Dark Ages, Magic was a weapon. Love was a mystery. Adventure was everywhere... And Dragons were real.

(Note: Disney/Paramount co-production)

Writers:

Hal Barwood, Matthew Robbins

Director:

Matthew Robbins

Premiere:

Jun 26, 1981, distributed by Paramount (US), Disney (International)

Length:

110 min

CONNECTIONS

Comic Strips:

Dragonslayer (Marvel Super Special #20, 1981)

COLLECTIONS

Video:

1981 Paramount

Laserdisc:

1981, 1995 Paramount

DVD:

- Paramount: 2003 (US)
- Disney: 2004 (UK)

Digital:

Amazon, Vudu

Soundtrack:

1983 (LP), 1990 (Australian CD), 2010 La-La Land Records (CD)

Condorman (1981)

An action adventure romantic comedy spy story.

Source:

The Game of X (1965) Robert Sheckley

Writers:

Marc Stirdivant

Director:

Charles Jarrott

Stars:

Michael Crawford, Oliver Reed, Barbara Carrera, James Hampton, Jean-Pierre Kalfon

Premiere:

Jul 2, 1981, UK

US Release:

Aug 7, 1981

Length:

90 min

CONNECTIONS

Comic Strips:

- *Condorman* (TCT, Nov 30, 1980 – Apr 12, 1981)
- *Condorman* (#1–3, Nov 1981 – Feb 1982)

COLLECTIONS

Video:

1981

DVD:

1999 Anchor Bay, 2003 Anchor Bay, 2009 Disney Movie Club Exclusive

Digital:

iTunes, Vudu

Soundtrack:

2012 Intrada Special Collection (CD)

The Fox and the Hound (1981)

A story of two friends who didn't know they were supposed to be enemies.

Source:

The Fox and the Hound (1967) Daniel P. Mannix

Writers:

Larry Clemmons, Ted Berman, David Michener, Peter Young, Burny Mattinson, Steve Hulett, Earl Kress, Vance Gerry

Directors:

Ted Berman, Richard Rich, Art Stevens

Premiere:

Jul 10, 1981

Re-releases:

1988

Length:

83 min

CONNECTIONS

Comic Strips:

- *The Fox and the Hound* (TCT, Apr 19 – Aug 30, 1981)
- *The Fox and the Hound* (#1-3, Aug – Oct 1981)

Movies:

The Fox and the Hound 2 (DTV, 2006) Sequel

Shorts:

The Fox and the Hound: A Lesson in Being Careful (1981) Educational

COLLECTIONS

Video:

1994

DVD*/Blu-ray:

2000 Gold Classic Collection*, 2006 25th Anniversary Edition*, 2011 2-Movie Collection, 2014 3-Movie Collection, 2017 2-Movie Collection

Digital:

Amazon, Vudu

Soundtrack:

1981 (LP)

Night Crossing (1982)

The East German border: 836 miles of barbed-wire walls, automated machine guns, armed guards, and deadly land mines. On September 15, 1979 two families tried to cross it. A true story.

Source:

True story

Writers:

John McGreevey

Director:

Delbert Mann

Premiere:

Feb 5, 1982

Length:

107 min

CONNECTIONS

Comic Strips:

Night Crossing (TCT, Sep 6, 1981 – Jan 17, 1982)

COLLECTIONS

Video:

1982

DVD:

2004

Digital:

iTunes, Vudu

Soundtrack:

1981 (LP), 1987 Intrada, 1994 Intrada, 2014 Intrada Special Collection

Tron (1982)

A world inside the computer where man has never been. Never before now.

AKA:

TRON, TRON: The Original Classic

Writers:

Bonnie MacBird (story), Steven Lisberger (story/screenplay)

Director:

Steven Lisberger

Stars:

Jeff Bridges, Bruce Boxleitner, David Warner, Cindy Morgan, Barnard Hughes

Premiere:

Jul 9, 1982

Length:

96 min

CONNECTIONS

Comic Strips:

- *Tron* (TCT, Jan 24 – Jun 6, 1982)
- *TRON: Ghost in the Machine* (#1-6, Apr 2006 – Sep 2008) [Collection > Trade Paperback (2009)]
- *TRON: Original Movie Adaptation* (#1-2, Nov 2010 – Feb 2011) [Collection > Trade Paperback (2011)]

Movies:

Tron: Legacy (2010) sequel

TV Series:

Tron: Uprising (2012–2013) Disney XD, 19 episodes [Collection > iTunes]

Video Games:

- *Tron* (1982) Arcade, X360S, Tomy Tutor
- *Tron: Deadly Disks* (1982) A2600, Aquarius, Intellivision
- *Tron: Maze-A-Tron* (1982) Intellivision
- *Adventures of Tron* (1982) A2600
- *Disc of Tron* (1983) Arcade, C64, GBA *TRON 2.0: Killer App* (2004), X360 Store
- *TRON Solar Sailer* (1983) Intellivision
- *TRON 2.0* (2003) Mac, PC, Xbox
- *TRON 2.0: Killer App* (2004) GBA, Xbox

COLLECTIONS

Video:

1982, 1993

Laserdisc:

1982, 1995 Archive Collection

DVD*/Blu-ray:

1998*, 2002 20th Anniversary Collector's Edition*, 2011 Special Edition + 2-Movie Collection

Digital:

iTunes, Vudu

Soundtrack:

1982, 2014 (LP), 2002 (CD)

Books:

- *The Art of Tron* (1982) Mike Bonifer
- *The Making of Tron: How Tron Changed Visual Effects and Disney Forever* (2011) William Kallay

Tex (1982)

His father's gone. His mother's a memory. His brother's moving on. But Tex McCormick isn't giving in.

Source:

Tex (1979) S.E. Hinton

Writers:

Charles S. Haas, Tim Hunter

Director:

Tim Hunter

Stars:

Matt Dillon, Jim Metzler, Meg Tilly, Bill McKinney, Ben Johnson

Premiere:

Jul 30, 1982

Length:

103 min

CONNECTIONS

Comic Strips:

Tex (TCT, Jun 13 – Sep 26, 1982)

COLLECTIONS

Video:

1983

Laserdisc:

1983

DVD:

2002 Anchor Bay, 2004

Digital:

Amazon, iTunes, Vudu

Trenchcoat (1983)

To write a great novel, you have to live a great novel. Too bad Mickey writes murder mysteries.

Writers:

Jeffrey Price, Peter S. Seaman

Director:

Michael Tuchner

Stars:

Margot Kidder, Robert Hays

Premiere:

Mar 11, 1983

Length:

91 min

COLLECTIONS

Video:

1983

DVD:

2012

Digital:

iTunes, Vudu

Something Wicked This Way Comes (1983)

What would you give a man who could make your deepest dreams come true?

AKA:

Ray Bradbury's Something Wicked This Way Comes

Source:

Something Wicked This Way Comes (1962) Ray Bradbury

Writers:

Ray Bradbury

Director:

Jack Clayton

Premiere:

Apr 29, 1983

Length:

95 min

COLLECTIONS

Video:

1983, 1993, 2000 Anchor Bay

Laserdisc:

1983, 1996

DVD:

1999 Anchor Bay, 2004

Soundtrack:

2009 Intrada Special Collection, 2015 Intrada Special Collection: Unused Score (CD)

Never Cry Wolf (1983)

THEY THOUGHT HE COULDN'T DO THE JOB. THAT'S WHY THEY CHOSE HIM. Assignment: The Lupus Project. Purpose: To study Alaskan wolves and determine if they were destroying the vanishing caribou deer. The man they chose expected to confront danger, adventure, solitude and, he hoped, the truth. But he never expected to embark upon a voyage of self-discovery. One that would ultimately transform his life. A TRUE STORY

Source:

Never Cry Wolf (1963) Farley Mowat

Writers:

- Curtis Hanson, Sam Hamm, Richard Kletter (screenplay)
- Charles Martin Smith, Eugene Corr, Christina Luescher (narration written by)

Director:

Carroll Ballard

Stars:

Charles Martin Smith, Brian Dennehy

Premiere:
Oct 6, 1983, Toronto

US Release:
Oct 7, 1983

Length:
105 min

COLLECTIONS

Video:
1984, 1993

Laserdisc:
1993

DVD:
2000 Anchor Bay, 2002 Anchor Bay / Full Screen Edition, 2004

Digital:
iTunes, Vudu

Soundtrack:
1983 *Film Music: Mark Isham* (LP/CD)

Where the Toys Come From (1984)

An Enchanting Tale Where Toys Come To Life And Talk.

Writers:
Theodore Thomas

Director:
Theodore Thomas

Premiere:
1984, DTV

Length:
58 min

COLLECTIONS

Video:
1984

DVD:
2002

Return to Oz (1985)

It's an all-new live-action fantasy—filled with Disney adventure and magic.

Source:
The Marvelous Land of Oz (1904) and *Ozma of Oz* (1907) L. Frank Baum

Writers:
Walter Murch, Gill Dennis

Director:
Walter Murch

Premiere:
Jun 21, 1985

Length:
109 min

CONNECTIONS

Comic Strips:
- *Return to Oz* (TCT, Apr 7 – Jul 14, 1985)
- *Walt Disney Pictures' Return to Oz* (1985)

Movies:
Oz the Great and Powerful (2013) Also set in Oz

COLLECTIONS

Video:
1985, 1999 Anniversary Edition / Anchor Bay

Laserdisc:
1985

DVD:
1999 Anchor Bay, 2004

Blu-ray:
2015 Disney Movie Club Exclusive / 30th Anniversary Edition

Digital:
iTunes, Vudu

Soundtrack:
1985, 2015 Intrada Special Collection (CD)

The Black Cauldron (1985)

Hidden by darkness. Guarded by witches. Discovered by a boy. Stolen by a king. Whoever owns it will rule the world. Or destroy it.

Source:

The Chronicles of Prydain (1964–1968) Lloyd Alexander

Writers:

David Jonas, Vance Gerry, Ted Berman, Richard Rich, Al Wilson, Roy Morita, Peter Young, Art Stevens, Joe Hale

Directors:

Ted Berman, Richard Rich

Premiere:

Jul 24, 1985

Length:

80 min

CONNECTIONS

Comic Strips:

- *The Black Cauldron* (TCT, Jul 21 – Oct 27, 1985)
- *Walt Disney Pictures' The Black Cauldron* (1985)

Video Games:

The Black Cauldron (1986) Amiga, Apple II, AST, PC

COLLECTIONS

Video:

1998 Masterpiece Collection

DVD:

2000 Gold Classic Collection, 2010 25th Anniversary Edition

Digital:

Amazon, Vudu

Soundtrack:

1985 (LP), 2007 (iTunes), 2012 Intrada, 2017 Varèse Encore / Ltd Edition (CD)

Breakin' Through (1985)

Director:

Peter Medak

Stars:

Ben Vereen

Premiere:

Sep 1985, DTV

Length:

73 min

COLLECTIONS

Video:

1985

The Journey of Natty Gann (1985)

Her name is Natty Gann. Two thousand miles of danger separate her from her father. Only love, hope and courage can help her find him.

Writers:

Jeanne Rosenberg

Director:

Jeremy Kagan

Stars:

Meredith Salenger, John Cusack, Ray Wise

Premiere:

Sep 8, 1985, Toronto

US Release:

Sep 27, 1985

Length:

101 min

CONNECTIONS

Comic Strips:

The Journey of Natty Gann (TCT, Nov 3 – Jan 26, 1986)

COLLECTIONS

Video:

1986, 2002

Laserdisc:

1986

DVD:

2002, 2012 Disney 4-Movie Collection: Dogs 2

Digital:

Amazon, Vudu

Soundtrack:

- 2000 Bootleg, 2008 *Elmer Bernstein: The Unused Scores* (Unused score) (CD)
- 2009 Intrada Special Collection (CD)

One Magic Christmas (1985)

COMING THIS HOLIDAY SEASON

Writers:

Thomas Meehan, Phillip Borsos, Barry Healey (story), Thomas Meehan (screenplay)

Director:

Phillip Borsos

Stars:

Mary Steenburgen

Premiere:

Nov 22, 1985

Length:

89 min

COLLECTIONS

Video:

1986

Laserdisc:

1992

DVD:

2004

Digital:

Amazon, iTunes, Vudu

The Great Mouse Detective (1986)

ALL NEW! ALL FUN!

AKA:

- *Basil the Great Mouse Detective* (UK)
- *The Adventures of the Great Mouse Detective* (1992 re-release)

Source:

Basil of Baker Street (1958–1982) Eve Titus, Paul Galdone

Writers:

Peter Young, Vance Gerry, Steve Hulett, Ron Clements, John Musker, Bruce Morris, Matthew O'Callaghan, Burny Mattinson, David Michener, Mel Shaw

Directors:

Ron Clements, Burny Mattinson, David Michener, John Musker

Premiere:

Jul 2, 1986

Re-releases:

1992

Length:

74 min

CONNECTIONS

Comic Strips:

The Great Mouse Detective (TCT, May 4 – Jul 27, 1986)

Video Games:

Basil the Great Mouse Detective (1987) ACPC, C64, ZXS, A8

COLLECTIONS

Video:

1992, 1999

Laserdisc:

1992

DVD*/Blu-ray:

2002*, 2010 Mystery in the Mist Edition*, 2012 Mystery in the Mist
Edition

Digital:

Amazon, Vudu

Soundtrack:

1992 (CD)

Books:

The Vault of Walt: Volume 3 (2014) Jim Korkis

Flight of the Navigator (1986)

Come along on the greatest adventure of the summer!

Writers:

Mark H. Baker (story), Michael Burton, Matt MacManus (screenplay)

Director:

Randal Kleiser

Premiere:

Jul 30, 1986

Length:

90 min

COLLECTIONS

Video:

1987, 1993

Laserdisc:

1986, 1993

DVD:

2004

Digital:

Amazon, iTunes, Vudu

Soundtrack:

1995 (CD)

Benji the Hunted (1987)

Source:

Third feature film sequel to non-Disney release *Benji* (1974)

Writers:

Joe Camp

Director:

Joe Camp

Premiere:

Jun 5, 1987, Dallas

Length:

88 min

CONNECTIONS (NON-DISNEY RELEASES)

Movies:

- *For the Love of Benji* (1977)
- *Oh Heavenly Dog* (1980)
- *Benji: Off the Leash!* (2004)
- *Benji* (2017)

Shorts:

- *Benji's Very Own Christmas Story* (TV, 1978)
- *Benji at Work* (TV, 1980)
- *Benji Takes a Dive at Marineland* (TV, 1981)

COLLECTIONS

Video:

1988, 1993

Laserdisc:

1993

DVD:

2006, 2012 Disney 4-Movie Collection: *Dogs 2*

Digital:

Amazon, iTunes, Vudu

The Brave Little Toaster (1987)

Plug into the Adventure!

(Note: Hyperion Pictures release, released by Disney on home video)

Source:

The Brave Little Toaster (1980) Thomas M. Disch

Writers:

Jerry Rees, Joe Ranft, Brian McEntee

Director:

Jerry Rees

Premiere:

Jul 10, 1987, Los Angeles

Length:

90 min

CONNECTIONS

Movies:

- *The Brave Little Toaster to the Rescue* (DTV, 1997) sequel
- *The Brave Little Toaster Goes to Mars* (DTV, 1998) sequel

COLLECTIONS

Video:

1991, 1994

Laserdisc:

1991

DVD:

2003

Soundtrack:

2005 (CD)

Return to Snowy River (1988)

They tried to destroy what they could not tame. But the man from Snowy River has returned to claim what is his. One man stands in his way. One woman lives in his heart. The legend continues

AKA:

The Man from Snowy River II, The Untamed (UK video)

Source:

- Sequel to non-Disney release *The Man from Snowy River* (1982)
- "The Man from Snowy River" (1890) Banjo Paterson

Writers:

Geoff Burrowes, John Dixon

Director:

Geoff Burrowes

Premiere:

Mar 24, 1988, Australia

US Release:

Apr 15, 1988

Length:

99 min

COLLECTIONS

Video:

1988, 1992

Laserdisc:

1988

DVD:

2003

Digital:

iTunes, Vudu

Soundtrack:

1988 (LP, CD)

Who Framed Roger Rabbit (1988)

It's the story of a man, a woman, and a rabbit in a triangle of trouble.

(Note: Touchstone Pictures release, featuring Disney characters)

Source:

Who Censored Roger Rabbit? (1981) Gary K. Wolf

Writers:

Jeffrey Price, Peter S. Seaman

Director:

Robert Zemeckis

Stars:

Bob Hoskins, Christopher Lloyd

Premiere:

Jun 21, 1988, New York

Length:

104 min

CONNECTIONS

Comic Books:

- *Who Framed Roger Rabbit* (Marvel Graphic Novel, 1989)
- *Roger Rabbit and the Resurrection of Doom* (Marvel Graphic Novel, 1989)
- *Roger Rabbit* (#1–18, 1990–1991)
- *Roger Rabbit's Toontown* (#1–5, 1991)
- *Roger Rabbit in 3-D* (1992)

Shorts:

- *Tummy Trouble* (1989)
- *Roller Coaster Rabbit* (1990)
- *Trail Mix-Up* (1993)

Theme Parks:

- Roger Rabbit's Car Toon Spin (DL 1994+), (TDL 1996+)
- *Hare Raising Havoc* (1991) Amiga, PC

COLLECTIONS

Video:

1989

Laserdisc:

1989, 1990, 1998

DVD*/Blu-ray:

1999*, 2003 Vista Series*, 2013 25th Anniversary Edition

Digital:

iTunes

Soundtrack:

1988 (LP), 1988, 2002, 2018 Intrada (CD)

Oliver & Company (1988)

Source:

Oliver Twist (1837–1839) Charles Dickens

Writers:

Jim Cox, Tim Disney, James Mangold (screenplay), Vance Gerry, Mike Gabriel, Joe Ranft, Jim Mitchell, Chris Bailey, Kirk Wise, David Michener, Roger Allers, Gary Trousdale, Kevin Lima, Michael Cedeno, Peter Young, Leon Joosen (story)

Director:

George Scribner

Premiere:

Nov 13, 1988, New York

Re-releases:

1996

Length:

74 min

CONNECTIONS

Video Games:

Oliver & Company (1989) Amiga, AST, PC

COLLECTIONS

Video:

1996 Masterpiece Collection

Laserdisc:

1997

DVD*/Blu-ray:

- 2002 Special Edition*, 2009 20th Anniversary Edition*, 2013 25th Anniversary Edition
- 2014 3-Movie Collection

Digital:

Amazon, iTunes, Vudu

Soundtrack:
1987 (LP), 1988, 1995, 2001 (CD)

Honey, I Shrunk the Kids (1989)

Writers:
Stuart Gordon, Brian Yuzna (story), Ed Naha, Tom Schulman (screenplay)

Director:
Joe Johnston

Stars:
Rick Moranis

Premiere:
Jun 23, 1989

Length:
93 min

CONNECTIONS

Movies:
- *Honey, I Blew Up the Kid* (1992) Sequel
- *Honey, We Shrunk Ourselves* (DTV, 1997) sequel

TV Series:
Honey, I Shrunk the Kids (1997–2000) Syndication, 66 episodes [Collection > iTunes]

Theme Parks:
- Honey, I Shrunk the Kids: Movie Set Adventure (HS 1990–2016)
- Honey, I Shrunk the Audience (E 1994–2010), (DL 1998–2010)
- MicroAdventure! (TDL 1997–2010)
- Chérie, j'ai rétréci le public (DP 1999–2010)

COLLECTIONS

Video:
1990

Laserdisc:
1990

DVD:
2002

Blu-ray:

2017 Disney Movie Club Exclusive

Digital:

Amazon, iTunes, Vudu

Soundtrack:

1999, 2009 Intrada Special Collection (CD)

Cheetah (1989)

In The Great Tradition of Disney's Adventure Classics Comes An All New Family Adventure

Source:

The Cheetahs (1970) Alan Caillou

Writers:

Erik Tarloff, John Cotter, Griff Du Rhone

Director:

Jeff Blyth

Premiere:

Aug 18, 1989

Length:

83 min

COLLECTIONS

Video:

1990

Laserdisc:

1990

DVD:

2002

Digital:

Amazon, iTunes, Vudu

The Little Mermaid (1989)

Somewhere under the sea and beyond your imagination is an adventure in fantasy.

Source:

"The Little Mermaid" (1837) Hans Christian Andersen

Writers:

Ron Clements, John Musker

Directors:

Ron Clements, John Musker

Premiere:

Nov 13, 1989, New York

Re-releases:

1997, 2006, 2013 (Limited)

Length:

83 min

CONNECTIONS

Comic Strips:

- *Walt Disney's The Little Mermaid* (1990) [Collection > *Disney Princess Comics Treasury* (2015)]
- *Disney's The Little Mermaid* (Limited Series, #1–4, Feb – June 1992) [Collection > Several stories in *Disney Princess Comics Treasury* (2015)]
- *Disney's The Little Mermaid* (#1–12, Sep 1994 – Aug 1995)
- *The Little Mermaid* (DHS, Nov 27 – Dec 24, 1997) [Collection > *Disney's Christmas Classics* (2017)]

Movies:

- *The Little Mermaid II: Return to the Sea* (DTV, 2000) sequel
- *The Little Mermaid: Ariel's Beginning* (DTV, 2008) prequel
- *The Little Mermaid* (TBC) live-action remake

Stage Musical:

- *The Little Mermaid* (2007+)
- *The Little Mermaid JR* (?) Disney Theatrical Licensing

TV Series:

- *The Little Mermaid* (1992-1995), CBS, 31 episodes [Collection > Episodes on *Disney Princess Party Vol 1* DVD (2004)]
- *Disney Princess Stories Vol 1–3* DVD (2004-2005)
- *Marsupilami* (1993-1994), CBS, 13 episodes, "Sebastian the Crab" segment

Theme Parks:

- Voyage of the Little Mermaid (HS 1992+)
- Ariel's Grotto (DL 1996-2008), (MK 2012+), (DCA 2001+), (TDS 2005+)
- King Triton's Carousel of the Sea (DCA 2001+)
- Mermaid Lagoon (TDS 2001+)
- Flounder's Flying Fish Coaster (TDS 2001+)
- Scuttle's Scooters (TDS 2001+)
- Ariel's Playground (TDS 2001+)
- Jumpin' Jellyfish (DL 2001+), (TDS 2001+)
- The Little Mermaid—Ariel's Undersea Adventure (DCA 2011+)
- Under the Sea~Journey of the Little Mermaid (MK 2012+)

Video Games:

- *Disney's The Little Mermaid* (1991) NES, GB
- *Disney's Ariel the Little Mermaid* (1992) GG, MD/G, SMS
- *Disney presents Ariel's Story Studio* (1997) PC, Mac
- *Disney's The Little Mermaid: Ariel's Undersea Adventure* (2006) DS

COLLECTIONS

Video:

1990, 1998 Masterpiece Collection

Laserdisc:

1990, 1998

DVD*/Blu-ray:

1999 Limited Issue*, 2006 Platinum Edition*, 2013 Diamond Edition + 3D

Soundtrack:

1989, 1990 *Sebastian from The Little Mermaid*, 1991 *Sebastian: Party Gras!*, 1992 *Songs from the Sea*, 1992 *Splash Hits*, 1994 *The Music Behind the Magic*, 1997, 1998 *Ariel's Favourites*, 2006 *The Little Mermaid and Friends*, 2006 Special Edition, 2009 *Songs and Story*, 2013 *Greatest Hits*, 2012 The Legacy Collection (CD), 2014 (LP)

Books:

- *The Art of the Little Mermaid* (1998) Jeff Kurtti
- *The Little Mermaid: From the Deep Blue Sea to the Great White Way* (2009) Michael Lassell

PART SIX

Movies: 1990–1994

DuckTales the Movie: Treasure of the Lost Lamp (1990)

Source:
Spun-off from *DuckTales* (1987-1992) TV series

Writers:
Alan Burnett

Director:
Bob Hathcock

Premiere:
Aug 3, 1990

Length
74 min

CONNECTIONS

Comic Book:
DuckTales the Movie (1990)

TV Series:

- *DuckTales* (1987–1992) Syndication, 100 episodes [Collection > Vols 1-3 DVD (2005–2007, 2013) 75 episodes]; iTunes Vol 1-6 (2016) 100 episodes
- *DuckTales* (2017+) Disney XD

Video Games:

- *DuckTales* (1989) NES, GB
- *Disney's DuckTales: The Quest for Gold* (1989) Amiga, AII, AST, C64, PC

- *DuckTales 2* (1993) NES, GB
- *DuckTales: Remastered* (2013) PS3, WU, PC, X360S, X360

COLLECTIONS

Video:
1991

Laserdisc:
1991

DVD:
2006 Disney Movie Club Exclusive, 2014

Digital:
Amazon, iTunes, Vudu

Soundtrack:
2017 Intrada Special Collection (CD)

Shipwrecked (1990)

A quest for survival that became the adventure of a lifetime.

AKA:
Haakon Haakonsen (Norway)

Source:
Haakon Haakonsen (1873) Oluf Vilhelm Falck-Ytter

Writers:
Nils Gaup, Bob Foss, Greg Dinner, Nick Thiel

Director:
Nils Gaup

Premiere:
Oct 3, 1990, Norway

US Release:
Mar 1, 1991

Length:
93 min

CONNECTIONS

Comic Book:
Shipwrecked! (1991)

COLLECTIONS
Video:
1991

Laserdisc:
1991

DVD:
2008

Digital:
iTunes, Vudu

Soundtrack:
1991 (CD)

The Rescuers Down Under (1990)

Source:
Sequel to *The Rescuers* (1977)

Writers:
Jim Cox, Karey Kirkpatrick, Byron Simpson, Joe Ranft

Directors:
Hendel Butoy, Mike Gabriel

Premiere:
Nov 16, 1990

Length:
77 min

CONNECTIONS
Comic Book:
The Rescuers Down Under (1990)

COLLECTIONS
Video:
1991, 2000 Gold Classic Collection

Laserdisc:
1991

DVD*/Blu-ray:

2000 Gold Classic Collection*, 2012 35th Anniversary Edition / 2-Movie Collection

Digital:

Amazon, Vudu

Soundtrack:

1991, 2002, 2016 Intrada Special Collection (CD)

White Fang (1991)

Where civilization ends, their journey begins.

Source:

White Fang (1906) Jack London

Writers:

Jeanne Rosenberg, Nick Thiel, David Fallon

Director:

Randal Kleiser

Premiere:

Jan 18, 1991

Length:

109 min

CONNECTIONS

Comic Book:

White Fang (Apr 1991)

Movies:

White Fang 2: Myth of the White Wolf (1994) sequel

Shorts:

White Fang (1995) educational

COLLECTIONS

Video:

1991

Laserdisc:

1991

DVD:

2002

Digital:

iTunes, Vudu

Soundtrack:

2012 Intrada Special Collection (CD)

Wild Hearts Can't Be Broken (1991)

When dreams take flight

Source:

A Girl and Five Brave Horses (1961) Sonora Webster Carver

Writers:

Matt Williams, Oley Sassone

Director:

Steve Miner

Premiere:

May 24, 1991

Length:

89 min

COLLECTIONS

Video:

1992

Laserdisc:

1992

DVD:

2006

Digital:

iTunes, Vudu

The Rocketeer (1991)

"Two Thumps Up!"—Siskel & Ebert

(Note: Released by Touchstone Pictures internationally)

Source:

Character of The Rocketeer (1982+) created by Dave Stevens

Writers:

William Dear (story), Danny Bilson, Paul De Meo (story/screenplay)

Director:

Joe Johnston

Premiere:

Jun 19, 1991, Hollywood

Length:

108 min

CONNECTIONS

Comic Books:

- *The Rocketeer: The Official Movie Adaptation* (Jun 1991)
- *The Rocketeer 3-D Comic* (Jun 1991)

Video Games:

The Rocketeer (1991) NES, PC, SNES

COLLECTIONS

Video:

1991, 1993

Laserdisc:

1992

DVD:

1999

Blu-ray:

2011 20th Anniversary Edition

Digital:

Amazon, iTunes, Vudu

Soundtrack:

1991, 2016 Intrada Special Collection (CD)

Beauty and the Beast (1991)

The most beautiful love story ever told.

Source:

"La Belle et la Bête" (1740) Gabrielle-Suzanne Barbot de Villeneuve

Writers:

Linda Woolverton (animation screenplay), Brenda Chapman, Chris Sanders, Burny Mattinson, Kevin Harkey, Brian Pimental, Bruce Woodside, Joe Ranft, Tom Ellery, Kelly Asbury, Robert Lense (story)

Director:

Gary Trousdale, Kirk Wise

Premiere:

Sep 29, 1991, New York Film Festival / Nov 10, 1991, Hollywood

Re-releases:

2002 (IMAX, Special Edition), 2012 (3D)

Length:

84 min (original), 84 min (work-in-progress), 90 mins (special edition)

CONNECTIONS

Comic Books:

- *Disney's Beauty and the Beast* (1991) [Collection > *Disney Princess Comics Treasury* (2015)]
- *Beauty and the Beast* (DHS, Nov 30 – Dec 25, 1992) [Collection > *Disney's Christmas Classics* (2017)]
- *Disney's Beauty and the Beast* (#1–13, Sep 1994 – Sep 1995)
- *Beauty and the Beast: Magical Memories* (Disney Comic Hits #5, Feb 1996)

Movies:

- *Beauty and the Beast: The Enchanted Christmas* (DTV 1997) midquel
- *Belle's Magical World* (DTV 1998) midquel
- *Belle's Tales of Friendship* (DTV 1999) midquel
- *Beauty and the Beast* (2017) live-action remake

Shorts:

Beauty and the Beast (1995) Educational videodisc

Stage Musical:

- *Beauty and the Beast* (1994+)
- *Beauty and the Beast JR* (?) Disney Theatrical Licensing

TV Series:

Disney's Sing Me a Story with Belle (1995–1997) Syndication, 26 episodes

Theme Parks:

Beauty and the Beast: Live on Stage! (HS 1991+)

Video Games:

- *Disney's Beauty and the Beast: Roar of the Beast* (1993) G/MD
- *Disney's Beauty and the Beast: Belle's Quest* (1993) G/MD
- *Disney's Beauty and the Beast* (1994) NES, SNES
- *Disney's Beauty and the Beast: A Board Game Adventure* (1999) GBC
- *Disney's Beauty and the Beast: Magical Ballroom* (2000) Mac, PC

COLLECTIONS

Video:

1992 (Original)

Laserdisc:

1992 (work-in-progress), 1993 (original)

DVD*/Blu-ray:

2002 Platinum Edition* (all versions), 2010 Diamond Edition + Gift Set (all versions), 2011 3D (All versions), 2012 The Royal Wedding Collection (all versions), 2016 25th Anniversary Edition / The Signature Collection (all versions)

Digital:

Amazon, iTunes, Vudu

Soundtrack:

1991, 1994 *The Music Behind the Magic*, 2001, 2010 + *Songs and Story*, 2018 Legacy Collection (CD), 2014 (LP)

Books:

- *Disney's Beauty and the Beast: A Celebration of the Broadway Musical* (1995) Donald Frantz
- *Tale As Old As Time: The Art and Making of Beauty and the Beast* (2010, 2017 updated edition) Charles Solomon

Newsies (1992)

A Thousand Voices. A Single Dream.

AKA:

The News Boys (UK)

Source:

Based on 1899 Newsboys Strike

Writers:
Bob Tzudiker, Noni White

Director:
Kenny Ortega

Premiere:
Apr 8, 1992, New York

Re-releases:
2001 (Limited)

Length:
121 min

CONNECTIONS

Movies:
Disney's Newsies: The Broadway Musical (2017) film version of stage musical

Stage Musical:
Newsies: The Musical (2011+)

COLLECTIONS

Video:
1992

Laserdisc:
1992

DVD:
2002 Collector's Edition

Blu-ray:
2012 20th Anniversary Edition

Digital:
Amazon, iTunes, Vudu

Soundtrack:
1992, 2001 (CD)

Books:
Newsies: Stories of the Unlikely Broadway Hit (2013) Ed. Ken Cerniglia

Honey, I Blew Up the Kid (1992)

Source:

Sequel to *Honey, I Shrunk the Kids* (1989)

Writers:

Thom Eberhardt, Peter Elbling, Garry Goodrow

Director:

Randal Kleiser

Stars:

Rick Moranis

Premiere:

Jul 17, 1992

Length:

89 min

COLLECTIONS

Video:

1993

Laserdisc:

1993

DVD:

2002, 2009 Double Feature

Blu-ray:

2017 Disney Movie Club Exclusive

Digital:

iTunes, Vudu

Soundtrack:

1992 Intrada, 2017 Intrada: Expanded (CD)

The Mighty Ducks (1992)

AKA:

Champions (UK), *The Mighty Ducks Are the Champions* (UK home media)

Writers:

Steven Brill

Director:

Stephen Herek

Premiere:

Sep 20, 1992, Westwood, California

Length:

100 min

CONNECTIONS

Movies:

- *D2: The Mighty Ducks* (1994) sequel
- *D3: The Mighty Ducks* (1996) sequel
- *Mighty Ducks the Movie: The First Face-Off* (DTV 1997) animated compilation

TV Series:

Mighty Ducks (1996–1997) ABC/Syndication, 26 episodes, animated spin-off

COLLECTIONS

Video:

1993

Laserdisc:

1993

DVD:

2000, 2002 Special 3-Pack

Blu-ray:

2017 Disney Movie Club Exclusive

Digital:

iTunes, Vudu

Aladdin (1992)

Imagine if you had three wishes, three hopes, three dreams and they all could come true.

Source:

"Aladdin and the Magic Lamp" (1710) Antoine Galland

Writers:

Ron Clements, John Musker, Ted Elliott, Terry Rossio (screenplay), Burny Mattinson, Roger Allers, Daan Jippes, Kevin Harkey, Sue C. Nichols, Francis Glebas, Darrell Rooney, Larry Leker, James Fujii, Kirk Hanson, Kevin Lima, Rebecca Rees, David S. Smith, Chris Sanders, Brian Pimenthal, Patrick A. Ventura

Director:

Ron Clements, John Musker

Premiere:

Nov 8, 1992, Hollywood

Re-releases:

2004

Length:

90 min

CONNECTIONS

Comic Strips:

- *Disney's Aladdin* (1992) [Collection > *Disney Princess Comics Treasury* (2015)]
- *The Return of Disney's Aladdin* (#1-2, May – Jun 1993)
- *Aladdin* (DHS, Nov 29 – Dec 25, 1993) [Collection > *Disney's Christmas Classics* (2017)]
- *Disney's Aladdin* (#1-11, Oct 1994 – Aug 1995)
- *Disney's Aladdin: Faking Thunderbirds* (Disney Comic Hits #6, Mar 1996)

Movies:

- *The Return of Jafar* (DTV 1994) sequel
- *Aladdin and the King of Thieves* (DTV 1996) sequel
- *Disney Princess Enchanted Tales: Follow Your Dreams* (DTV 2007) [Section: "More Than a Peacock Princess"]
- *Aladdin* (2019) live-action remake

Stage Musical:

- *Aladdin* (2011+)
- *Aladdin JR.* (?) Disney Theatrical Licensing

TV Series:

- *Aladdin* (1994–1995) Disney Channel, 86 episodes [Collection > Episodes on: *Disney Princess Stories Vol 1-3* DVD (20042005)]
- *Disney Princess Party Vol 2* DVD (2005)
- *Jasmine's Enchanted Tales: Journey of a Princess* DVD (2005)

Theme Parks:

- Adventureland Bazaar (DP 1992+)
- Le Passage Enchanté d'Aladdin (DP 1993+)
- Arabian Coast (TDS 2001+)
- Caravan Carousel (TDS 2001+)
- The Magic Lamp Theater (TDS 2001+)
- The Magic Carpets of Aladdin (MK 2001+)
- Flying Carpets Over Agrabah (WDS 2002+)
- Disney's Aladdin: A Musical Spectacular (DCA 2003-2016)
- Jasmine's Flying Carpets (TDS 2011+)

Video Games:

- *Disney's Aladdin* (1993) G/MD, SNES, NES, Amiga, SMS, GG, GB, GBC, PC, GBA
- *Disney's Math Quest with Aladdin* (1998) PC, Mac
- *Disney's Aladdin in Nasira's Revenge* (2001) PS, PC
- *Disney's Aladdin Chess Adventures* (2004) PC

COLLECTIONS

Video:

1993

Laserdisc:

1994

DVD*/Blu-ray:

2004 Platinum Edition* + Collector's Gift Set*, 2015 Diamond Edition

Digital:

Amazon, iTunes

Soundtrack:

1992, 1994 *The Music Behind the Magic*, 2001, 2004 Special Edition (CD), 2014 (LP)

Books:

- *Disney's Aladdin: The Making of an Animated Film* (1992) John Culhane
- *Disney's Aladdin: A Whole New World – The Road to Broadway and Beyond* (2017) Michael Lassell

The Muppet Christmas Carol (1992)

Source:

A Christmas Carol (1843) Charles Dickens

Writers:

Jerry Juhl

Director:

Brian Henson

Stars:

The Muppets

Premiere:

Dec 11, 1992

Length:

85 min (original), 89 min (extended)

COLLECTIONS

Video:

1993 (Extended)

Laserdisc:

1993 (Extended)

DVD:

2002 (Extended), 2005 Kermit's 50th Anniversary Edition (original and extended)

Blu-ray:

2012 It's Not Easy Being Scrooge Special Edition / 20th Anniversary (original)

Digital:

Amazon, iTunes, Vudu

Soundtrack:

1993, 2005 Special Anniversary Edition (CD)

Homeward Bound: The Incredible Journey (1993)

In the classic tradition of Walt Disney Pictures comes a story about courage, adventure and friendship.

Source:

- *The Incredible Journey* (1961) Sheila Burnford
- Remake of *The Incredible Journey* (1963)

Writers:

Caroline Thompson, Linda Woolverton

Director:

Duwayne Dunham

Premiere:

Feb 3, 1993

Length:

84 min

CONNECTIONS

Movies:

Homeward Bound II: Lost in San Francisco (1996)

COLLECTIONS

Video:

1993

Laserdisc:

1993

DVD:

2000, 2008 2-Movie Collection, 2013 2-Movie Collection

Digital:

Amazon, iTunes, Vudu

Soundtrack:

1993 Intrada, 2015 Intrada Special Collection (CD)

A Far-Off Place (1993)

A far off land. A far off journey. A far off adventure.

Source:

A Story Like the Wind (1972) and *A Far-Off Place* (1974) Laurens van der Post

Writers:

Robert Caswell, Jonathan Hensleigh, Sally Robinson

Director:

Mikael Salomon

Premiere:

Mar 12, 1993

Length:

108 min

COLLECTIONS

Video:

1993

Laserdisc:

1993

DVD:

2004

Soundtrack:

1993 Intrada, 2014 Intrada Special Collection

The Adventures of Huck Finn (1993)

For anyone who has ever dreamed of running away from it all.

Source:

Adventures of Huckleberry Finn (1884) Mark Twain

Writers:

Stephen Sommers

Director:

Stephen Sommers

Premiere:

Mar 25, 1993, Los Angeles

Length:
108 min

CONNECTIONS

Movies:
Tom and Huck (1995) Adapts same source material

TV Movie:
Back to Hannibal: The Return of Tom Sawyer and Huckleberry Finn (1990) Disney Channel Premiere Film, adapts same source material

COLLECTIONS

Video:
1993

Laserdisc:
1993

DVD:
2002, 2009 Double Feature

Digital:
Amazon, Vudu

Soundtrack:
1993 Varese Sarabande (CD)

Hocus Pocus (1993)

Writers:
David Kirschner (story), Mick Garris (story/screenplay), Neil Cuthbert (screenplay)

Director:
Kenny Ortega

Stars:
Bette Midler, Sarah Jessica Parker, Kathy Najimy

Premiere:
Jul 16, 1993

Length:
96 min

COLLECTIONS

Video:

1994

Laserdisc:

1994

DVD*/Blu-ray:

2002*, 2012

Digital:

Amazon, iTunes, Vudu

Soundtrack:

1993, 2013 Intrada Special Collection (CD)

Books:

Hocus Pocus in Focus: The Thinking Fan's Guide to Disney's Halloween Classic (2016) Aaron Wallace

Cool Runnings (1993)

One dream. Four Jamaicans. Twenty below zero. Inspired by the True Story of the First Jamaican Olympic Bobsled Team

Source:

True story of 1988 Jamaican Olympic bobsled team

Writers:

Michael Ritchie (story), Lynn Siefert (story/screenplay), Tommy Swerdlow, Michael Goldberg (screenplay)

Director:

Jon Turteltaub

Premiere:

Oct 1, 1993

Length:

98 min

COLLECTIONS

Video:

1994

Laserdisc:

1994

DVD:

1999

Blu-ray:

2017 Disney Movie Club Exclusive

Digital:

iTunes, Vudu

Soundtrack:

1993 (CD)

The Nightmare Before Christmas (1993)

(Note: Touchstone Pictures release, later released by Disney on re-release and home media.)

AKA:

Tim Burton's The Nightmare Before Christmas

Source:

Story and characters by Tim Burton

Writers:

Michael McDowell (adaptation), Caroline Thompson (screenplay)

Director:

Henry Selick

Premiere:

Oct 9, 1993, New York

Re-releases:

2000, 2006 (3D), 2007 (3D), 2009 (3D)

Length:

76 min

CONNECTIONS

Comic Books:

- *Disney Tim Burton's the Nightmare Before Christmas* (Halloween ComicFest / Special Collector's Manga Oct 2016)
- *Disney Manga: Tim Burton's The Nightmare Before Christmas* (Sep 2017)

Video Games:

- *Tim Burton's The Nightmare Before Christmas: Oogie's Revenge* (2005) PS2, Xbox
- *Tim Burton's The Nightmare Before Christmas: The Pumpkin King* (2005) GBA

COLLECTIONS

Video:

1994

Laserdisc:

1994 + Deluxe Edition, 1997

DVD*/Blu-ray:

1997*, 2000 Special Edition*, 2006 Collector's Edition*, 2008 Collector's Edition + Limited Edition Ultimate Collector's DVD Set, 2010 Collector's Edition, 2011 3D, 2013 20th Anniversary Edition + 3D

Digital:

Amazon, iTunes, Vudu

Soundtrack:

1993, 2006 Special Edition, 2008 *Nightmare Revisited* (CD), 2003, 2016 (LP)

Books:

Tim Burton's The Nightmare Before Christmas: The Film, the Art, the Vision (1993) Frank Thompson

The Three Musketeers (1993)

A PLACE OF BETRAYAL. THE FATE OF A KING. A TIME FOR HEROES.

Source:

The Three Musketeers (1844) Alexandre Dumas

Writers:

David Loughery

Director:

Stephen Herek

Stars:

Charlie Sheen, Keifer Sutherland, Chris O'Donnell, Oliver Platt, Tim Curry, Rebecca De Mornay

Premiere:

Nov 12, 1993

Length:

105 min

CONNECTIONS

Comic Books:

Disney's The Three Musketeers (#1–2, Jan – Feb 1994)

Movies:

The Three Musketeers (DTV 2004) Animation, adapted from same source

COLLECTIONS

Video:

1994

Laserdisc:

1994

DVD:

1999

Blu-ray:

2018 25th Anniversary Edition, Disney Movie Club Exclusive

Digital:

iTunes, Vudu

Soundtrack:

1993 (CD)

Iron Will (1994)

It's not a question of age. Or strength. Or ability. It's a matter of will. Inspired by the incredible true story.

Source:

Based on a true story

Writers:

John Michael Hayes, Djordje Milicevic, Jeff Arcg

Director:

Charles Haid

Premiere:

Jan 14, 1994

Length:

109 min

COLLECTIONS

Video:

1994

Laserdisc:

1994

DVD:

2002

Soundtrack:

1994 Varese Sarabande (CD)

Blank Check (1994)

When Preston Waters sees an opportunity, he takes it. He knew what to do with a million bucks.

AKA:

Blank Cheque

Writers:

Blake Snyder, Colby Carr

Director:

Rupert Wainwright

Premiere:

Feb 11, 1994

Length:

93 min

COLLECTIONS

Video:

1994

Laserdisc:

1994

DVD:

2003

Digital:

Amazon, iTunes, Vudu

D2: The Mighty Ducks (1994)

THE PUCK STOPS HERE! THE MIGHTY DUCKS ARE BACK!

AKA:

The Mighty Ducks (UK, Australia), *The Mighty Ducks 2*

Source:

First sequel to *The Mighty Ducks* (1992)

Writers:

Steven Brill

Director:

Sam Weisman

Stars:

Emilio Estevez

Premiere:

Mar 25, 1994

Length:

106 min

COLLECTIONS

Video:

1994

Laserdisc:

1994

DVD:

2002 + Three Pack

Blu-ray:

2017 Disney Movie Club Exclusive

Digital:

iTunes, Vudu

Soundtrack:
1994 (CD)

White Fang 2: Myth of the White Wolf (1994)

AN ANCIENT MYTH. A LAND OF MYSTERY. AN EXTRAORDINARY ADVENTURE.

Source:
Sequel to *White Fang* (1991)

Writers:
David Fallon

Director:
Ken Olin

Premiere:
Apr 15, 1994

Length:
106 min

COLLECTIONS

Video:
1994

Laserdisc:
1994

DVD:
2002

Digital:
iTunes, Vudu

Soundtrack:
1994 *The Film Music of John Debney Volume 1* (CD)

The Return of Jafar (1994)

AKA:
Aladdin: The Return of Jafar

Source:
First sequel to *Aladdin* (1992)

Writers:

Duana Capizzi, Douglas Langadle, Mark McCorkle, Robert Schooley, Tad Stones (story), Kevin Campbell, Mirith J. Colao, Bill Motz, Steve Roberts, Dev Ross, Bob Roth, Jan Strnad, Brain Swenlin (screenplay)

Directors:

Toby Shelton, Tad Stones, Alan Zaslove

Premiere:

May 20, 1994, Video

Length:

69 min

CONNECTIONS

Comic Strips:

The Return of Jafar (Disney Adventures Digest Vol 4 #8, Jun 1994) [Collection > *Disney Princess Comics Treasury* (2015)]

COLLECTIONS

Video:

1994

Laserdisc

1994

DVD*Blu-ray:

2005 + Aladdin II & III Collection*, 2016 Disney Movie Club Exclusive / 2-Movie Collection

Digital:

Amazon, iTunes, Vudu

Soundtrack:

1996 *Aladdin and the King of Thieves* (CD)

The Lion King (1994)

Writers:

Irene Mecchi, Jonathan Roberts, Linda Woolverton (screenplay), Burny Mattinson, Barry Johnson, Lorna Cook, Thom Enriquez, Andy Gaskill, Gary Trousdale, Jim Capobianco, Kevin Harkey, Jorgen Klubien, Chris Sanders, Tom Sito, Larry Leker, Joe Ranft, Rick Maki, Ed Gombert, Francis Glebas, Mark Kausler

Directors:

Roger Allers, Rob Minkoff

Premiere:

Jun 15, 1994, New York/Los Angeles

Re-releases:

2002 (IMAX), 2011 (3D)

Length:

88 min (original), 90 min (special edition)

CONNECTIONS

Comic Strips:

- *Disney's The Lion King* (#1–2, Jul – Aug 1994)
- *The Lion King* (DHS, Nov 28 – Dec 24, 1994) Collection > *Disney's Christmas Classics* (2017)]
- *The Lion King's Timon & Pumbaa* (Disney Comic Hits #2, 8, 14, Nov 1995 – Nov 1996)
- *Timon and Pumbaa: Mall I Want for Christmas* (Disney Comics Hits #5, Feb 1996)

Movies:

- *The Lion King II: Simba's Pride* (DTV 1998) sequel
- *The Lion King 1½* (DTV 2004) prequel/midquel
- *The Lion King* (2019) CGI remake

Shorts:

- *Disney's Timon and Pumbaa in Stand By Me* (1995)
- *Wild About Safety* (2008-2012) Educational, 9 shorts
- *One by One* (2004) [Collection > *The Lion King II: Simba's Pride* DVD (2004)]

Stage Musical:

- *The Lion King* (1997+)
- *The Lion King Experience JR Edition* (?) Disney Theatrical Licensing
- *The Lion King Experience KIDS Edition* (?) Disney Theatrical Licensing

TV Movie:

The Lion Guard: Return of the Roar (2015) Pilot for *The Lion Guard* TV series

TV Series:

- *The Lion King's Timon & Pumbaa* (1995-1997) CBS/Syndication, 85 episodes
- *The Lion Guard* (2015+) Disney Junior/Disney Channel

Theme Parks:

- The Legend of the Lion King (MK 1994-2002), (DP 2004-2009)
- The Lion King Celebration (DL 1994-1997) parade
- *Circle of Life: An Environmental Fable* (E 1995+)
- Festival of the Lion King (AK 1998+), (HKD 2005+)

Video Games:

- *The Lion King* (1994) SNES, G/MG, GB, NES, GG, PC, Amiga, SMS
- *Disney's Timon & Pumbaa's Jungle Games* (1995) PC, SNES, Mac
- *Disney's The Lion King: Simba's Mighty Adventure* (2000) PS, GBC

COLLECTIONS

Video:

1995 Masterpiece Collection (original)

Laserdisc:

1995 + Deluxe Edition / Masterpiece Collection (original)

DVD*/Blu-ray:

2003 Platinum Edition* + Collector's Gift Set* (special edition), 2011 Diamond Edition + 3D (original), 2017 The Circle of Life Edition / The Signature Collection (original)

Soundtrack:

1994, 2014 (LP), 1994, 1995 *Rhythm of the Pride Lands*, 2003 Special Edition, 2011 *Songs and Story*, 2011 *Best of The Lion King*, 2014 The Legacy Collection (CD)

Books:

- *The Art of The Lion King* (1994) Christopher Finch
- *The Lion King: Pride Rock on Broadway* (1997) Julie Taymor
- *The Lion King: Twenty Years on Broadway and Around the World* (2017) Michael Lassell

Angels in the Outfield (1994)

Ya Gotta Believe! It Could Happen.

Source

Remake of MGM's *Angels in the Outfield* (1951)

Writers:

Dorothy Kingsley, George Wells, Holly Goldberg Sloan

Director:

William Dear

Stars:

Danny Glover, Tony Danza, Christopher Lloyd

Premiere:

Jul 10, 1994, Pittsburgh

Length:

103 min

CONNECTIONS

TV Movies:

- *Angels in the Endzone* (1997) ABC, *The Wonderful World of Disney*
- *Angels in the Infield* (2000) ABC, *The Wonderful World of Disney*

COLLECTIONS

Video:

1995

Laserdisc:

1995

DVD:

2002, 2009 Double Feature, 2012 Disney 4-Movie Collection: Game Changers

Soundtrack:

1994 (CD)

Squanto: A Warrior's Tale (1994)

AKA:

The Last Great Warrior

Writers:

Darlene Craviotto

Director:

Xavier Koller

Premiere:

Oct 28, 1994

Length:

102 min

COLLECTIONS

Video:

1995

Laserdisc:

1995

DVD:

2004

Digital:

iTunes, Vudu

Soundtrack:

2011 Intrada Special Collection (CD)

The Santa Clause (1994)

Scott Calvin must become Santa. No ifs or ands…just one big butt.

Writers:

Leo Benvenuti, Steve Rudnick

Director:

John Pasquin

Stars:

Tim Allen

Premiere:

Nov 11, 1994

Length:

97 min

CONNECTIONS
Movies:
- *The Santa Clause 2* (2002) sequel
- *The Santa Clause 3: The Escape Clause* (2006) sequel

COLLECTIONS
Video:
1995

Laserdisc:
1995

DVD:
1998, 2002 Special Edition, 2007 The Santa Clause Holiday Collection

Blu-ray:
2012 + The Santa Clause: The Complete 3-Movie Collection

Digital:
Amazon, iTunes, Vudu

Soundtrack:
1994 (CD)

The Jungle Book (1994)

From one of the greatest novels ever written comes a thrilling new motion picture classic. Born of men. Raised by animals. Destined for adventure.

AKA:
Rudyard Kipling's The Jungle Book

Source:
The Jungle Book (1894) Rudyard Kipling

Writers:
Ron Yanover, Mark Geldman (story/screenplay), Stephen Sommers (screenplay)

Director:
Stephen Sommers

Premiere:
Dec 26, 1994, Iceland

US Release:

Dec 29, 1994, New York

Length:

111 min

CONNECTIONS

Video Games:

The Jungle Book (1996) PC

COLLECTIONS

Video:

1995

Laserdisc:

1995

DVD:

2002

Digital:

Vudu

Soundtrack:

1994 (CD)

PART SEVEN

Movies: 1995–1999

Gargoyles the Movie: The Heroes Awaken (1995)

From Disney Animators!

Source:

Edited from *Gargoyles* (1994–1997) TV series: "Awakening Parts 1–5"

Writers:

Eric Luke (story), Michael Reaves (story/screenplay)

Directors:

Saburo Hashimoto, Kazuo Terada, Takamitsu Kawamura

Premiere:

Jan 31, 1995, Video/Laserdisc

Length:

80 min

CONNECTIONS

Comic Books:

- *Gargoyles* (#1–11, Feb – Dec 1995) Marvel
- *Gargoyles: Clan-Building* (#1–8, Jun 2006 – Mar 2008) SLG Publishing [Collection > *Gargoyles: Clan-Building Vol. 1* (2007) & *Vol. 2* (2009)]
- *Gargoyles: Bad Guys* (#1-4, Nov 2007 – Aug 2008) SLG Publishing [Collection > *Gargoyles: Bad Guys* (2009)]

TV Series:

- *Gargoyles* (1994-1996) ABC/Syndication, 65 episodes [Collection > *Gargoyles: The Complete First Season* DVD (2004)]
- *Gargoyles: Season 2, Vol 1* DVD (2005)

- *Gargoyles: Season 2, Vol 2* DVD (2013 Disney Movie Club Exclusive, 2015)
- *Gargoyles Vol 1–4* iTunes (2017)
- *Gargoyles: The Goliath Chronicles* (1996-1997), ABC/Syndication, 13 episodes [Collection > *Gargoyles Vol 5* iTunes (2017)]

Video Games:
Gargoyles (1995) G/MD

COLLECTIONS
Video:
1995

Laserdisc:
1995

Heavyweights (1995)

From the Creator of "The Mighty Ducks." They don't run the fastest. They don't jump the highest. But they sure are getting the last laugh. They never met a hot dog they didn't like... until now.

Writers:
Judd Apatow, Steven Brill

Director:
Steven Brill

Premiere:
Feb 17, 1995

Length:
98 min

COLLECTIONS
Video:
1995

Laserdisc:
1995

DVD:
2003

Blu-ray:
2012

Digital:

Amazon, iTunes, Vudu

Man of the House (1995)

Jack wants to marry Ben's mother. But there are strings attached.

Writers:

David E. Peckinpah, Richard Jefferies (story), James Orr, Jim Cruickshank (screenplay)

Director:

James Orr

Stars:

Chevy Chase, Jonathan Taylor Thomas

Premiere:

Mar 3, 1995

Length:

96 min

COLLECTIONS

Video:

1995

Laserdisc:

1995

DVD:

2004

Digital:

iTunes, Vudu

Tall Tale (1995)

A journey into a world where legends come to life, dreams come true, and every boy is a hero.

AKA:

- *Tall Tale: The Unbelievable Adventures of Pecos Bill*
- *Tall Tale: The Unbelievable Adventure*

Source:

Based on various western heroes

Writers:

Steve Bloom, Robert Rodat

Director:

Jeremiah S. Chechik

Premiere:

Mar 24, 1995

Length:

97 min

COLLECTIONS

Video:

1995

Laserdisc:

1995

DVD:

2008

Digital:

Amazon, iTunes, Vudu

Soundtrack:

1995 (CD)

A Goofy Movie (1995)

It's hard to be cool when your Dad is Goofy.

Source:

Spin-off from *Goof Troop* (1992-1993) TV series

Writers:

Jymn Magon (story/screenplay), Chris Matheson, Brian Pimental (screenplay)

Director:

Kevin Lima

Premiere:

Apr 7, 1995

Length:

77 min

CONNECTIONS

Movies:

An Extremely Goofy Movie (DTV 2000) Sequel

TV Series:

Goof Troop (1992-1993) Disney Channel/Syndication, 78 episodes [Collection > 54 Episodes on *Goof Troop Vol 1-2* DVD (2013)] All episodes on iTunes (2017)

TV Special:

A Goof Troop Christmas/Have Yourself a Goofy Little Christmas (1992) [Collection > DVD (2015)]

Video Games:

Goof Troop (1993) SNES

COLLECTIONS

Video:

1995

Laserdisc:

1996

DVD:

2000 Gold Classic Collection

Digital:

Amazon, Vudu

Soundtrack:

1995, 2001 (CD), 2016 (LP)

Pocahontas (1995)

An American Legend Comes to Life.

Source:

Inspired by historical events

Writers:

Carl Binder, Susannah Grant, Philip LaZebnik (screenplay), Glen Keane, Joe Grant, Ralph Zondag, Burny Mattinson, Ed Gombert, Kaan Kalyon, Francis Glebas, Rob Gibbs, Bruce Morris, Todd Kurosawa, Duncan Marjoribanks, Chris Buck (story)

Directors:

Mike Gabriel, Eric Goldberg

Premiere:

Jun 10, 1995, New York

Length:

81 min (original), 84 min (10th Anniversary Edition)

CONNECTIONS

Comic Strips:

- *Pocahontas* (Jul 1995) [Collection > *Disney Princess Comics Treasury* (2015)]
- *Pocahontas* (Disney Comic Hits #1, 3, 7, Oct 1995 – Apr 1996)
- *Pocahontas* (DHS, Nov 27 – Dec 23, 1995) [Collection > *Disney's Christmas Classics* (2017)]
- *Pocahontas: Holiday Harmony* (Disney Comic Hits #5, Feb 1996)

Movies:

Pocahontas II: Journey to a New World (DTV 1998) Sequel

Video Games:

Disney's Pocahontas (1996) GB, G/MD, PS

COLLECTIONS

Video:

1996 Masterpiece Collection

Laserdisc:

1996 + Deluxe Edition / Masterpiece Collection, 1997

DVD*/Blu-ray:

2000 Gold Classic Collection*, 2005 10th Anniversary Edition*, 2012 2-Movie Collection / Special Edition, 2016 Disney Movie Club Exclusive

Digital:

Amazon, Vudu

Soundtrack:

1995, 2012 *Songs and Story*, 2015 Legacy Collection (CD)

Books:

The Art of Pocahontas (1995) Stephen Rebello

Operation Dumbo Drop (1995)

When you weight four tons, it's hard to be a secret weapon. A story about big dreams and small miracles.

Source:

Based on a true story.

Writers:

Gene Quintano, Jim Kouf (screenplay), James Morris (story)

Director:

Simon Wincer

Stars:

Danny Glover, Ray Liotta, Denis Leary, Doug E. Doug, Corin Nemec

Premiere:

Jul 28, 1995

Length:

108 min

COLLECTIONS

Video:

1996

Laserdisc:

1996

DVD:

2003

Blu-ray:

2016 Disney Movie Club Exclusive / 20th Anniversary Edition

Digital:

iTunes, Vudu

Soundtrack:

1995, 2017 *Good Morning, Vietnam/Operation Dumbo Drop* Intrada Special Collection (CD)

A Kid in King Arthur's Court (1995)

Calvin Fuller is about to break curfew...by 1500 years. JOUST DO IT.

Source:

A Connecticut Yankee in King Arthur's Court (1889) Mark Twain

Writers:
Michael Part, Robert L. Levy

Director:
Michael Gottlieb

Premiere:
Aug 11, 1995

Length:
89 min

CONNECTIONS

Movies:
A Kid in Aladdin's Palace (DTV 1997) Sequel released by Trimark Pictures

COLLECTIONS

Video:
1996

Laserdisc:
1996

DVD:
2003

Digital:
Amazon, Vudu

Soundtrack:
1995 (CD)

The Big Green (1995)

The Biggest Kick Of The Year!

Writers:
Holly Goldberg Sloan

Director:
Holly Goldberg Sloan

Premiere:
Sep 29, 1995

Length:
100 min

COLLECTIONS

Video:

1996

Laserdisc:

1996

DVD:

2004

Digital:

Amazon, iTunes, Vudu

Soundtrack:

1995 (CD)

Frank and Ollie (1995)

Their friendship changed the face of animation.

Writers:

Theodore Thomas

Director:

Theodore Thomas

Stars:

Frank Thomas, Ollie Johnston

Preview:

Jan 22, 1995, Sundance Festival

Premiere:

Oct 20, 1995, Los Angeles (Limited)

Length:

89 min

COLLECTIONS

Video:

1998

DVD:

2003 Special Edition

Digital:

iTunes, Vudu

Books:

- *The Illusion of Life: Disney Animation* (1981) Frank Thomas & Ollie Johnston
- *Too Funny For Words!* (1987) Frank Thomas & Ollie Johnston
- *The Disney Villains* (1993) Frank Thomas & Ollie Johnston

Toy Story (1995)

Writers:

John Lasseter, Pete Docter, Joe Ranft (story), Andrew Stanton (story/screenplay), Joss Whedon, Joel Cohen, Alec Sokolow (screenplay)

Director:

John Lasseter

Premiere:

Nov 19, 1995, Hollywood

Re-releases:

2009 (3D)

Length:

81 min

CONNECTIONS

Comic Strips:

- *Disney's Toy Story* (1995)
- *Toy Story: Mysterious Stranger* (#1–4, May – Jul 2009)
- *Toy Story* (#0–7, Nov 2009 – Sep 2010)
- *Toy Story: Tales from the Toy Chest* (#1–4, Jul – Oct 2010)
- *Toy Story* (#1–4, May – Aug 2012)

Movies:

- *Toy Story 2* (1999) sequel
- *Toy Story 3* (2010) sequel
- *Toy Story 4* (2019) sequel

Shorts:

Toy Story Treats (1996) x 15 [Collection > *Toy Story* DVD/Blu-ray (2005+)]

Stage Musical:

Toy Story: The Musical (2008–2016) Disney Wonder Cruise Ship

Theme Parks:

- Buzz Lightyear's Space Ranger Spin (MK 1998+)
- Buzz Lightyear's Astro Blasters (TDL 2004+), (DL 2005+), (HKD 2005+)
- Buzz Lightyear Laser Blast (DP 2006+)
- Toy Story Midway Mania! (HS 2008+), (DCA 2008+), (TDS 2012+)
- RC Racer (WDS 2010+), (HKD 2011+)
- Toy Story Parachute Drop (WDS 2010+), (HKD 2011+)
- Slinky Dog Zigzag Spin (WDS 2010+)
- Slinky Dog Spin (HKD 2011+)
- Buzz Lightyear Planet Rescue (SD 2016+)

Video Games:

Disney's Toy Story (1995) SNES, G/MD, GB, PC

COLLECTIONS

Video:

1996, 2002

Laserdisc:

1996 + Deluxe Edition

DVD*/Blu-ray:

2000 2 Pack* + Ultimate Toy Box: Collector's Edition*, 2005 10th Anniversary Edition*, 2010 Special Edition + Ultimate Toy Box Collection, 2011 3D, 2015, 2016 3D

Digital:

Amazon, iTunes, Vudu

Soundtrack:

1995, 2002, 2009 *Songs and Story*, 2015 The Legacy Collection (CD), 2015 (LP)

Books:

- *Toy Story: The Art and Making of the Animated Film* (1995) Steve Daly, John Lasseter
- *Toy Story Sketchbook* (2000)
- *The Toy Story Films: An Animated Journey* (2012) Charles Solomon

Tom and Huck (1995)

A lot of kids get into trouble. These too invented it. THE ORIGINAL BAD BOYS.

Source:

The Adventures of Tom Sawyer (1876) Mark Twain

Writers:

Stephen Sommers, David Loughery

Director:

Peter Hewitt

Stars:

Jonathan Taylor Thomas, Brad Renfro

Premiere:

Dec 22, 1995

Length:

97 min

COLLECTIONS

Video:

1996

Laserdisc:

1996

DVD:

2003, 2009 Double Feature

Digital:

iTunes, Vudu

Soundtrack:

1995 (CD)

Muppet Treasure Island (1996)

Source:

Treasure Island (1883) Robert Louis Stevenson

Writers:

Jerry Juhl, Kirk R. Thatcher, James V. Hart

Director:

Brian Henson

Premiere:

Feb 16, 1996

Length:

99 min

CONNECTIONS

Video Games:

Muppet Treasure Island (1997) Mac, PC

COLLECTIONS

Video:

1996

Laserdisc:

1997

DVD*/Blu-ray:

2002*, 2005 Kermit's 50th Anniversary Edition*, 2013 Of Pirates & Pigs Collection

Digital:

Amazon, iTunes, Vudu

Soundtrack:

1996 (CD)

Homeward Bound II: Lost in San Francisco (1996)

Source:

Sequel to *Homeward Bound: The Incredible Journey* (1993)

Writers:

Chris Hauty, Julie Hickson

Director:

David R. Ellis

Premiere:

Mar 8, 1996

Length:

89 min

COLLECTIONS

Video:

1996

Laserdisc:

1996

DVD:

2002, 2008 2-Movie Collection, 2013 2-Movie Collection

Digital:

Amazon, iTunes, Vudu

Soundtrack:

1996, 2016 Intrada Special Collection (CD)

James and the Giant Peach (1996)

Source:

James and the Giant Peach (1961) Roald Dahl

Writers:

Karey Kirkpatrick, Jonathan Roberts, Steve Bloom

Director:

Henry Selick

Premiere:

Apr 12, 1996

Length:

79 min

COLLECTIONS

Video:

1996

Laserdisc:

1997

DVD*/Blu-ray:

2000 Special Edition*, 2010 Special Edition

Digital:

Amazon, iTunes, Vudu

Soundtrack:

1996 (CD)

Books:

James and the Giant Peach: The Book and Movie Scrapbook (1996) Lucy Dahl

The Hunchback of Notre Dame (1996)

Source:

Notre-Dame de Paris (1831) Victor Hugo

Writers:

Irene Mecchi, Bob Tzudiker, Noni White, Jonathan Roberts (screen-play), Tab Murphy (story/screenplay), Kevin Harkey, Gaëtan Brizzi, Paul Brizzi, Ed Gombert, Brenda Chapman, Jeff Snow, Jim Capobianco, Denis Rich, Burny Mattinson, John Sanford, Kelly Wightman, James Fuji, Geefwee Boedoe, Floyd Norman, Francis Glebas, Kirk Hanson, Christine Blum, Sue C. Nichols

Directors:

Gary Trousdale, Kirk Wise

Premiere:

Jun 19, 1996

Length:

91 min

CONNECTIONS

Comic Strips:

- *Disney's The Hunchback of Notre Dame* (Jul 1996)
- *Disney's The Hunchback of Notre Dame* (Disney Comic Hits #10-11, Jul-Aug 1996)
- *The Hunchback of Notre Dame* (DHS, Dec 2 – 28 1996) [Collection > *Disney's Christmas Classics* (2017)]

Movies:

The Hunchback of Notre Dame II (DTV 2002) Sequel

Stage Musical:

- *Der Glöckner von Notre Dame* (1999-2002) Berlin
- *The Hunchback of Notre Dame* (2014+)

Theme Parks:
- Hunchback of Notre Dame – A Musical Spectacular (MGM 1996-2002)
- The Hunchback of Notre Dame Festival of Fools (DL 1996-1998)

Video Games:

Disney's The Hunchback of Notre Dame: Topsy Turvy Games (1996) GB, PC

COLLECTIONS

Video:

1997 Masterpiece Collection

Laserdisc:

1997 + Deluxe Edition

DVD*/Blu-ray:

2002*, 2013 2-Movie Collection / Special Edition

Digital:

Google Play

Soundtrack:

1996 (CD), 2016 (LP)

Books:

The Art of The Hunchback of Notre Dame (1996) Stephen Rebello

Aladdin and the King of Thieves (1996)

The Must-Own Spectacular Conclusion To The Aladdin Movie Trilogy!

Source:

Second sequel to *Aladdin* (1992)

Writers:

Mark McCorkle, Robert Schooley

Director:

Tad Stones

Stars:

Robin Williams

Premiere:

Aug 13, 1996, Video

Length:

80 min

CONNECTIONS

Comic Strips:

- *Aladdin and the King of Thieves* (Disney Adventures #96-12, Dec 1996)
- *Aladdin and the King of Thieves* (unknown provenance) [Collection > *Disney Princess Comics Treasury* (2015)]

COLLECTIONS

Video:

1996

Laserdisc:

1997

DVD*/Blu-ray:

2005 + Aladdin II & III Collection*, 2015*, 2016 Disney Movie Club Exclusive / 2-Movie Collection

Digital:

iTunes, Vudu

Soundtrack:

1996 (CD)

First Kid (1996)

He's young. He's wild. He's fun. And he's the one protecting the president's son.

Writers:

Tim Kelleher

Director:

David M. Evans

Stars:

Sinbad

Premiere:

Aug 30, 1996

Length:

101 min

COLLECTIONS

Video:
1997

Laserdisc:
1997

DVD:
2003

Digital:
iTunes, Vudu

Soundtrack:
1996 (CD)

D3: The Mighty Ducks (1996)
DUCK SEASON OPENS OCT. 4

Source:
Second sequel to *The Mighty Ducks* (1992)

Writers:
Kenneth Johnson (story), Jim Burnstein (story/screenplay), Steven Brill (screenplay)

Director:
Robert Lieberman

Stars:
Emilio Estevez

Premiere:
Oct 4, 1996

Length:
104 min

COLLECTIONS

Video:
1997

Laserdisc:
1997

DVD:

2002 + Three-Pack

Blu-ray:

2017 Disney Movie Club Exclusive

Digital:

Amazon, iTunes, Vudu

Soundtrack:

1996 (CD)

Mr. Toad's Wild Ride (1996)

(Note: Allied Filmmakers film initially distributed by Columbia Pictures in US home media distribution by Disney.)

AKA:

The Wind in the Willows (Original title)

Source:

The Wind in the Willows (1908) Kenneth Grahame

Writers:

Terry Jones

Director:

Terry Jones

Stars:

Steve Coogan, Eric Idle, Terry Jones, John Cleese

Premiere:

Oct 18, 1996, UK & Ireland

US Release:

Oct 31, 1997 (Columba Pictures)

Length:

88 min

COLLECTIONS

Video:

1998

DVD:

2004, 2012 Disney 4-Movie Collection: Thrills and Chills

101 Dalmatians (1996)

So many dogs. So little time.

Source:

- Remake of *One Hundred and One Dalmatians* (1961)
- *The Hundred and One Dalmatians* (1956) Dodie Smith

Writers:

John Hughes

Director:

Stephen Herek

Stars:

Glenn Close

Premiere:

Nov 18, 1996, New York

Length:

103 min

CONNECTIONS

Movies:

102 Dalmatians (2000) sequel

Video Games:

101 Dalmatians: Escape from DeVil Manor (1997) PC

COLLECTIONS

Video:

1997

Laserdisc:

1997

DVD:

2000, 2001 2-Pack, 2008

Digital:

Vudu

Soundtrack:

1996 (CD)

Books:

101 Dalmatians Scrapbook: Behind the Scenes of the Live-Action Movie (1997) Lucy Dahl

That Darn Cat (1997)

This FBI agent is putting his life on the line. Fortunately, he's got nine.

Source:

- Remake of *That Darn Cat!* (1965)
- *Undercover Cat* (1963) The Gordons

Writers:

Scott Alexander, Larry Karaszewski

Director:

Bob Spiers

Stars:

Christina Ricci, Doug E. Doug

Premiere:

Feb 14, 1997

Length:

89 min

COLLECTIONS

Video:

1997

Laserdisc:

1997

DVD:

2003, 2009 Double Feature

Digital:

Amazon, iTunes, Vudu

Soundtrack:

1997 (CD)

Jungle 2 Jungle (1997)
GET A LITTLE SAVAGE

Source:

Remake of *Un indien dans la ville* (1994)

Writers:

Bruce A. Evans, Raynold Gideon

Director:

John Pasquin

Stars:

Tim Allen

Premiere:

Mar 7, 1997

Length:

105 min

COLLECTIONS

Video:

1997

Laserdisc:

1997

DVD:

2002

Blu-ray:

2018 20th Anniversary Edition / Disney Movie Club Exclusive

Digital:

iTunes, Vudu

Soundtrack:

1997 (CD)

Honey, We Shrunk Ourselves (1997)
ALL-NEW FULL-LENGTH MOTION PICTURE!

Source:

Second sequel to *Honey, I Shrunk the Kids* (1989)

Writers:

Karey Kirkpatrick, Nell Scovell, Joel Hodgson

Director:

Dean Cundey

Stars:

Rick Moranis

Premiere:

Mar 18, 1997, Video

Length:

74 min

COLLECTIONS

Video:

1997

Laserdisc:

1997

DVD:

2002, 2009 Double Feature

Digital:

iTunes, Vudu

Mighty Ducks the Movie: The First Face-Off (1997)

Source:

Edited from episodes of *The Mighty Ducks* (1996–1997) TV series: "The First Face-Off Parts 1–2" and "Duck Hard"

Writers:

Garfield Reeves-Stevens, Judith Reeves-Stevens, David Wise

Directors:

Joe Barruso, Doug Murphy, Blair Peters, Baekyup Sung

Premiere:

Apr 8, 1997, Video

Length:

66 min

CONNECTIONS

TV Series:

Mighty Ducks (1996–1997) ABC/Syndication, 26 episodes

COLLECTIONS

Video:

1997

The Brave Little Toaster to the Rescue (1997)

Complete Your "Brave Little Toaster" Collection With The Fun-Filled Final Chapter!

Source:

First sequel to *The Brave Little Toaster* (1987)

Writers:

Willard Carroll

Director:

Robert C. Ramirez

Premiere:

May 25, 1997, Video

Length:

74 min

COLLECTIONS

Video:

1997

DVD:

2003

Digital:

Vudu

Hercules (1997)

Source:

Greek mythology

Writers:

Ron Clements, John Musker, Don McEnery, Bob Shaw, Irene Mecchi (screenplay), Kaan Kalyon, Kelly Wightman, Randy Cartwright, John Ramirez, Jeff Snow, Vance Gerry, Kirk Hanson, Tamara Lusher-Stocker, Francis Glebas, Mark Kennedy, Bruce Morris, Don Dougherty, Thom Enriquez

Directors:

Ron Clements, John Musker

Premiere:

Jun 14, 1997, New York

Length:

93 min

CONNECTIONS

Movies:

Hercules: Zero to Hero (DTV 1999) prequel

TV Series:

Hercules (1998-1999) syndication, 65 episodes

Video Games:

- *Disney's Hercules: Action Game* (1997) PS, PC, PS3
- *Disney's Hades Challenge* (1998) Mac, PC

COLLECTIONS

Video:

1998 Masterpiece Collection

Laserdisc:

1998 Masterpiece Collection

DVD*/Blu-ray:

1999 Limited Issue*, 2000 Gold Classic Collection*, 2014 Special Edition

Digital:

iTunes, Vudu

Soundtrack:

1997 (CD), 2017 (LP)

Books:

The Art of Hercules: The Chaos of Creation (1997) S. Rebello & J. Healey

Air Bud (1997)

He Sits. He Stays. He Shoots. He Scores. The Dog Is In The House.

Source:

Inspired by Buddy, a golden retriever trained by Kevin DiCicco

Writers:

Paul Tamasy, Aaron Mendelsohn

Director:

Charles Martin Smith

Premiere:

Aug 1, 1997

Length:

98 min

CONNECTIONS

Movies:

- *Air Bud: Golden Receiver* (1998) sequel
- *Air Bud: World Pup* (DTV 2000) sequel
- *Air Bud: Seventh Inning Fetch* (DTV 2002) sequel
- *Air Bud: Spikes Back* (DTV 2003) sequel
- *Air Buddies* (DTV 2006) spin-off

COLLECTIONS

Video:

1997

Laserdisc:

1997

DVD:

1998, 2009 Special Edition

Digital:

Amazon, iTunes, Vudu

Soundtrack:

1997 (CD)

Pooh's Grand Adventure:
The Search for Christopher Robin (1997)

THE ALL-NEW MOVIE

AKA:

Winnie the Pooh's Most Grand Adventure

Writers:

Karl Geurs, Carter Crocker

Director:

Karl Geurs

Premiere:

Aug 5, 1997, Video

Length:

76 min

COLLECTIONS

Video:

1997

Laserdisc:

1998

DVD:

2006 Special Edition

Digital:

Amazon, iTunes, Vudu

Soundtrack:

1997 + *The Many Songs of Winnie the Pooh*

George of the Jungle (1997)

Source:

George of the Jungle (1967) TV series

Writers:

Dana Olsen (story/screenplay), Audrey Wells (screenplay)

Director:

Sam Weisman

Stars:

Brendan Fraser

Premiere:

Jul 16, 1997

Length:

92 min

CONNECTIONS

Movies:

George of the Jungle 2 (DTV 2003)

COLLECTIONS

Video:

1997

Laserdisc:

1997

DVD:

1997, 2010 Double Feature

Digital:

Amazon, iTunes, Vudu

Soundtrack:

1997 (CD)

RocketMan (1997)

He's just taking up space.

Writers:

Oren Aviv (story), Craig Mazin, Greg Erb (story/screenplay)

Director:

Stuart Gillard

Premiere:

Oct 10, 1997

Length:

95 min

COLLECTIONS

Video:

1998

Laserdisc:

1998

DVD:

2005

Blu-ray:

2018 20th Anniversary Edition, Disney Movie Club Exclusive

Digital:

iTunes, Vudu

Beauty and the Beast: The Enchanted Christmas (1997)

All The Magic of Disney's Legendary Classic Continues.

Source:

Spin-off from *Beauty and the Beast* (1991)

Writers:

Flip Kobler, Cindy Marcus, Bill Motz, Bob Roth

Director:

Andrew Knight

Premiere:

Nov 11, 1997, Video

Length:

72 min

COLLECTIONS

Video:

1997

Laserdisc:

1998

DVD*/Blu-ray:

1998*, 2002 Special Edition*, 2011 Special Edition, 2016 Disney Movie Club Exclusive

Digital:

Amazon, iTunes, Vudu

Soundtrack:

1997 (CD)

Flubber (1997)

Source:

- Remake of *The Absent-Minded Professor* (1961)
- "A Situation of Gravity" in *Liberty* (1943) Samuel W. Taylor

Writers:

John Hughes, Bill Walsh

Director:

Les Mayfield

Stars:

Robin Williams

Premiere:

Nov 16, 1997, New York

Length:

94 min

COLLECTIONS

Video:

1998

Laserdisc:

1998

DVD:

1998

Digital:

Amazon, iTunes, Vudu

Soundtrack:

1997 (CD)

Mr. Magoo (1997)

The eighth blunder of the world.

Source:

Mr. Magoo, created in 1949 by UPA Productions

Writers:

Pat Proft, Tom Sherohman

Director:

Stanley Tong

Stars:

Leslie Nielsen

Premiere:

Dec 25, 1997

Length:

87 min

COLLECTIONS

Video:

1998

Laserdisc:

1998

DVD:

2000

Digital:

Amazon, Vudu

Belle's Magical World (1998)

Sections:

The Perfect World[1], *Fifi's Folly*[2], *The Broken Wing*[3], *Mrs. Potts' Party*[4]

Source:

Spin-off from *Beauty and the Beast* (1991)

Writers:

[3] Chip Hand (story), [1,4] Richard Cray, [2] Alice Brown, [2,3] Carter Crocker, [3] Sheree Guitar, [4] Nancy Greystone

Directors:

Bob Kline, [1,4] Cullen Blaine, [2] Dale Case, [2] Daniel de la Vega, [3] Barbara Dourmashkin, [4] Rick Leon, [3] Burt Medall, [1] Mitch Rochon

Premiere:

Feb 16, 1998, Video

Length:

70 min ([1,2,3] original), 92 min ([1,2,3,4] special edition)

CONNECTIONS

Movies:

Belle's Tales of Friendship (DTV 1999) [4] taken from this film for special edition

COLLECTIONS

Video:

1998

DVD:

2003 Special Edition, 2011 Special Edition

Meet the Deedles (1998)

TO PROTECT AND SURF.

Writers:

Jim Herzfeld

Director:

Steve Boyum

Premiere:

Mar 27, 1998

Length:

94 min

COLLECTIONS

Video:

1998

Laserdisc:

1998

DVD:
2005 (UK)

Digital:
Amazon, iTunes, Vudu

Soundtrack:
1998 (CD)

The Brave Little Toaster Goes to Mars (1998)

An All-New, Feature-Length Animated Movie!

Source:

- Second sequel to *The Brave Little Toaster* (1987)
- *The Brave Little Toaster Goes to Mars* (1988) Thomas M. Disch

Writers:
Willard Carroll

Director:
Robert C. Ramirez

Premiere:
May 18, 1998, Video

Length:
73 min

COLLECTIONS

Video:
1998

DVD:
2003

Digital:
Amazon, Vudu

Mulan (1998)

Source:
Chinese legend of Hua Mulan, 6th century

Writers:

Rita Hsiao, Chris Sanders, Philip LaZebnik, Raymond Singer, Eugenia Bostwick-Singer (screenplay), Robert D. San Souci, Dean DeBlois, John Sanford, Tim Hodge, Chris Williams, Julius Aguimatang, Burny Mattinson, Lorna Cook, Barry Johnson, Thom Enriquez, Ed Gombert, Joe Grant, Floyd Norman

Directors:

Tony Bancroft, Barry Cook

Premiere:

Jun 5, 1998

Length:

88 min

CONNECTIONS

Comic Books:

Mulan (Dec 1998) [Collection > *Disney Princess Comics Treasury* (2015)]

Movies:

- *Mulan II* (DTV 2004) sequel
- *Mulan* (2020) live-action remake

Stage Musical:

Mulan JR. (?) Disney Theatrical Licensing

Video Games:

- *Disney's Mulan* (1998) GB
- *Disney's Story Studio: Mulan* (1999) PS

COLLECTIONS

Video:

1999

DVD*/Blu-ray:

1999 Gold Collection*, 2004 Special Edition*, 2013 2-Movie Collection / Special Edition, 2016 Disney Movie Club Exclusive, 2017 2-Movie Collection

Digital:

Amazon, Vudu

Soundtrack:

1998, 2013 *Songs and Story* (CD)

Books:

- *The Art of Mulan* (1998) Jeff Kurtti
- *Disney's Mulan: Special Collectors Edition* (1998) Russell Schroeder & Kathleen Weidner Zoehfeld
- *The Legend of Mulan: A Folding Book Inspired by the Disney Animated Film* (1998)

The Parent Trap (1998)

Source:

- Remake of *The Parent Trap* (1961)
- *Lottie and Lisa* (1949) Erich Kästner

Writers:

David Swift, Nancy Meyers, Charles Shyer

Director: Nancy Meyers

Premiere:

Jul 20, 1998

Length:

128 min

COLLECTIONS

Video:

1998

DVD:

2004, 2005 Special Double Trouble Edition

Blu-ray:

2018 20th Anniversary Edition, Disney Movie Club Exclusive

Digital:

Amazon, iTunes, Vudu

Soundtrack:

1998 Score + Soundtrack (CD)

Air Bud: Golden Receiver (1998)

The Timber Wolves are about to unleash their secret weapon.

(Note: Dimension Films theatrical release, Disney home media release.)

AKA:

Air Bud 2

Source:

First sequel to *Air Bud* (1997)

Writers:

Paul Tamasy, Aaron Mendelsohn

Director:

Richard Martin

Premiere:

Aug 14, 1998

Length:

90 min

COLLECTIONS

Video:

1998

Laserdisc:

1999

DVD:

2000, 2010 Special Edition

Digital:

iTunes, Vudu

Pocahontas II: Journey to a New World (1998)

A NEW JOURNEY BEGINS!

AKA:

Pocahontas 2: Journey to a New World

Source:

Sequel to *Pocahontas* (1995)

Writers:

Allen Estrin, Cindy Marcus, Flip Kobler

Directors:

Tom Ellery, Bradley Raymond

Premiere:

Aug 25, 1998, Video

Length:

72 min

COLLECTIONS

Video:

1998, 2000 Gold Classic Collection

DVD*/Blu-ray:

2000 Gold Classic Collection*, 2012 Special Edition / 2-Movie Collection, 2017 2-Movie Collection

Digital:

Amazon, iTunes, Vudu

Soundtrack:

2009 (Digital)

Summer of the Monkeys (1998)

Own Disney's All-New Heartwarming Adventure! In The Great Disney Tradition Of Old Yeller...

(Note: Edge Productions release, distributed on home media by Disney.)

Source:

Summer of the Monkeys (1976) Wilson Rawls

Writers:

Greg Taylor, Jim Strain

Director:

Michael Anderson

Premiere:

Sep 13, 1998, Toronto International Film Festival

US Release:

Dec 18, 1998, Video

Length:

101 min

COLLECTIONS

Video:

1998

DVD:
2003

The Jungle Book: Mowgli's Story (1998)
ALL-NEW FEATURE-LENGTH MOVIE!

Source:
The Jungle Book (1894) Rudyard Kipling

Writers:
Jose Rivera, Jim Herzfeld

Director:
Nick Marck

Premiere:
Sep 29, 1998, Video

Length:
77 min

COLLECTIONS

Video:
1998

Digital:
Amazon, Vudu

The Lion King II: Simba's Pride (1998)
THE CIRCLE OF LIFE CONTINUES...

AKA:
The Lion King 2: Simba's Pride

Source:
First sequel to *The Lion King* (1994)

Writers:
Flip Kobler, Cindy Marcus

Directors:
Darrell Rooney, Rob LaDuca (co-director)

Premiere:
Oct 26, 1998, Video

Length:

81 min

COLLECTIONS

Video:

1998

DVD*/Blu-ray:

1999 Limited Issue*, 2004 Special Edition*, 2011 Trilogy Set, 2012 + Special Edition, 2017

Soundtrack:

1998 *Return to Pride Rock*, 2004 (CD)

I'll Be Home For Christmas (1998)

This Yule, be cool.

Writers:

Tom Nursall and Harris Goldberg (screenplay), Michael Allin (story)

Directors:

Arlene Sanford

Stars:

Jonathan Taylor Thomas

Premiere:

Nov 13, 1998

Length:

86 min

COLLECTIONS

Video:

1999

DVD:

2002

Digital:

Amazon, iTunes, Vudu

A Bug's Life (1998)

From the creators of "toy story"

AKA:

a bug's life

Writers:

John Lasseter, Joe Ranft (story), Andrew Stanton (story/screenplay), Don McEnery, Bob Shaw (screenplay)

Directors:

John Lasseter, Andrew Stanton (co-director)

Premiere:

Nov 14, 1998

Length:

95 min

CONNECTIONS

Theme Parks:

- It's Tough to Be a Bug! (AK 1998+), (DCA 2001+)
- A Bug's Land (DCA 2002+)

Video Games:

A *Bug's Life* (1998) PS, N64, PS3, Vita, GBC, PC, PSP

COLLECTIONS

Video:

1999

DVD*/Blu-ray:

1999 + Collector's Edition*, 2000 Gold Classic Collection*, 2003 Collector's Edition*, 2009, 2010 + Disney/Pixar: The Ultimate Blu-ray Collection, 2016

Digital:

Amazon, iTunes, Vudu

Soundtrack:

1998 (CD)

Books:

- *A Bug's Life: Special Collector's Edition* (1998) Jeff Kurtti
- *A Bug's Life: The Art and Making of an Epic of Miniature Proportions* (1998) Jeff Kurtti

Mighty Joe Young (1998)

SURVIVAL IS AN INSTINCT.

Source:

Remake of RKO's *Mighty Joe Young* (1949)

Writers:

Mark Rosenthal, Lawrence Konner

Director:

Ron Underwood

Premiere:

Dec 25, 1998

Length:

115 min

COLLECTIONS

Video:

1999

Laserdisc:

1999

DVD:

1999

Blu-ray:

2018 20th Anniversary Edition, Disney Movie Club Exclusive

Digital:

Amazon, iTunes, Vudu

Soundtrack:

1998 (CD)

Endurance (1999)

IN THE HEART OF AN OLYMPIC CHAMPION IS THE COURAGE TO ENDURE.

Source:

Biopic of Haile Gebrselassie

Writers:

Leslie Woodhead

Directors:

Leslie Woodhead, Bud Greenspan

Premiere:

Feb 5, 1999, Pan-African Film Festival

Length:

83 min

COLLECTIONS

Video:

2000

DVD:

2012 Generations Collection

Digital:

iTunes, Vudu

Soundtrack:

1999 (CD)

My Favorite Martian (1999)

YOUR FAVORITE PLANET.

Source:

My Favorite Martian (1963–1966) CBS TV series

Writers:

Sherri Stoner, Deanna Oliver

Director:

Donald Petrie

Premiere:

Feb 12, 1999

Length:

93 min

COLLECTIONS

Video:

1999

Laserdisc:

1999

DVD:

1999, 2003

Digital:

Amazon, iTunes, Vudu

Soundtrack:

2000 (Promo CD)

Doug's 1st Movie (1999)

Source:

Spin-off from *Doug* (1991–1999) TV series

Writers:

Ken Scarborough

Director:

Maurice Joyce

Premiere:

Mar 19, 1999

Length:

77 min

CONNECTIONS

TV Series:

- *Doug* (1991–1994) Nickelodeon, 52 episodes [Collection > Digital (2008), DVD (2014)]
- *Brand Spanking New Doug / Disney's Doug* (1996-1999) ABC, 65 episodes

Theme Parks:

Doug Live! (MGM 1999–2002)

Video Games:

Disney's Doug: Doug's Big Game (2000) GBC

COLLECTIONS

Video:

1999

DVD:

2012 Disney Movie Club Exclusive

Digital:

Amazon, iTunes, Vudu

The Straight Story (1999)

Source:

Based on a true story.

Writers:

John Roach, Mary Sweeney

Director:

David Lynch

Premiere:

May 21, 1999, Cannes Film Festival

US Release:

Oct 11, 1999, Hollywood

Length:

112 min

COLLECTIONS

Video:

2000

DVD:

2000

Digital:

iTunes, Vudu

Soundtrack:

1999 (CD)

Tarzan (1999)

Source:

Tarzan of the Apes (1912) Edgar Rice Burroughs

Writers:

Tab Murphy, Bob Tzudiker, Noni White (screenplay), Stephen J. Anderson, Mark Kennedy, Carole Holliday, Gaëtan Brizzi, Don Dougherty, Ed Gombert, Randy Haycock, Don Hall, Kevin Harkey, Glen Keane, Burny Mattinson, Frank Nissen, John Norton, Jeff

Snow, Michael Surrey, Chris Ure, Mark Walton, Stevie Wermers, Kelly Wightman, John Ramirez (story)

Directors:
Chris Buck, Kevin Lima

Premiere:
Jun 12, 1999, Los Angeles

Length:
88 min

CONNECTIONS

Comic Strips:
Disney's Tarzan (#1–2, Jun 1999)

Movies:
- *Tarzan & Jane* (DTV 2002) sequel
- *Tarzan II* (DTV 2005) prequel

Stage Musical:
Tarzan (2006+)

TV Series:
The Legend of Tarzan (2001-2003) UPN/ABC, 39 episodes

Theme Parks:
Tarzan's Treehouse (DL 1999+), (HKD 2005+)

Video Games:
- *Disney's Tarzan* (1999) GBC, PS, N64, PC
- *Disney's Tarzan Untamed* (2001) PS2, GC
- *Disney's Tarzan: Return to the Jungle* (2002) GBA

COLLECTIONS

Video:
2000

DVD*/Blu-ray:
2000 + Collector's Edition*, 2005 Special Edition*, 2014 Special Edition

Digital:
Amazon, iTunes, Vudu

Soundtrack:
1999 (CD)

Books:

- *The Tarzan Chronicles* (1999) Howard Green
- *Tarzan: Special Collector's Edition* (1999) Russell Schroeder & Victoria Saxon
- *Tarzan: The Broadway Adventure* (2007) Michael Lassell

Inspector Gadget (1999)

THEY'VE GOT GIZMOS UP THE WAZOO.

Source:

Inspector Gadget (1982-1986) Syndicated TV Series

Writers:

Dana Olsen (story), Kerry Ehrin (story/screenplay), Zak Penn (screenplay)

Director:

David Kellogg

Stars:

Matthew Broderick, Rupert Everett

Premiere:

Jul 18, 1999

Length:

78 min

CONNECTIONS

Movies:

Inspector Gadget 2 (DTV 2003) Sequel

COLLECTIONS

Video:

1999

Laserdisc:

1999

DVD:

2003

Digital:

iTunes, Vudu

Soundtrack:
1999 (CD)

Madeline: Lost in Paris (1999)

(Note: DIC Entertainment production, released on video by Disney.)

AKA:
The Madeline Movie: Lost in Paris

Source:
Madeline (1939) Ludwig Bemelmans

Director:
Stan Phillips, Marija Miletic Dail

Re-releases:
Aug 2, 1999, Video

Length:
74 min

COLLECTIONS

Video:
1999

DVD:
2010 (Shout Factory)

Digital:
iTunes

Belle's Tales of Friendship (1999)

Charming Storybook Adventures

Sections:
Includes *Mrs. Potts' Party*

Source:
Spin-off from *Beauty and the Beast* (1991) and *Sing Me a Story with Belle* (1995-1997) TV series

Writers:
Alice Brown, Richard Cray

Director:
Jimbo Marshall

Premiere:

Aug 17, 1999, Video

Length:

70 min

CONNECTIONS

Movies:

Belle's Magical World (DTV 1998) Mrs. Potts' Party edited into Special Edition

COLLECTIONS

Video:

1999

Hercules: Zero to Hero (1999)

Three Superhuman Adventures

Source:

Edited from episodes of *Hercules* (1998-1999) TV series: "Hercules and the First Day of School"[1], "Hercules and the Grim Avenger"[2], "Hercules and the Visit from Zeus"[3]

Writers:

[1]Bob Schooley, [1]Mark McCorkle, [2]Greg Weisman, [3]Gary Sperling

Director:

[1]Tad Stones, [1,2]Phil Weinstein, [3]Bob Kline

Premiere:

Aug 31, 1998, Video

Length:

70 min

CONNECTIONS

TV Series:

Hercules (1998-1999) Syndication, 65 episodes

COLLECTIONS

Video:

1998

The Hand Behind the Mouse:
The Ub Iwerks Story (1999)

An intimate biography of Ub Iwerks, the man Walt Disney called "the greatest animator in the world."

Writers:

Leslie Iwerks

Director:

Leslie Iwerks

Premiere:

Oct 8, 1999, Los Angeles (Limited)

Length:

90 min

COLLECTIONS

Video:

2001

DVD:

2007 *WD Treasures: The Adventures of Oswald the Lucky Rabbit*

Digital:

Vudu

Books:

The Hand Behind the Mouse: The Ub Iwerks Story (2001) Leslie Iwerks & John Kenworthy

The Duke (1999)

Royalty goes to the dogs.

(Note: Keystone Pictures production, released by Disney on home media.)

Writers:

Craig Detweiler (story/screenplay), Anne Vince, Robert Vince

Director:

Philip Spink

Premiere:

Oct 30, 1999, Iceland

US Release:

Apr 18, 2000, Video

Length:

88 min

COLLECTIONS

Video:

1999

DVD:

2003, 2013 (Phase 4 Films)

Digital:

Google Play

Mickey's Once Upon a Christmas (1999)

MICKEY, DONALD & GOOFY STAR IN A AN ALL-NEW MOVIE

Sections:

Donald Duck: Stuck on Christmas[1], *A Very Goofy Christmas*[2], *Mickey and Minnie's Gift of the Magi*[3]

Sources:

[1] "Christmas Every Day" (1892) William Dean Howells, [3] "The Gift of the Magi" (1905) O. Henry

Writers:

[1] Charlie Cohen, [1] Alex Mann, [2] Scott Spencer Gordon, [2] Tom Nance, [2] Carter Crocker, [3] Richard Cray, [3] Temple Mathews, Thomas Hart, Eddie Guzelian

Directors:

[1] Alex Mann, [1] Bradley Raymond, [2] Jun Falkenstein, [2] Bill Speers, [3] Toby Shelton

Premiere:

Nov 9, 1999, Video

Length:

66 min

CONNECTIONS

Movies:

Mickey's Twice Upon a Christmas (DTV 2004)

COLLECTIONS

Video:

1999

DVD*/Blu-ray:

2003 Gold Classic Collection*, 2014 Special Edition / 2-Movie Collection

Digital:

Amazon, iTunes, Vudu

Winnie the Pooh: Seasons of Giving (1999)

A New Full-Length Adventure

Source:

Edited from *A Winnie the Pooh Thanksgiving*[1] (1998) TV special and episodes of *The New Adventures of Winnie the Pooh* (1988-1992): "Groundpiglet Day"[2] and "Find Her, Keep Her"[3]

Writers:

[2]Jimmy Danelli, [2,3]Mark Zaslove (story) Barbara Slade, [1,2]Carter Crocker, [3]Larry Bernard, [3]Doug Hutchinson, [3]Mark Zaslove (screenplay)

Directors:

[1]Jun Falkenstein, [2,3]Karl Geurs, Gary Katona, Ed Wexler

Premiere:

Nov 9, 1999, Video

Length:

70 min

COLLECTIONS

Video:

1999, 2000

DVD:

2003, 2009 10th Anniversary + Gift Set

Toy Story 2 (1999)

THE TOYS ARE BACK!

Source:

First sequel to *Toy Story* (1995)

Writers:

John Lasseter, Pete Docter, Ash Brannon (story), Andrew Stanton (story/screenplay) Rita Hsiao, Doug Chamberlin, Chris Webb (screenplay)

Directors:

John Lasseter, Ash Brannon (co-director), Lee Ukrich (co-director)

Stars:

Tom Hanks, Tim Allen

Premiere:

Nov 13, 1999, Hollywood

Re-releases:

2009 (3D)

Length:

92 min

CONNECTIONS

Comic Strips:

Disney Comics Collection: Toy Story 2 (2009)

Movies:

Buzz Lightyear of Star Command: The Adventure Begins (DTV 2000)

TV Series:

Buzz Lightyear of Star Command (2000-2001) UPN/Syndication, 65 episodes

Video Games:

- *Toy Story 2* (1999) GBC
- *Toy Story 2: Buzz Lightyear to the Rescue!* (1999) PS, PSP, DC, N64, PS3, PC, Vita
- *Disney/Pixar Toy Story Racer* (2001) GBC, PS3, PSP
- *Toy Story Mania!* (2009) Wii, PS3, X360, PS3, X360S

COLLECTIONS

Video:

2000

DVD*/Blu-ray:

2000 2-Pack + Ultimate Toy Box: Collector's Edition*, 2005 Special Edition*, 2010 Special Edition + Ultimate Toy Box Collection, 2011 3D, 2015

Digital:

Amazon, iTunes, Vudu

Soundtrack:

1999, 2000 *Woody's Roundup*, 2002 Sing-Along Songs, 2010 *Toy Story Favorites + Songs and Story* (CD)

Books:

The Toy Story Films: An Animated Journey (2012) Charles Solomon

Fantasia/2000 (1999)

Sections:

Symphony No. 5[1], *Pines of Rome*[2], *Rhapsody in Blue*[3], *Piano Concerto No. 2*[4], *The Carnival of the Animals*[5], *The Sorcerer's Apprentice*[6], *Pomp and Circumstance*[7], *The Firebird Suite*[8]

Source:

Sequel to *Fantasia* (1940) [1] Beethoven, [2] Respighi, [3] Gershwin, [4] Shostakovich, [5] Saint-Saëns, [6] Dukas, [7] Elgar, [8] Stravinsky, [4] 'The Steadfast Tin Soldier' (1838) Hans Christian Andersen, [7] Book of Genesis: Noah's Ark

Writers:

[3,5] Eric Goldberg, [5] Joe Grant, [6] Perce Pearce, [6] Carl Fallberg, [8] Gaëtan Brizzi, [8] Paul Brizzi, [2] Brenda Chapman, Don Hahn, David Reynolds, Irene Mecchi, Elena Driskill

Directors:

[6] James Algar, [8] Gaëtan Brizzi, [8] Paul Brizzi, [2,4] Hendel Butoy, [7] Francis Glebas, [3,5] Eric Goldberg, [1] Pixote Hunt, Don Hahn

Premiere:

Dec 17, 1999, New York

Re-releases:

Jan 1, 2000 (IMAX)

Length:

75 min

CONNECTIONS

Movies:

Fantasia (1940) [6] taken from original film

COLLECTIONS

Video:

2000

DVD*/Bu-ray:

2000 + The Fantasia Anthology: Collector's Edition*, 2010 2-Movie Collection / Special Edition

Digital:

Netflix

Soundtrack:

1999 (CD)

Books:

Fantasia/2000: A Vision of Hope (1999) John Culhane

PART EIGHT

Movies: 2000–2004

The Tigger Movie (2000)

Source:

Characters created by A.A. Milne

Writers:

Eddie Guzelian (story), Jun Falkenstein (screenplay)

Director:

Jun Falkenstein

Premiere:

Feb 11, 2000

Length:

77 min

CONNECTIONS

Video Games:

Tigger's Honey Hunt (2000) PS, N64, PC

COLLECTIONS

Video:

2000

DVD*/Blu-ray:

2000*, 2009 10th Anniversary Edition*, 2012 Bounce-a-Rrrific Special Edition

Digital:

Amazon, iTunes, Vudu

Soundtrack:

2000 *Songs and Story + The Tigger Movie...and More!* (CD)

An Extremely Goofy Movie (2000)

Source:

Sequel to *A Goofy Movie* (1995)

Writers:

Scott Spencer Gordon, Hillary Carlip

Director:

Douglas McCarthy

Premiere:

Feb 28, 2000, Video

Length:

79 min

COLLECTIONS

Video:

2000

DVD:

2000

Digital:

iTunes, Vudu

Soundtrack:

2000 *Dance Party!* (CD)

Whispers: An Elephant's Tale (2000)

The True-Life Adventure Of A Big Little Hero

Writers:

Beverly Joubert (story), Dereck Joubert (story/screenplay), Jordan Moffet, Holly Goldberg Sloan (screenplay)

Director:

Dereck Joubert

Premiere:

Mar 10, 2000 / Oct 13, 2000 (Limited)

Length:

72 min

COLLECTIONS
Video/DVD:
2001

Digital:
Google Play

The Little Mermaid II: Return to the Sea (2000)
Making A Splash On Video and Disney DVD

AKA:
The Little Mermaid 2: Return to the Sea

Source:
Sequel to *The Little Mermaid* (1989)

Writers:
Elizabeth Anderson, Temple Mathews (screenplay), Elise D'Haene, Eddie Guzelian (additional screenplay material)

Director:
Jim Kammerud, Brian Smith (co-director)

Premiere:
Mar 17, 2000, UK

US Release:
Sep 19, 2000, Video

Length:
75 min

CONNECTIONS
Video Games:
- *Disney's The Little Mermaid II: Pinball Frenzy* (2000) GBC
- *Disney's The Little Mermaid II* (2000) PS, PS3

COLLECTIONS
Video:
2000

DVD*/Blu-ray:
2000*, 2008 Special Edition*, 2013 2-Movie Collection

Soundtrack:

2000, 2013 *The Little Mermaid: Greatest Hits* (CD)

Perfect Game (2000)

They Beat The Odds—One Base Hit At A Time

(Note: Produced by Up to Bat Productions, released on home media by Disney)

Writers:

Dan Guntzelman

Director:

Dan Guntzelman

Stars:

Edward Asner, Patrick Duffy, Cameron Finley

Premiere:

Apr 18, 2000, video

Length:

99 min

COLLECTIONS

Video:

2000

DVD:

2012 Disney 4-Movie Collection: Game Changers

Dinosaur (2000)

Writers:

Thom Enriquez, Ralph Zondag (story), John Harrison, Robert Nelson Jacobs (story/screenplay), Walon Green (earlier screenplay)

Directors:

Eric Leighton, Ralph Zondag

Premiere:

May 13, 2000

Length:

82 min

CONNECTIONS

Theme Parks:

DINOSAUR (AK 1998+)

Video Games:

Dinosaur (2000) GBC, PS, DC, PS2, PC

COLLECTIONS

Video:

2001

DVD*/Blu-ray:

2001 + Collector's Edition*, 2006, 2007 Blu-ray 4-Pack: Disney Movies, 2011

Digital:

Amazon, iTunes, Vudu

Soundtrack:

2000 + *Dinosaur Song Factory* (CD)

Books:

Dinosaur: The Evolution of an Animated Feature (2000) Jeff Kurtti

Disney's The Kid (2000)

Nobody ever grows up quite like they imagined.

AKA:

The Kid

Writers:

Audrey Wells

Director:

Jon Turteltaub

Stars:

Bruce Willis

Premiere:

Jun 25, 2000

Length:

104 min

COLLECTIONS

Video/DVD:

2001

Digital:

Google Play

Buzz Lightyear of Star Command: The Adventure Begins (2000)

Never Fear, Buzz Is Here...

Source:

Spin-off from *Toy Story 2* (1999), pilot for *Buzz Lightyear of Star Command* TV series

Writers:

Mark McCorkle, Robert Schooley, Bill Motz, Bob Roth

Director:

Tad Stones

Stars:

Tim Allen

Premiere:

Aug 8, 2000, Video

Length:

70 min

CONNECTIONS

TV Series:

Buzz Lightyear of Star Command (2000-2001) UPN/syndication, 65 episodes

Video Games:

Disney/Pixar's Buzz Lightyear of Star Command (2000) GBC, PS, DC, PS3, PC, PSP

COLLECTIONS

Video:

2000

DVD:

2000

Remember the Titans (2000)

History is written by the winners.

Source:

Based on a true story

Writers:

Gregory Allen Howard

Director:

Boaz Yakin

Stars:

Denzel Washington

Premiere:

Sep 23, 2000

Length:

113 min (original), 120 min (director's cut)

COLLECTIONS

Video:

2001

DVD*/Blu-ray:

2001*, 2006 Director's Cut*, 2007, 2011

Digital:

Amazon, iTunes, Vudu

Soundtrack:

2001 (CD)

102 Dalmatians (2000)

THE DALMATIANS REIGN

Source:

Sequel to *101 Dalmatians* (1996)

Writers:

Kristen Buckley, Brian Regan (story/screenplay), Bob Tzudiker, Noni White

Director:

Kevin Lima

Stars:

Glenn Close

Premiere:

Nov 22, 2000

Length:

100 min

CONNECTIONS

Video Games:

Disney's 102 Dalmatians: Puppies to the Rescue (2000) PS, DC, GBC, PC

COLLECTIONS

Video:

2001

DVD:

2001 + 2-Pack, 2008

Digital:

Amazon, iTunes, Vudu

Soundtrack:

2000 (CD)

The Emperor's New Groove (2000)

IT'S ALL ABOUT... ME

AKA:

Kingdom in the Sun (working title)

Writers:

Chris Williams, Mark Dindal (story), David Reynolds (screenplay), Roger Allers, Matthew Jacobs (original story)

Director:

Mark Dindal

Premiere:

Dec 10, 2000

Length:

78 min

CONNECTIONS

Movies:

- *The Sweatbox* (2002) behind-the-scenes documentary
- *Kronk's New Groove* (DTV 2005) sequel

TV Series:

The Emperor's New School (2006-2008) Disney Channel/ABC Kids, 52 episodes

Video Games:

The Emperor's New Groove (2000) PS, PS3, GBC, PC

COLLECTIONS

Video:

2001

DVD*/Blu-ray:

2001 + The Ultimate Groove: Collector's Edition*, 2005 The New Groove Edition*, 2013 Special Edition / 2-Movie Collection

Digital:

Amazon, Vudu

Soundtrack:

2000 (CD)

Air Bud 3: World Pup (2000)

A New Breed Of Soccer Dad!

Source:

Second sequel to *Air Bud*

Writers:

Mick Whiting, Robert Vince, Anne Vince

Director:

Bill Bannerman

Premiere:

Dec 12, 2000, Video

Length:

83 min

COLLECTIONS

Video:

2000

DVD:

2000, 2010 Special Edition

Digital:

iTunes, Vudu

Recess: School's Out (2001)

SAVING THE WORLD ONE PLAYGROUND AT A TIME

Source:

Spin-off of *Recess* (1997–2001) TV series

Writers:

Paul Germain, Joe Ansolabehere (story), Jonathan Greenberg (story/ screenplay)

Director:

Chuck Sheetz

Premiere:

Feb 10, 2001

Length:

82 min

CONNECTIONS

Movies:

- *Recess Christmas: Miracle on Third Street* (DTV 2001) sequel
- *Recess: All Growed Down* (DTV 2003) sequel
- *Recess: Taking the Fifth Grade* (DTV 2003) sequel

TV Series:

Recess (1997–2001) ABC/UPN, 127 episodes

COLLECTIONS

Video:

2001

DVD:

2001

Digital:

Amazon, iTunes, Vudu

Soundtrack:

2001 (CD)

Lady and the Tramp II: Scamp's Adventure (2001)

A New Pup Arrives

AKA:

Lady and the Tramp 2: Scamp's Adventure

Source:

Sequel to *Lady and the Tramp* (1955)

Writers:

Bill Motz, Bob Roth

Directors:

Darrell Rooney, Jeannine Roussel (co-director)

Premiere:

Feb 27, 2001, Video

Length:

70 min

COLLECTIONS

Video:

2001

DVD*/Blu-ray:

2001*, 2006*, 2012 Special Edition, 2018 Disney Movie Club Exclusive

Atlantis: The Lost Empire (2001)

Source:

The legend of Atlantis

Writers:

Tab Murphy (story/screenplay), Kirk Wise, Gary Trousdale, Joss Whedon, Bryce Zabel, Jackie Zabel (story), David Reynolds (additional material)

Directors:

Gary Trousdale, Kirk Wise

Premiere:

Jun 8, 2001, Los Angeles/New York

Length:

95 min

CONNECTIONS

Comic Book:

Atlantis: The Lost Empire (2001)

Movies:

Atlantis: Milo's Return (DTV 2003) Sequel

Video Games:

- *Disney's Atlantis: The Lost Empire* (2001) PC, PS, GBC, GBA
- *Disney's Atlantis: The Lost Empire: Trial by Fire* (2001) PC
- *Disney's Atlantis: The Lost Empire: Search for the Journal* (2001) PC

COLLECTIONS

Video:

2002

DVD*/Blu-ray:

2002 + Collector's Edition*, 2013 Special Edition / 2-Movie Collection

Digital:

Amazon, iTunes, Vudu

Soundtrack:

2001 (CD)

Books:

- *Atlantis: The Lost Empire – The Illustrated Script* (2001)
- *Subterranean Tours: Atlantis – A Traveler's Guide to the Lost City* (2001) Jeff Kurtti
- *Milo's Journal – Atlantis: The Lost Empire* (2001) Jeff Kurtti

- *The Mythical World of Atlantis: From Plato to Disney – Theories of Lost Empire* (2001) Jeff Kurtti

The Book of Pooh: Stories from the Heart (2001)

An All-New Full-Length Adventure

Source:

Edited from *The Book of Pooh* (2001-2003) TV series: "Over the Hill," "Tigger's Replacement," "Kessie Wises Up," "Eeyore's Tailiversary," "Greenhorn with a Green Thumb," "Night of the Waking Tigger"

Writers:

Mitchell Kriegman, Andy Yerkes, Jymn Magon, Claudia Silver, Mark Zaslove

Directors:

Dean Gordon, Mitchell Kriegman

Premiere:

Jul 16, 2001, Video

Length:

76 min

CONNECTIONS

TV Series:

The Book of Pooh (2001–2003) Playhouse Disney, 24 episodes

COLLECTIONS

Video:

2001

DVD:

2001

Digital:

iTunes

Soundtrack:

2002 *Songs from The Book of Pooh* (CD)

The Princess Diaries (2001)

SHE ROCKS. SHE RULES. SHE REIGNS.

Source:

The Princess Diaries (2000) Meg Cabot

Writers:

Gina Wendkos

Director:

Garry Marshall

Stars:

Julie Andrews, Anne Hathaway

Premiere:

Jul 29, 2001

Length:

111 min

CONNECTIONS

Movies:

The Princess Diaries 2: Royal Engagement (2004) sequel

COLLECTIONS

Video:

2001

DVD*/Blu-ray:

2001*, 2004 Special Edition Collector's Set*, 2012 10th Anniversary Edition / 2-Movie Collection

Digital:

Amazon, iTunes, Vudu

Soundtrack:

2001 Soundtrack + Score (CD)

Max Keeble's Big Move (2001)

HIS WORLD. HIS RULES.

Writers:

David L. Watts (story), Jonathan Bernstein, Mark Blackwall, James Greer (story/screenplay)

Director:

Tim Hill

Premiere:

Oct 5, 2001

Length:

86 min

COLLECTIONS

Video:

2002

DVD:

2002

Digital:

iTunes, Vudu

Monsters, Inc. (2001)

From the Creators of Toy Story

Writers:

Pete Docter, David Silverman (co-director), Lee Unkrich (co-director)

Director:

Andrew Stanton, Daniel Gerson (screenplay), Pete Docter, Jill Culton, Jeff Pidgeon, Ralph Eggleston (story)

Premiere:

Oct 28, 2001, Los Angeles

Re-releases:

2012 (3D)

Length:

92 min

CONNECTIONS

Comic Books:

- *Monsters, Inc.* (Oct 2001)
- *Monsters, Inc.: Laugh Factory* (#1–4, Jun – Nov 2009)
- *Monsters, Inc.* (#1–2, Feb 2013)*
- *Monsters, Inc.: The Humanween Party* (Apr 2013)*

- *Monsters, Inc.: A Perfect Date* (2013)* 9 [*Collection > *Monsters, Inc.: Scary Stories* (2013)]

Movies:

Monsters University (2013) Prequel

Shorts:

Mike's New Car (DTV 2002)

Theme Parks:

- Monsters, Inc. Mike and Sulley to the Rescue! (DCA 2005+)
- Monsters, Inc. Laugh Floor (MK 2007+)
- Monsters, Inc. Ride & Go Seek (TDL 2009+)

Video Games:

- *Monsters, Inc. Scream Team* (2001) PS, PC, PS2, PS3, PSP
- *Disney/Pixar's Monsters, Inc.* (2002) GBA, PS2, GBC
- *Monsters, Inc. Scream Arena* (2002) GC
- *Disney/Pixar's Monsters. Inc.: Wreck Room Arcade* (2002) PC

COLLECTIONS

Video:

2002

DVD*/Blu-ray:

2002 Collector's Edition*, 2009, 2010 + Disney/Pixar: The Ultimate Blu-ray Collection, 2013 Collector's Edition + Ultimate Collector's Edition (3D), 2016 Ultimate Collector's Edition (3D) 2017

Digital:

Amazon, iTunes, Vudu

Soundtrack:

2001, 2002 *Scream Factory Favorites*, 2012 *Songs and Story* (CD)

Books:

The Art of Monsters, Inc. (2001)

Mickey's Magical Christmas: Snowed in at the House of Mouse (2001)

Source:

Spin-off of *Disney's House of Mouse* (2001-2003) TV series; includes shorts: *Pluto's Christmas Tree* (1952), *Mickey's Christmas Carol* (1983), and *Donald on Ice* & *The Nutcracker* from *Mickey Mouse Works* (1999-2000) TV series

Writers:

Thomas Hart

Directors:

Tony Craig, Roberts Gannaway

Premiere:

Nov 6, 2001, Video

Length:

65 min

CONNECTIONS

Movies:

Mickey's House of Villains (DTV 2002)

TV Series:

Disney's House of Mouse (2001-2003) ABC/Toon Disney, 52 episodes

COLLECTIONS

Video:

2001

DVD:

2001, 2009

Digital:

Amazon, iTunes, Vudu

Recess Christmas: Miracle on Third Street (2001)

Full-Length Holiday Movie

Source:

Edited from episodes of *Recess* (1997-2001) TV series: "Principal for a Day," "The Great Can Drive," "Weekend at Muriel's" "Yes Mikey, Santa Does Shave"

Writers:

Joseph Purdy, Michael Kramer, Phil Walsh, Mark Drop, Holly Huckins

Directors:

Chuck Sheetz, Susie Dietter

Premiere:

Nov 6, 2001, Video

Length:

63 min

CONNECTIONS

TV Series:

Recess (1997-2001) ABC/UPN, 127 episodes

COLLECTIONS

Video:

2001

DVD:

2001

The Other Side of Heaven (2001)

Based on a true story

(Note: Excel Entertainment theatrical release, Disney home media release)

Source:

In the Eye of the Storm (1993) John H. Groberg

Writers:

Mitch Davis

Director:

Mitch Davis

Stars:

Christopher Gorham, Anne Hathaway

Premiere:

Dec 14, 2001 (Limited)

Length:

113 min

COLLECTIONS

Video/DVD:

2003

Digital:

Amazon, iTunes, Vudu

Soundtrack:

2001 (CD)

Return to Never Land (2002)

AN ALL-NEW ADVENTURE ONLINE IN THEATERS

Source:

Sequel to *Peter Pan* (1953)

Writers:

Temple Matthews (screenplay), Carter Crocker (additional material)

Directors:

Robin Budd, Donovan Cook (co-director)

Stars:

Peter Pan

Premiere:

Feb 10, 2002

Length:

72 min

COLLECTIONS

Video:

2002

DVD*/Blu-ray:

2002*, 2007 Pixie-Powered Edition*, 2013 Special Edition

Soundtrack:

2002 (CD)

Air Bud: Seventh Inning Fetch (2002)

He's A Natural Baseball Player With Major League Talent!

AKA:

Air Bud: 7th Inning Fetch

Source:

Third sequel to *Air Bud* (1997)

Writers:

Robert Vince (story), Sara Sutton, Stephanie Isherwood, Anne Vince, Anna McRoberts (screenplay)

Director:

Robert Vince

Premiere:

Jun 18, 2002, Video

Length:

93 min

COLLECTIONS

Video:

2002

DVD:

2002, 2008 Double Feature, 2013 Golden Edition

Digital:

Amazon, iTunes, Vudu

Snow Dogs (2002)

GET READY FOR MUSH HOUR!

Source:

Winterdance: The Fine Madness of Running the Iditarod (1994) Gary Paulsen

Writers:

Jim Kouf, Tommy Swerdlow, Michael Goldberg, Mark Gibson, Philip Halprin

Director:

Brian Levant

Stars:

Cuba Gooding, Jr., James Coburn

Premiere:

Jan 18, 2002

Length:

99 min

COLLECTIONS

Video:

2002

DVD:

2002

Blu-ray:

2018 Disney Movie Club Exclusive

Digital:

Amazon, iTunes, Vudu

The Hunchback of Notre Dame II (2002)

AKA:

The Hunchback of Notre Dame II: The Secret of the Bell

Source:

Sequel to *The Hunchback of Notre Dame* (1996)

Writers:

Jule Selbo, Flip Kobler, Cindy Marcus

Director:

Bradley Raymond

Premiere:

Feb 5, 2002, Video, Italy

US Release:

Mar 19, 2002, Video

Length:

68 min

COLLECTIONS

Video:

2002

DVD*/Blu-ray:

2002*, 2013 Special Edition / 2-Movie Collection

Digital:

iTunes, Vudu

Cinderella II: Dreams Come True (2002)

The Magic Didn't End At Midnight

Sections:

Aim to Please[1], *Tall Tail*[2], *An Uncommon Romance*[3]

Source:

Sequel to *Cinderella* (1950)

Writers:

[1] Jill E. Blotevogel, [1, 2, 3] Tom Rogers, [2] Jule Selbo

Director:

John Kafka

Premiere:

Feb 23, 2002, Video

Length:

73 min

COLLECTIONS

Video:

2002

DVD*/Blu-ray:

2002*, 2007 Special Edition*, 2012 Special Edition / 2-Movie Collection + 3-Movie Jewelry Box Collection

Soundtrack:

2002 *Disney's Princess Favorites* (CD)

The Rookie (2002)

IT'S NEVER TOO LATE TO BELIEVE IN YOUR DREAMS.

Source:

Based on a true story

Writers:

Mike Rich

Director:

John Lee Hancock

Stars:

Dennis Quaid

Premiere:

Mar 26, 2002, New York

Length:

128 min

COLLECTIONS

Video:

2002

DVD*/Blu-ray:

2002*, 2008 2-Pack, 2011

Digital:

Amazon, iTunes, Vudu

Soundtrack:

2002 (CD)

Lilo & Stitch (2002)

There's one in every family.

Writers:

Chris Sanders, Dean DeBlois

Directors:

Dean DeBlois, Chris Sanders

Premiere:

Jun 16, 2002

Length:

85 min

CONNECTIONS

Comic Strips:

Lilo & Stitch: The Series (#1–3, Jun 2004 – Mar 2005)

Movies:

- *Stitch! The Movie* (DTV 2003) sequel/TV series pilot
- *Lilo & Stitch 2: Stitch Has a Glitch* (DTV 2005) sequel
- *Leroy & Stitch* (DTV 2006+) sequel/TV series finale

Shorts:

The Origin of Stitch (DTV 2005)

TV Series:

- *Lilo & Stitch: The Series* (2003–2003) Disney Channel/ABC, 65 episodes [Collection > *Lilo & Stitch: The Series Box 1-4* DVD (Japan)]
- *Stitch!* (2008–2011) TV Tokyo/TV Asahi/Disney Channel Japan, 83 episodes
- *Stitch & Ai* (2017) CCTV-1/CCTV-14, 13 episodes

TV Specials:

- *Challenge from Piko* (*Stitch vs. Penny*) (2009) Disney Channel Japan
- *Brother of the Universe* (*Son of Sprout*) (2010) Disney Channel Japan
- *Ace's Back* (*Heroes are Hard*) (2011) Disney Channel Japan
- *Stitch and the Planet of Sand* (2012) Disney Channel Japan
- *Stitch! A Perfect Memory* (2015) Disney Channel Japan

Theme Parks:

- Stitch's Great Escape! (MK 2004+)
- Stitch Encounter (HKD 2006-2016), (TDL 2015+), (SD 2016+)
- Stitch Live! (WDS 2008+)
- The Enchanted Tiki Room: Stitch Presents Aloha E Komo Mai! (TDL 2008+)
- Stitch's Supersonic Celebration (MK 2009)

Video Games:

- *Disney's Lilo & Stitch* (2002) GBA, PS, PC, PS3
- *Disney's Lilo & Stitch: Trouble in Paradise* (2002) PS, PC, PS3
- *Disney's Stitch: Experiment 626* (2002) PS2, PS3
- *Disney's Lilo & Stitch: Hawaiian Adventure* (2002) PC
- *Disney's Stitch Jam* (Japan, 2010) DS
- *Motto! Stitch! DS: Rhythm de Rakugaki Daisakusen* (Japan, 2010) DS
- *Bomberman: Disney Stitch Edition* (Japan, 2010) DS

COLLECTIONS

Video:

2002

DVD*/Blu-ray:

2002*, 2009 Big Wave Edition*, 2013 Special Edition / 2-Movie Collection, 2017 2-Movie Collection

Digital:

Amazon, iTunes, Vudu

Soundtrack:

2002, 2006 *Lilo & Stitch Hawaiian Album* (Japan), 2008 *Lilo & Stitch Hawaiian Album: Stitch's Ohana Village* (Japan), 2010 *Rock Stitch!* (Japan) (CD), 2016 (LP)

Books:

Lilo and Stitch: Collected Stories from the Film's Creators (2002) Ed. Hiro Clark Wakabayashi

Tarzan & Jane (2002)

Source:

- Sequel to *Tarzan* (1999)
- Edited from episodes of *The Legend of Tarzan* (2001-2003) TV series: "Tarzan and the British Invasion,"[1] "Tarzan and the Volcanic Diamond Mine,"[2] and "Tarzan and the Flying Ace"[3]

Writers:

Bill Motz, Bob Roth, [1] Mirith J. Colao, [2] John Behnke, [2] Rob Humphrey, [2] Jim Peterson (screenplay), [3] Jess Winfield (story/screenplay), [3] Dave Bullock, [3] Adam Van Wyk (story)

Directors:

Steve Loter, Lisa Schaffer (co-director), [2,3] Victor Cook, [1] Don MacKinnon

Premiere:

Jul 23, 2002, Video

Length:

75 min

COLLECTIONS

Video:

2002

DVD:

2002

Digital:

Netflix

Mickey's House of Villains (2002)

Sections:

Trick or Treat (1952)[1], *Mickey's Mechanical House*[2], *How to Haunt a House*[3], *Lonesome Ghosts* (1937)[4], *Dance of the Goofys*[5], *Donald Duck and the Gorilla* (1944)[6], *Donald's Halloween Scare*[7], *Hansel & Gretel*[8]

Source:

- Spin-off of *Disney's House of Mouse* (2001–2003) TV series
- [8] 'Hansel and Gretel' (1812) Brothers Grimm

Writers:

[2,3] Thomas Hart, [3] Kevin Campbell, [3] Elizabeth Stonecipher, [5,8] Roberts Gannaway, [7] Henry Gilroy, [7] Jymn Magon

Directors:

Jamie Mitchell, [7] Rick Calabash, [2,3,5,8] Tony Craig, [2,3,5,8] Roberts Gannaway, [7] Mike Moon

Premiere:

Sep 3, 2002, Video

Length:

70 min

CONNECTIONS

Movies:

Mickey's Magical Christmas: Snowed in at the House of Mouse (DTV 2001)

TV Series:

Disney's House of Mouse (2001-2003) ABC/Toon Disney, 52 episodes

COLLECTIONS

Video:

2002

DVD:

2002

Digital:

Amazon, iTunes, Vudu

Tuck Everlasting (2002)

Source:
Tuck Everlasting (1975) Natalie Babbitt

Writers:
Jeffrey Lieber, James V. Hart

Director:
Jay Russell

Stars:
Alexis Bledel, Ben Kingsley, Sissy Spacek, Jonathan Jackson, William Hurt

Premiere:
Sep 8, 2002, Toronto International Film Festival

US Release:
Oct 5, 2002, Hollywood

Length:
90 min

COLLECTIONS

Video:
2003

DVD:
2003

Digital:
iTunes, Vudu

Soundtrack:
2002 (CD)

The Country Bears (2002)

They're Legends. Bearly. THE HIBER NATION TOUR BEGINS THIS SUMMER.

Source:
Country Bear Jamboree theme park attraction

Writers:
Mark Perez

Director:

Peter Hastings

Premiere:

Jul 21, 2002

Length:

88 min

CONNECTIONS

Theme Parks:

Country Bear Jamboree (MK 1971+), (DL 1972-2001), (TDL 1983+)

COLLECTIONS

Video:

2002

DVD:

2002, 2012 Disney 4-Movie Collection: Thrills and Chills

Digital:

Amazon, Vudu

Soundtrack:

2002 (CD)

The Adventures of Tom Thumb & Thumbelina (2002)

The Most Magical Pairing in Fairy Tale History

(Note: Hyperion Pictures production, video release by Buena Vista Home Entertainment.)

Source:

- *The History of Tom Thumb* (1621) Richard Johnson
- "Thumbelina" (1835) Hans Christian Andersen

Writers:

Willard Carroll

Director:

Glenn Chaika

Premiere:

Aug 6, 2002, Video

Length:

75 min

COLLECTIONS

Video:

2002

DVD:

2015 (Lionsgate Films)

Digital:

Vudu

The Santa Clause 2 (2002)

AKA:

The Santa Clause 2: The Mrs. Clause

Source:

First sequel to *The Santa Clause* (1994)

Writers:

Leo Benvenuti, Steve Rudnick (story), Don Rhymer, Cinco Paul, Ken Daurio, Ed Decter, John J. Strauss (screenplay)

Director:

Michael Lembek

Stars:

Tim Allen

Premiere:

Oct 27, 2002

Length:

104 min

COLLECTIONS

Video:

2003

DVD:

2003, 2007 The Santa Clause Holiday Collection

Blu-ray:

2012 10th Anniversary + The Santa Clause: The Complete 3-Movie Collection

Digital:

Amazon, iTunes, Vudu

Soundtrack:

2002 (CD)

Treasure Planet (2002)

ROBERT LOUIS STEVENSON'S GREATEST ADVENTURE "TREASURE ISLAND" AS IT HAS NEVER BEEN SEEN BEFORE

Source:

Treasure Island (1883) Robert Louis Stevenson

Writers:

Ron Clements, John Musker (story/screenplay), Rob Edwards (screenplay), Ted Elliott, Terry Rossio (story)

Directors:

Ron Clements, John Musker

Premiere:

Nov 5, 2002, Paris

US Release:

Nov 17, 2002

Length:

95 min

CONNECTIONS

Video Games:

- *Disney's Treasure Planet* (2002) GBA, PS, PS2
- *Disney's Treasure Planet: Battle at Procyon* (2002) PC
- *Disney's Treasure Planet Collection* (2002) PC, Mac

COLLECTIONS

Video:

2003

DVD*/Blu-ray:

2003*, 2012 10th Anniversary Edition

Digital:

Amazon, iTunes, Vudu

Soundtrack:

2002 (CD)

Books:

Treasure Planet: A Voyage of Discovery (2002) Jeff Kurtti

Winnie the Pooh: A Very Merry Pooh Year (2002)

A Brand-New Full-Length Adventure

Sections:

Winnie the Pooh and Christmas Too[1] (TV 1991), *Happy Pooh Year*[2]

Writers:

Ted Henning, [1,2] Karl Geurs, [2] Brian Hohlfeld, [1] Mark Zaslove

Directors:

Gary Katona, Ed Wexler, [2] Jamie Mitchell

Premiere:

Nov 11, 2002, Video

Length:

65 min

COLLECTIONS

Video:

2002

DVD*/Blu-ray:

2002*, 2013 Gift of Friendship Edition

Digital:

Amazon, iTunes, Vudu

101 Dalmatians II: Patch's London Adventure (2003)

AKA:

101 Dalmatians 2: Patch's London Adventure

Source:

Sequel to *One Hundred and One Dalmatians* (1961)

Writers:

Dan Root, Garrett K. Schiff (story), Jim Kammerud, Brian Smith (story/screenplay)

Directors:

Jim Kammerud, Brian Smith

Premiere:

Jan 20, 2003, Video

Length:

74 min

CONNECTIONS

Video Games:

Disney's 101 Dalmatians II: Patch's London Adventure (2003) PS

COLLECTIONS

Video:

2003

DVD*/Blu-ray:

2003*, 2008 Special Edition*, 2015 Special Edition

Digital:

iTunes, Vudu

The Jungle Book 2 (2003)

Baloo is Back Only In Theaters This February

Source:

Sequel to *The Jungle Book* (1967)

Writers:

Karl Geurs (screenplay), Carter Crocker, Evan Spiliotopoulos, David Reynolds, Roger S.H. Schulman, Tom Rogers (additional material)

Director:

Steve Trenbirth

Stars:

John Goodman, Haley Joel Osment

Premiere:
Feb 5, 2003

US Release:
Feb 9, 2003

Length:
72 min

COLLECTIONS

Video:
2003

DVD*/Blu-ray:
2003*, 2008 Special Edition, 2014

Soundtrack:
2003 (CD)

Inspector Gadget 2 (2003)

Gadget Meets His Match

Source:
Sequel to *Inspector Gadget* (1999)

Writers:
Ron Anderson, William Robertson, Alex Zamm

Director:
Alex Zamm

Stars:
French Stewart

Premiere:
Mar 3, 2003, Video

Length:
89 min

COLLECTIONS

Video:
2003

DVD:
2003

Digital:

Amazon, iTunes, Vudu

Piglet's Big Movie (2003)

A tale you'll never forget.

Source:

Winnie the Pooh (1926) and *The House at Pooh Corner* (1928) A.A. Milne

Writers:

Brian Hohlfeld (screenplay), Ted Henning (additional material)

Director:

Francis Glebas

Premiere:

Mar 16, 2003

Length:

75 min

CONNECTIONS

Video Games:

Piglet's Big Game (2003) PS2, GC

COLLECTIONS

DVD:

2003

Digital:

iTunes

Soundtrack:

2003 (CD)

Ghosts of the Abyss (2003)

UNSCRIPTED. GROUNDBREAKING. HEROIC. AN IMMERSIVE 3D ADVENTURE

AKA:

Titanic3D: Ghosts of the Abyss

Director:

James Cameron

Premiere:

Mar 31, 2003, IMAX + 3D

Length:

61 min (original), 92 min (extended)

COLLECTIONS

DVD*/Blu-ray:

2004 (original)*, 2012 3D (extended)

Digital:

iTunes, Vudu

Soundtrack:

2003 (CD)

Holes (2003)

SOME SECRETS ARE TOO BIG TO KEEP HIDDEN. THE AWARD WINNING NOVEL COMES TO LIFE. THE ADVENTURE IS DOWN THERE... START DIGGING

Source:

Holes (1998) Louis Sachar

Writers:

Louis Sachar

Director:

Andrew Davis

Stars:

Sigourney Weaver, Jon Voight, Patricia Arquette

Premiere:

Apr 11, 2003

Length:

117 min

COLLECTIONS

Video:

2003

DVD:

2003

Blu-ray:

2018 15th Anniversary Edition, Disney Movie Club Exclusive

Digital:

Amazon, iTunes, Vudu

Soundtrack:

2003 (CD)

Atlantis: Milo's Return (2003)

The All-New Adventures

Source:

Sequel to *Atlantis: The Lost Empire* (2001)

Writers:

Thomas Hart, Henry Gilroy, Kevin Hopps, Tad Stones, Steve Englehart, Marty Isenberg

Directors:

Victor Cook, Toby Shelton, Tad Stones

Premiere:

Apr 23, 2003, Video, Denmark/Sweden

US Release:

May 19, 2003, Video

Length:

70 min

COLLECTIONS

Video:

2003

DVD*/Blu-ray:

2003*, 2013 Special Edition / 2-Movie Collection

Digital:

iTunes, Vudu

The Lizzie McGuire Movie (2003)

The Only Risk In Taking An Adventure Is Not Taking It At All.

Source:

Spin-off of *Lizzie McGuire* (2001–2004) TV series

Writers:

Susan Estelle Jansen, Ed Decter, John J. Strauss

Director:

Jim Fall

Stars:

Hilary Duff

Premiere:

Apr 26, 2003

Length:

94 min

CONNECTIONS

TV Series:

Lizzie McGuire (2001–2004) Disney Channel, 65 episodes [Collection >
Lizzie McGuire Box Set: Vol 1 (2004) iTunes]

Video Games:

- *Lizzie McGuire: On The Go!* (2003) GBA
- *Lizzie McGuire 2: Lizzie Diaries* (2004) GBA
- *Lizzie McGuire 3: Homecoming Havoc* (2005) GBA

COLLECTIONS

Video:

2003

DVD:

2003, 2009 Double Feature

Digital:

Amazon, Vudu

Soundtrack:

2003 (CD)

Where the Red Fern Grows (2003)

(Note: Crusader Entertainment, Elixir Films & Bob Yari Productions film,
Disney home media release)

Source:

Where the Red Fern Grows (1961) Wilson Rawls

Writers:

Douglas C. Stewart, Eleanor Lamb, Lyman Dayton, Sam Pillsbury

Directors:

Lyman Dayton, Sam Pillsbury

Stars:

Dabney Coleman, Dave Matthews

Premiere:

May 3, 2003, Tribeca Film Festival

Length:

86 min

COLLECTIONS

Video:

2004

DVD:

2004, 2012 Disney 4-Movie Collection: Dogs 2

Digital:

Amazon, iTunes, Vudu

Finding Nemo (2003)

Sea it in theaters.

Writers:

Andrew Stanton (story/screenplay), Bob Peterson, David Reynolds (screenplay)

Directors:

Andrew Stanton, Lee Unkrich (co-director)

Premiere:

May 30, 2003

Re-releases:

2012 (3D)

Length:

100 min

CONNECTIONS

Comic Books:

- *Finding Nemo: Reef Rescue* (#1–4, May – Oct 2009) [Collection > *Finding Nemo: Reef Rescue* (2009)]
- *Finding Nemo* (#1–4, Jul – Oct 2010) [Collection > *Finding Nemo: Losing Dory* (2010)]

Movies:

Finding Dory (2016) sequel

Short:

Exploring the Reef (2003)

Stage Musical:

Finding Nemo—The Musical (2006+) Disney's Animal Kingdom

Theme Parks:

- Turtle Talk with Crush! (E 2004+), (DCA 2005+), (HKD 2008), (TDS 2009+) (Children's Hospital of Orange Country 2013+)
- Finding Nemo Submarine Voyage (DL 2007+)
- The Seas with Nemo & Friends (E 2007+)
- Crush's Coaster (WDS 2007+)
- Nemo & Friends SeaRider (TDS 2017+)

Video Games:

- *Disney/Pixar's Finding Nemo* (2003) GBA, GC, PC, Mac, PS2, Xbox
- *Finding Nemo: Nemo's Underwater World of Fun* (2003) Mac, PC
- *Finding Nemo: Escape to the Big Blue* (2006) DS, 3DS
- *Nemo's Reef* (2012) PC, iPhone, iPad, Android

COLLECTIONS

Video:

2003

DVD*/Blu-ray:

2003 Collector's Edition*, 2012 Ultimate Collector's Edition (3D) + Collector's Edition, 2013, 2016 + Ultimate Collector's Edition (3D)

Digital:

Amazon, Vudu

Soundtrack:

2003 + Ocean Favorites (CD)

Books:
The Art of Finding Nemo (2003) Mark Cotta Vaz

Air Bud: Spike's Back (2003)
He's Got The Golden Touch.

Source:
Fourth sequel to *Air Bud* (1997)

Writers:
Robert Vince (story), Anne Vince, Anna McRoberts (screenplay)

Director:
Mike Southon

Premiere:
Jun 24, 2003, Video

Length:
87 min

COLLECTIONS
Video:
2003

DVD:
2003, 2008 Double Feature

Digital:
Amazon, iTunes, Vudu

Pirates of the Caribbean: The Curse of the Black Pearl (2003)

Source:
Pirates of the Caribbean theme park attraction

Writers:
Ted Elliott, Terry Rossio (story/screenplay), Stuart Beattie, Jay Wolpert (story)

Director:
Gore Verbinski

Stars:
Johnny Depp, Geoffrey Rush, Orlando Bloom, Keira Knightley

Premiere:

Jun 28, 2003, Disneyland

Length:

143 min

CONNECTIONS

Comic Books:

Disney Pirates of the Caribbean (Sep 2016+)

Movies:

- *Pirates of the Caribbean: Dead Man's Chest* (2006) sequel
- *Pirates of the Caribbean: At World's End* (2007) sequel
- *Pirates of the Caribbean: On Stranger Tides* (2011) sequel
- *Pirates of the Caribbean: Dead Men Tell No Tales* (2017) squel

Shorts:

Tales of the Code: Wedlocked (DTV 2011) Prequel

Theme Parks:

- Pirates of the Caribbean (DL 1967+), (MK 1973+), (TDL 1983+), (DP 1992+), (SD 2016+)
- The Legend of Captain Jack Sparrow (HS 2012–2014)
- Pirates of the Caribbean: Battle for the Sunken Treasure (SD 2016+)

Video Games:

- *Pirates of the Caribbean: The Curse of the Black Pearl* (2003) GBA
- *Pirates of the Caribbean: The Legend of Jack Sparrow* (2006) PS2, PC
- *LEGO Pirates of the Caribbean: The Video Game* (2011) Wii, PSP, PS3, 3DS, PC, DS, X360, X360S, PS3, Mac

COLLECTIONS

Video:

2003

DVD*/Blu-ray:

2003 Collector's Edition*, 2004 Special Edition Gift Set*, 2007 + Blu-ray 4-Pack: Family Movies, 2008 Trilogy, 2011 + Ultimate Trilogy Collection + Four-Movie Collection

Digital:

Amazon, iTunes, Vudu

Soundtrack:
2003, 2007 *Soundtrack Treasures Collection* (CD)

Books:
- *Pirates of the Caribbean: From the Magic Kingdom to the Movies* (2005) Jason Surrell
- *Bring Me That Horizon: The Making of Pirates of the Caribbean* (2007) Michael Singer
- *The Art of Pirates of the Caribbean* (2007) Timothy Shaner & Christopher Meason
- *Pirates of the Caribbean: The Price of Freedom* (Novel, 2011) A.C. Crispin

Freaky Friday (2003)
Every teenager's nightmare...turning into her mother.

Source:
- Remake of *Freaky Friday* (1976) and *Freaky Friday* (TV 1995)
- *Freaky Friday* (1972) Mary Rodgers

Writers:
Heather Hach, Leslie Dixon

Director:
Mark Waters

Stars:
Jamie Lee Curtis, Lindsay Lohan

Premiere:
Aug 4, 2003, Hollywood

Length:
97 min

COLLECTIONS
Video:
2003

DVD:
2003

Blu-ray:
2018 15th Anniversary Edition, Disney Movie Club Exclusive

Digital:

Amazon, iTunes, Vudu

Soundtrack:

2003 (CD)

George of the Jungle 2 (2003)

Watch Out For That Sequel!

Source:

Sequel to *George of the Jungle* (1997)

Writers:

Jordan Moffet

Director:

David Grossman

Premiere:

Aug 18, 2003, Video, UK

US Release:

Oct 20th 2003, Video

Length:

87 min

COLLECTIONS

Video:

2003

DVD:

2003, 2010 Double Feature

Digital:

iTunes, Vudu

Stitch! The Movie (2003)

Stitch was experiment 626...meet the other 625!

Source:

Sequel to *Lilo & Stitch* (2002)

Writers:

Jess Winfield, Roberts Gannaway

Director:

Tony Craig, Roberts Gannaway

Premiere:

Aug 25, 2003, Video

Length:

60 min

CONNECTIONS

TV Series:

Lilo & Stitch: The Series (2003–2006) Disney Channel/ABC, 65 episodes

COLLECTIONS

Video:

2003

DVD:

2003

Digital:

iTunes, Vudu

Recess: Taking the Fifth Grade (2003)

Taking Recess To The Next Level

Sections:

No More School[1], *A Recess Halloween*[2], *Grade Five Club*[3]

Source:

Spin-off of episodes of *Recess* (1997–2001) TV series

Writers:

[1]David Pilik, [1,2,3]Bart Jennett, [2]Peter Gaffney, Elijah Aron, Holly Huckins

Director:

Howy Parkins

Premiere:

Aug 26, 2003, DVD, UK

US Release:

Dec 9, 2003, DVD

Length:

62 min

CONNECTIONS

TV Series:

Recess (1997–2001) ABC/UPN, 127 episodes

COLLECTIONS

DVD:

2003

Digital:

iTunes, Vudu

Brother Bear (2003)

Nature Calls

Writers:

Tab Murphy, Lorne Cameron, David Hoselton, Steve Bencich, Ron J. Friedman (screenplay), Stephen J. Anderson, Stevie Wermers, Kevin Deters, John Puglisis, Woody Woodyman, Thom Enriquez, Kevin Harkey, Broose Johnson, John Norton

Directors:

Aaron Blaise, Robert Walker

Premiere:

Oct 20, 2003

Length:

85 min

CONNECTIONS

Movies:

Brother Bear 2 (DTV 2006) sequel

Video Games:

Disney's Brother Bear (2003) GBA, PC

COLLECTIONS

Video:

2004

DVD*/Blu-ray:

2004 Special Edition*, 2013 Special Edition / 2-Movie Collection

Digital:

Amazon, iTunes, Vudu

Soundtrack:

2003 (CD)

Books:

Brother Bear: A Transformation Tale (2003) Ed. Wendy Lefkon

The Haunted Mansion (2003)

Check Your Pulse At The Door...If You Have One.

Source:

The Haunted Mansion theme park attraction

Writers:

David Berenbaum

Director:

Rob Minkoff

Stars:

Eddie Murphy

Premiere:

Nov 26, 2003

Length:

88 min

CONNECTIONS

Comic Books:

- *Haunted Mansion* (#1–7, Oct 2005 – Oct 2007)
- *Haunted Mansion* (#1–5, May – Sep 2016) [Collection > *Haunted Mansion* (2016)]

Theme Parks:

- Haunted Mansion (DL 1969+), (MK 1971+), (TDL 1983+)
- Phantom Manor (DP 1992+)
- Mystic Manor (HKD 2013+)

Video Games:

Disney's The Haunted Mansion (2003) PS2, GC, Xbox

COLLECTIONS

Video:

2004

DVD:

2004, 2012 Disney 4-Movie Collection: Thrills and Chills

Blu-ray:

2006

Digital:

Amazon, Vudu

Soundtrack:

2003 *The Haunted Hits*, 2016 Intrada Special Collection (CD)

Books:

- *The Haunted Mansion: From the Magic Kingdom to the Movies* (2003/2009) Jason Surrell
- *The Unauthorized Story of Walt Disney's Haunted Mansion* (2016) Jeff Baham

Recess: All Growed Down (2003)

The Kindergarten Years

Source:

Spin-off of *Recess* (1997-2001) TV series

Writers:

Bart Jennett, Elijah Aron

Directors:

Howy Parkins, Brenda Piluso

Premiere:

Dec 9, 2003, DVD

Length:

61 min

CONNECTIONS

TV Series:

Recess (1997–2001) ABC/UPN, 127 episodes

COLLECTIONS

DVD:

2003

The Young Black Stallion (2003)

THE GREATEST STORY OF FRIENDSHIP EVER TOLD.

Source:

The Young Black Stallion (1989) Walter Farley and Steven Farley

Writers:

Jeanne Rosenberg

Director:

Simon Wincer

Premiere:

Dec 25, 2003, IMAX

Length:

50 min

COLLECTIONS

Video:

2004

DVD:

2004

Digital:

Amazon, Vudu

Miracle (2004)

FROM THE STUDIO THAT BROUGHT YOU "THE ROOKIE" AND "REMEMBER THE TITANS." IF YOU BELIEVE IN YOURSELF, ANYTHING CAN HAPPEN. THE STORY OF THE GREATEST MOMENT IN SPORTS HISTORY.

Source:

Based on a true story

Writers:

Eric Guggenheim

Director:

Gavin O'Connor

Stars:

Kurt Russell

Premiere:

Feb 2, 2004

Length:

135 min

COLLECTIONS

Video:

2004

DVD*/Blu-ray:

2004*, 2008 2-Pack*, 2012

Digital:

iTunes, Vudu

Soundtrack:

2004 (CD)

The Lion King 1½ (2004)

You Don't Know The ½ Of It!

AKA:

The Lion King 3: Hakuna Matata

Source:

Prequel/midquel to *The Lion King* (1994)

Writers:

Tom Rogers (screenplay), Roger Allers, Irene Mecchi, Bill Steinkellner, Evan Spiliotopoulos (additional material)

Director:

Bradley Raymond

Premiere:

Feb 10, 2004, Video/DVD

Length:

77 min

CONNECTIONS

Video Games:

The Lion King 1½ (2003) GBA

COLLECTIONS

Video:

2004

DVD*/Blu-ray:

2004*, 2011 The Lion King Trilogy, 2012 Special Edition, 2017

Soundtrack:

2004 (CD)

Confessions of a Teenage Drama Queen (2004)

So much drama, so little time.

Source:

Confessions of a Teenage Drama Queen (1999) Dyan Sheldon

Writers:

Gail Parent

Director:

Sara Sugarman

Stars:

Lindsay Lohan

Premiere:

Feb 17, 2004

Length:

89 min

COLLECTIONS

Video:

2004

DVD:

2004, 2009 Double Feature

Digital:

iTunes, Vudu

Soundtrack:

2004 (CD)

Winnie the Pooh: Springtime with Roo (2004)

Source:

Characters created by A.A. Milne

Writers:

Tom Rogers

Directors:

Saul Blinkoff, Elliot M. Bour

Premiere:

Mar 8, 2004, Video/DVD

Length:

65 min

COLLECTIONS

Video:

2004

DVD*/Blu-ray:

2004*, 2014 Hippity Hoppity Roo Edition

Digital:

iTunes, Vudu

Home on the Range (2004)

BUST A MOO

Writers:

Will Finn, John Sanford (story/screenplay), Michael LaBash, Sam Levine, Mark Kennedy, Robert Lence (story)

Directors:

Will Finn, John Sanford

Premiere:

Mar 21, 2004, Los Angeles

Length:

76 min

CONNECTIONS
Shorts:
A Dairy Tale (DTV 2004) Spin-off
Video Games:
Disney's Home on the Range (2004) GBA
COLLECTIONS
Video:
2004
DVD*Blu-ray:
2004*, 2012
Digital:
Amazon, iTunes, Vudu
Soundtrack:
2004 (CD)
Books:
Home on the Range: The Adventures of a Bovine Goddess (2004) Monique Peterson

Sacred Planet (2004)
Discover The Magic Of The Place Everyone Calls Home.
Writers:
Karen Fernandez Long, Jon Long
Director:
Jon Long
Stars:
Robert Redford
Premiere:
Apr 12, 2004, Universal City, CA, IMAX
Length:
47 min
COLLECTIONS
DVD:
2005

Digital:

iTunes, Vudu

America's Heart & Soul (2004)

Director:

Louie Schwartzberg

Premiere:

May 1, 2004, Tribeca Film Festival

Length:

88 min

COLLECTIONS

DVD:

2005, 2008 Classroom Edition

Digital:

iTunes, Vudu

Soundtrack:

2004 (CD)

Around the World in 80 Days (2004)

THE RACE BEGINS

(Note: Distributed by Disney in the US, but not internationally)

Source:

Around the World in 80 Days (1873) Jules Verne

Writers:

David N. Titcher, David Benullo, David Andrew Goldstein

Director:

Frank Coraci

Stars:

Jackie Chan

Premiere:

Jun 13, 2004, Los Angeles

Length:

120 min

CONNECTIONS
Video Games:
Around the World in 80 Days (2004) GBA

COLLECTIONS
Video:
2004

DVD:
2004

Digital:
iTunes, Vudu

Soundtrack:
2004 (CD)

The Princess Diaries 2: Royal Engagement (2004)
She needs the rock to rule.

Source:
Sequel to *The Princess Diaries* (2001)

Writers:
Gina Wendkos (story), Shonda Rhimes (story/screenplay)

Director:
Garry Marshall

Stars:
Julie Andrews, Anne Hathaway

Premiere:
Aug 7, 2004, Disneyland

Length:
113 min

COLLECTIONS
Video:
2004

DVD*/Blu-ray:
2004*, 2912 10th Anniversary Edition / 2-Movie Collection

Digital:

Amazon, Vudu

Soundtrack:

2004 (CD)

Mickey, Donald, Goofy: The Three Musketeers (2004)

AKA:

The Three Musketeers

Source:

The Three Musketeers (1844) Alexandre Dumas

Writers:

Evan Spiliotopoulos, David Mickey Evans

Director:

Donovan Cook

Premiere:

Aug 16, 2004, Video/DVD

Length:

68 min

CONNECTIONS

Comic Books:

Mickey, Donald, Goofy: The Three Musketeers (Sep 2004)

COLLECTIONS

Video:

2004

DVD*/Blu-ray:

2004*, 2014 10th Anniversary Edition

Digital:

Amazon, Vudu

Soundtrack:

2004, 2018 Intrada Special Collection (CD)

Mulan II (2004)

The Epic Journey Continues

AKA:

Mulan 2

Source:

Sequel to *Mulan* (1998)

Writers:

Michael Lucker, Chris Parker, Roger S.H. Schulman

Directors:

Darrell Rooney, Lynne Southerland

Premiere:

Nov 3, 2004, Video/DVD, Italy/Norway

US Release:

Jan 31, 2005, Video/DVD

Length:

79 min

COLLECTIONS

Video:

2005

DVD*/Blu-ray:

2005*, 2013 Special Edition / 2-Movie Collection

Digital:

iTunes, Vudu

Soundtrack:

2005 (CD)

The Incredibles (2004)

FROM THE CREATORS OF FINDING NEMO. SAVE THE DAY

Writers:

Brad Bird

Director:

Brad Bird

Premiere:

Oct 27, 2004, London Film Festival

US Release:

Nov 5, 2004

Length:

115 min

CONNECTIONS

Comic Strips:

- *The Incredibles* (#1–4, Nov 2004 – Feb 2005) Dark Horse Comics [Collection > *The Incredibles* (2005)]
- *The Incredibles: Family Matters* (#1–4, Mar – Jun 2009) [Collection > *The Incredibles: Family Matters* (2009) Boom Studios]
- *The Incredibles* (#0–15, Jul 2009 – Oct 2010) Boom Studios [Collection > *The Incredibles Vol 1–4* (2009–2011)]

Movies:

Incredibles 2 (2018) sequel

Shorts:

- *Jack Jack Attack* (DTV 2005)
- *Mr. Incredible and Pals* (DTV 2005)

Video Games:

- *The Incredibles* (2004) PS2, Mac, PC, GBA, GC, Xbox, DS, PS3
- *The Incredibles: When Danger Calls* (2004) PC, Mac
- *The Incredibles: Rise of the Underminer* (2005) PS2, GC, DS, GBA, Xbox, Mac, PC

COLLECTIONS

Video:

2005

DVD*/Blu-ray:

2005 Collector's Edition*, 2011, 2016

Digital:

Amazon, iTunes, Vudu

Soundtrack:

2004 (CD)

Books:

The Art of the Incredibles (2004) Mark Cotta Vaz

National Treasure (2004)

IN ORDER TO BREAK THE CODE, ONE MAN WILL HAVE TO BREAK ALL THE RULES.

Writers:

Oren Aviv, Charles Segars (story), Jim Kouf (story/screenplay), Cormac Wibberley, Marianne Wibberley (screenplay)

Director:

Jon Turteltaub

Stars:

Nicolas Cage

Premiere:

Nov 8, 2004, Pasadena

Length:

131 min

CONNECTIONS

Movies:

National Treasure: Book of Secrets (2007) Sequel

COLLECTIONS

Video:

2005

DVD*/Blu-ray:

2005 + Premium Pack*, 2007 Collector's Edition*, 2008 Collector's Edition, 2011 Collector's Edition

Digital:

Amazon, iTunes, Vudu

Soundtrack:

2004 (CD)

Mickey's Twice Upon a Christmas (2004)
Two Times The Christmas Fun!

Sections:
Belles on Ice[1], *Christmas: Impossible*[2], *Christmas Maximus*[3], *Donald's Gift*[4], *Mickey's Dog-Gone Christmas*[5]

Source:
Sequel to *Mickey's Once Upon a Christmas* (DTV 1999)

Writers:
[3] Theresa Cullen, [5] Colin Goldman, [5] Matthew O'Callaghan (story) [1] Peggy Holmes, [2] Chad Fiveash, [2] James Patrick Stoteraux, [4] Carole Holliday (story/screenplay), [1,3] Bill Motz, [1,3] Bob Roth, [2] Matthew O'Callaghan, [3] Shirley Pierce, [4] Jim Peronto, [5] Michael Shipley, [5] Jim Bernstein, [5] Shirley Pierce (screenplay)

Directors:
Carole Holliday, Matthew O'Callaghan, [3] Theresa Cullen

Premiere:
Nov 9, 2004, Video/DVD

Length:
68 min

CONNECTIONS
Comic Book:
Mickey's Twice Upon a Christmas (2004)

COLLECTIONS
Video:
2004

DVD*/Blu-ray:
2004*, 2014 Special Edition / 2-Movie Collection

Digital:
iTunes, Vudu

PART NINE

Movies: 2005–2009

Aliens of the Deep (2005)

The search for life beyond begins below.

Directors:
James Cameron, Steven Quale

Premiere:
Jan 28, 2005, IMAX/3D

Length:
47 min (IMAX), 99 min (DVD)

COLLECTIONS

DVD:
2005

Digital:
iTunes, Vudu

Pooh's Heffalump Movie (2005)

Heffa nice day.

Source:
Characters created by A.A. Milne

Writers:
Brian Hohlfeld, Evan Spiliotopoulos

Director:
Frank Nissen

Premiere:
Feb 4, 2005, Iceland/Poland

US Release:
Feb 11, 2005

Length:
68 min

CONNECTIONS

Movies:
Pooh's Heffalump Halloween Movie (DTV 2005) sequel

COLLECTIONS

Video:
2005

DVD:
2005

Digital:
iTunes

Soundtrack:
2005 *The Best of Pooh & Heffalumps Too* (CD)

The Pacifier (2005)
PREPARE FOR BOTTLE.

Writers:
Thomas Lennon, Robert Ben Garant

Director:
Adam Shankman

Stars:
Vin Diesel

Premiere:
Mar 1, 2005, Hollywood

Length:
95 min

COLLECTIONS

Video:
2005

DVD:

2005

Digital:

Vudu

Ice Princess (2005)

From small town Mathlete, to big time Athlete. Big things happen to those who dream BIG.

Writers:

Meg Cabot (story), Hadley Davis (story/screenplay)

Director:

Tim Fywell

Premiere:

Mar 18, 2005

Length:

98 min

COLLECTIONS

Video:

2005

DVD:

2005

Digital:

Amazon, iTunes, Vudu

Soundtrack:

2005 (CD)

Valiant (2005)

FEATHERWEIGHT HEROES.

(Note: Vanguard Animation and Ealing Studios production, released by Disney in US)

Writers:

George Webster (story/screenplay), Jordan Katz, George Melrod (screenplay)

Director:

Gary Chapman

Premiere:

Mar 20, 2005, Festival du Film d'Aventures de Valenciennes, France

US Release:

Aug 19, 2005

Length:

76 min

COLLECTIONS

DVD:

2005

Digital:

Amazon, iTunes, Vudu

Soundtrack:

2005 (CD)

Tarzan II (2005)

THE LEGEND BEGINS

AKA:

Tarzan 2

Source:

Prequel to *Tarzan* (1999)

Writers:

Jim Kammerud, Brian Smith, Bob Tzudiker, Noni White (screenplay), Evan Spiliotopoulos, Rhett Reese (additional material)

Director:

Brian Smith

Premiere:

Jun 13, 2005, Video/DVD

Length:

72 min

COLLECTIONS
Video/DVD:

2005

Digital:

Amazon, iTunes, Vudu

Herbie Fully Loaded (2005)

Source:

Sequel to *The Love Bug* (1969)

Writers:

Mark Perez (story), Thomas Lennon, Robert Ben Garant (story/screen-play) Alfred Gough, Miles Millar (screenplay)

Director:

Angela Robinson

Stars:

Lindsay Lohan

Premiere:

Jun 19, 2005, Los Angeles

Length:

101 min

CONNECTIONS
Video Games:

Herbie: Fully Loaded (2005) GBA

COLLECTIONS
Video:

2005

DVD:

2005

Digital:

Amazon, iTunes, Vudu

Soundtrack:

2005 (CD)

Sky High (2005)

SAVING THE WORLD… ONE HOMEWORK ASSIGNMENT AT A TIME. BRAINS, BRAWN AND BEYOND.

Writers:

Paul Hernandez, Robert Schooley, Mark McCorkle

Director:

Mike Mitchell

Premiere:

Jul 24, 2005, Hollywood

Length:

100 min

COLLECTIONS

DVD:

2005

Blu-ray:

2006

Digital:

Amazon, iTunes, Vudu

Soundtrack:

2005, 2017 Intrada Special Collection (CD)

Lilo & Stitch 2: Stitch Has a Glitch (2005)

Source:

Sequel to *Lilo & Stitch* (2002)

Writers:

Tony Leondis, Michael LaBash, Eddie Guzelian, Alexa Junge

Directors:

Michael LaBash, Tony Leondis

Premiere:

Aug 15, 2005, Video/DVD

Length:

68 min

CONNECTIONS

Video Games:

Disney's Lilo & Stitch 2: Hamsterviel Havoc (2004) GBA

COLLECTIONS

Video:

2005

DVD*/Blu-ray:

2005*, 2013 Special Edition / 2-Movie Collection, 2017 2-Movie Collection

Digital:

iTunes, Vudu

Soundtrack:

2005 *Island Favorites* (CD)

Pooh's Heffalump Halloween Movie (2005)

Celebrate Lumpy's First Halloween

Source:

Sequel to *Pooh's Heffalump Movie* (2005)

Writers:

Brian Hohlfeld, Evan Spiliotopoulos

Directors:

Saul Blinkoff, Elliot M. Bour

Premiere:

Sep 12, 2005, Video/DVD

Length:

67 min

COLLECTIONS

Video/DVD:

2005

The Greatest Game Ever Played (2005)

FROM THE STUDIO THAT BROUGHT YOU "REMEMBER THE TITANS", "THE ROOKIE," AND "MIRACLE"

Source:

The Greatest Game Ever Played (2002) Mark Frost

Writers:

Mark Frost

Director:

Bill Paxton

Premiere:

Sep 30, 2005

Length:

120 min

COLLECTIONS

DVD:

2006

Blu-ray:

2009, 2011

Digital:

Amazon, iTunes, Vudu

Soundtrack:

2005 (CD)

Chicken Little (2005)

The end is near! This time the sky really is falling.

Source:

"Chicken Little" folk tale

Writers:

Mark Dindal, Mark Kennedy (story), Steve Bencich, Ron J. Friedman, Ron Anderson (screenplay), Robert L. Baird, Daniel Gerson, Sara Parriott, Josann McGibbon, David Reynolds, Sandra Tsing Log (additional material)

Director:

Mark Dindal

Premiere:

Oct 30, 2005, Los Angeles + 3D

Length:

81 min

CONNECTIONS

Video Games:

- *Disney's Chicken Little* (2005) PS2, GBA, GC, Xbox, PC
- *Disney's Chicken Little: Ace in Action* (2006) PS2, DS, Wii

COLLECTIONS

DVD*/Blu-ray:

2006*, 2007 + Blu-ray 4-Pack: Disney Movies, 2011 + 3D

Digital:

Amazon, Vudu

Soundtrack:

2005 (CD)

Books:

Chicken Little: From Hen House to Hollywood (2005) Monique Peterson

Kronk's New Groove (2005)

Source:

Sequel to *The Emperor's New Groove* (2000)

Writers:

Tony Leondis, Michael LaBash (story), Tom Rogers (story/screenplay)

Directors:

Saul Blinkoff, Elliot M. Bour

Premiere:

Dec 5, 2005, Video/DVD, UK

US Release:

Dec 12, 2005, Video/DVD

Length:

75 min

COLLECTIONS

Video:

2005

DVD*/Blu-ray:

2005*, 2013 Special Edition / 2-Movie Collection

Digital:

iTunes, Vudu

The Chronicles of Narnia: The Lion, the Witch and the Wardrobe (2005)

The beloved masterpiece comes to life

Source:

The Lion, the Witch and the Wardrobe (1950) C.S. Lewis

Writers:

Ann Peacock, Andrew Adamson, Christopher Markus, Stephen McFeely

Director:

Andrew Adamson

Premiere:

Dec 7, 2005, Switzerland/Spain

US Release:

Dec 9, 2005

Length:

143 min (Original), 150 min (Extended)

CONNECTIONS

Movies:

- *The Chronicles of Narnia: Prince Caspian* (2008) sequel
- *The Chronicles of Narnia: The Voyage of the Dawn Treader* (2010) sequel, produced by 20th Century Fox

Video Games:

The Chronicles of Narnia: The Lion, the Witch and the Wardrobe (2005) GBA, DS, Xbox, PC, GC, PS2, PS3

COLLECTIONS

DVD*/Blu-ray:

2006 + Collector's Edition* + Extended Edition*, 2008 + Classroom Edition*, 2010

Digital:

Amazon, Vudu

Soundtrack:

2005 + Special Edition + *Music Inspired By* (CD)

Glory Road (2006)

THE ICNREDIBLE STORY OF THE TEAM THAT CHANGED THE GAME FOREVER. WINNING CHANGES EVERYTHING

Source:

Glory Road (2005) Don Haskins & Daniel Wetzel

Writers:

Christopher Cleveland, Bettina Gilois

Director:

James Gartner

Premiere:

Jan 13, 2006

Length:

118 min

COLLECTIONS

DVD/Blu-ray:

2006

Digital:

iTunes, Vudu

Soundtrack:

2006 (CD)

Bambi II (2006)

A Son's Courage. A Father's Love.

Source:

Sequel to *Bambi* (1942)

Writers:

Alicia Kirk (screenplay), Brian Pimental, Jeanne Rosenberg (story), Nick Thiel, Roger S.H. Schulman (additional material)

Director:

Brian Pimental

Premiere:

Jan 26, 2006, Argentina

US Release:

Feb 6, 2006, Video/DVD

Length:

75 min

COLLECTIONS

Video:

2006

DVD*/Blu-ray:

2006*, 2011 Special Edition, 2017 Disney Movie Club Exclusive

Digital:

Amazon, iTunes, Vudu

Soundtrack:

2006 (CD)

Roving Mars (2006)

A WHOLE NEW WORLD AWAITS.

Writers:

George Butler, Robert Andrus

Director:

George Butler

Premiere:

Jan 27, 2006, IMAX

Length:

40 min

COLLECTIONS
DVD/Blu-ray:
2007

Digital:
iTunes, Vudu

Soundtrack:
2006 (CD)

Books:
Roving Mars: Spirit, Opportunity, and the Exploration of the Red Planet (2006) Steve Squyres

Eight Below (2006)
THE MOST AMAZING STORY OF SURVIVAL, FRIENDSHIP, AND ADVENTURE EVER TOLD. INSPIRED BY A TRUE STORY

Source:
Suggested by Japanese film *Nankyoku Monogatari* (1983)

Writers:
David DiGilio

Director:
Frank Marshall

Stars:
Paul Walker

Premiere:
Feb 17, 2006

Length:
120 min

COLLECTIONS
DVD:
2006

Blu-ray:
2006, 2007 Blu-ray 4-Pack: Family Movies

Digital:
iTunes, Vudu

The Shaggy Dog (2006)

RAISE THE WOOF.

Source:

Remake of *The Shaggy Dog* (1959)

Writers:

Cormac Wibberley, Mariane Wibberley, Geoff Rodkey, Jack Amiel, Michael Begler

Director:

Brian Robbins

Stars:

Tim Allen

Premiere:

Mar 10, 2006

Length:

98 min

COLLECTIONS

DVD:

2006, 2012 Disney 4-Movie Collection: Dogs 1

Digital:

Vudu

Soundtrack:

2006 (CD)

Cars (2006)

Writers:

John Lasseter, Joe Ranft, Jorgen Klubien (story/screenplay), Dan Fogelman, Kiel Murray, Phil Lorin (screenplay), Steve Pucell (additional material)

Directors:

John Lasseter, Joe Ranft (co-director)

Premiere:

Mar 26, 2006, Charlotte, North Carolina

Length:

117 min

CONNECTIONS

Comic Strips:

- *Cars: The Rookie* (#1–4, Mar – Jun 2009) [Collection > *Cars: The Rookie* (2009)]
- *Cars: Radiator Springs* (#1–4, Jul – Oct 2009) [Collection > *Cars: Radiator Springs* (2009)]
- *Cars* (#0–7, Nov 2009 – Jun 2010) [Collection > *Cars: Rally Race* (2010) & *Cars: Route 66 Dash* (2010)]
- *Cars: Adventures of Tow Mater* (#1–4, Jul – Oct 2010) [Collection > *Cars: Rust Bucket Derby* (2011)]

Movies:

- *Cars 2* (2011) sequel
- *Planes* (2013) spin-off
- *Cars 3* (2017) sequel

Shorts:

- *Mater and the Ghostlight* (DTV 2006)
- *Tokyo Mater* (2008)
- *Cars Toons: Mater's Tall Tales* [*Rescue Squad Mater* (TV 2008) Toon Disney, *Mater the Greater* (TV 2008) Toon Disney, *El Materdor* (TV 2008) Toon Disney, *Unidentified Flying Mater* (TV 2009) Disney Channel, *Monster Truck Mater* (TV 2010) Disney Channel, *Heavy Metal Mater* (TV 2010) Disney Channel, *Moon Mater* (DTV 2010), *Mater's Private Eye* (DTV 2010), *Air Mater* (DTV 2011), *Time Travel Mater* (TV 2012) Disney Channel]
- *Cars Toons: Tales from Radiator Springs* [*Hiccups* (TV 2013) Disney Channel, *Bugged* (TV 2013) Disney Channel, *Spinning* (TV 2013) Disney Channel, *The Radiator Springs 500½* (TV 2014) Disney Channel]

Theme Parks:

- Cars Quatre Roues Rallye (WDS 2007+)
- Cars Land (DCA 2012+)
- Radiator Springs Racers (DCA 2012+)
- Luigi's Flying Tyres (DCA 2012-2015)
- Luigi's Rollickin' Roadsters (DCA 2016+)

Video Games:

- *Cars* (2006) PSP, Xbox, GC, PC, Mac, DS, GBA, PS2, X360, Wii, X360S, PS3

- *Disney/Pixar Cars: Radiator Springs Adventures* (2006) PC, Mac
- *Disney/Pixar Cars: Mater-national Championship* (2007) DS, X360, X360S, GBA, PS2, PS3, Wii, PC
- *Cars: Race-O-Rama* (2009) PSP, Wii, X360, PS3, PS2, DS, X360S

COLLECTIONS

DVD*/Blu-ray:

2006*, 2007, 2009 Ultimate Gift Set, 2010 Disney/Pixar: The Ultimate Blu-ray Collection, 2011 + Cars Director's Edition, 2013 Ultimate Collector's Edition / 3D, 2017

Digital:

Amazon, iTunes, Vudu

Soundtrack:

2006 + *Lightning McQueen's Fast Tracks*, 2007, 2009 *Mater's Car Tunes*, 2010 *Songs and Story* (CD)

Books:

- *The Art of Cars* (2006) Michael Wallis
- *Poster Art of Cars* (2017) Victoria Saxton

The Wild (2006)

START SPREADING THE NEWSPAPER.

Writers:

Mark Gibson, Philip Halprin (story/screenplay), Ed Decter, John J. Strauss (screenplay), Bill Wolkoff, David Collard, Matt Lopez, Lloyd Taylor, Steve "Spaz" Williams (additional material)

Director:

Steve 'Spaz' Williams

Premiere:

Apr 12, 2006, Belgium/Spain/France

US Release:

Apr 14, 2006

Length:

85 min

CONNECTIONS
Video Games:
The Wild (2006), GBA

COLLECTIONS
DVD:
2006

Blu-ray:
2006, 2007 Blu-ray 4-Pack: Disney Movies, 2011

Digital:
Vudu

Soundtrack:
2006 (CD)

Leroy & Stitch (2006)

Source:
Sequel to *Lilo & Stitch* (2002) and *Lilo & Stitch: The Series* (2003-2006)

Writers:
Roberts Gannaway, Jess Winfield

Directors:
Roberts Gannaway, Tony Craig

Premiere:
Jun 23, 2006, Disney Channel

Re-releases:
Jun 27, 2006, DVD

Length:
73 min

COLLECTIONS
DVD:
2006

Digital:
Amazon, iTunes, Vudu

Pirates of the Caribbean: Dead Man's Chest (2006)

Source:
Sequel to *Pirates of the Caribbean: The Curse of the Black Pearl* (2003)

Writers:
Ted Elliott, Terry Rossio

Director:
Gore Verbinski

Stars:
Johnny Depp, Orlando Bloom, Keira Knightley

Premiere:
Jun 24, 2006, Disneyland

Length:
151 min

CONNECTIONS

Comic Books:
Disney Manga: Pirates of the Caribbean: Dead Man's Chest (Jan 2018)

Video Games:
Pirates of the Caribbean: Dead Man's Chest (2006) GBA, DS, PSP

COLLECTIONS

DVD*/Blu-ray:
2006 + Collector's Edition*, 2007 + Blu-ray 4-Pack: Family Movies, 2008 Trilogy + Ultimate Trilogy Collection, 2011 + 4-Movie Collector's Edition

Digital:
Amazon

Soundtrack:
2006, 2007 Soundtrack Treasures Collection + *Swashbuckling Sea Songs* (CD)

Books:
- *Bring Me That Horizon: The Making of Pirates of the Caribbean* (2007) Michael Singer
- *The Art of Pirates of the Caribbean* (2007) Timothy Shaner & Christopher Meason

Brother Bear 2 (2006)

The Moose Are On The Loose

Source:

Sequel to *Brother Bear* (2003)

Writers:

Rich Burns (screenplay), Ben Gluck (additional screenplay)

Director:

Ben Gluck

Premiere:

Aug 17, 2006, Germany/Mexico, DVD

US Release:

Aug 28, 2006, DVD

Length:

73 min

COLLECTIONS

DVD*/Blu-ray:

2006*, 2013 Special Edition / 2-Movie Collection

Digital:

iTunes, Vudu

Soundtrack:

2006 (Digital)

Invincible (2006)

IN 1978, A 30-YEAR OLD BARTENDER, WHO PLAYED ONLY ONE YEAR OF HIGH SCHOOL FOOTBALL, TRIED TO BECOME THE NFL'S MOST UNLIKELY ROOKIE. DREAMS ARE NOT LIVED ON THE SIDELINES

Source:

Inspired by the true story of Vince Papale

Writers:

Brad Gann

Director:

Ericson Core

Stars:

Mark Wahlberg

Premiere:

Aug 25, 2006

Length:

105 min

COLLECTIONS

DVD:

2006

Blu-ray:

2006, 2007 Blu-ray 4-Pack: Family Movies, 2011

Digital:

iTunes

Soundtrack:

2006 (CD)

The Santa Clause 3: The Escape Clause (2006)

'Twas The Fight Before Christmas…

Source:

Second sequel to *The Santa Clause* (1994)

Writers:

Ed Decter, John J. Strauss

Director:

Michael Lembeck

Stars:

Tim Allen, Martin Short

Premiere:

Nov 3, 2006

Length:

97 min

COLLECTIONS

DVD:

2007 + The Santa Clause Holiday Collection

Blu-ray:

2007, 2011, 2012 The Santa Clause: The Complete 3-Movie Collection

Digital:

Amazon, iTunes, Vudu

The Fox and the Hound 2 (2006)

Old Friends. New Adventure.

Source:

Midquel to *The Fox and the Hound* (1981)

Writers:

Rich Burns, Roger S.H. Schulman

Director:

Jim Kammerud

Premiere:

Nov 9, 2006, Australia, DVD

US Release:

Dec 11, 2006, DVD

Length:

69 min

COLLECTIONS

DVD*/Blu-ray:

2006*, 2011 30th Anniversary Edition / 2-Movie Collection, 2017 2-Movie Collection

Digital:

Vudu

Soundtrack:

2006 (CD)

Air Buddies (2006)

They Shoot. They Score. They TALK!

Source:

Spin-off from *Air Bud* (1997)

Writers:

Robert Vince, Anna McRoberts, Phil Hanley

Director:

Robert Vince

Premiere:

Dec 12, 2006, DVD

Length:

80 min

CONNECTIONS

Movies:

- *Snow Buddies* (DTV 2008)
- *Space Buddies* (DTV 2009)
- *Santa Buddies* (DTV 2009)
- *The Search for Santa Paws* (DTV 2010)
- *Spooky Buddies* (DTV 2011)
- *Treasure Buddies* (DTV 2012)
- *Santa Paws 2: The Santa Pups* (DTV 2012)
- *Super Buddies* (DTV 2013)

COLLECTIONS

DVD:

2006, 2009 4-Movie Collection

Digital:

iTunes, Vudu

Cinderella III: A Twist in Time (2007)

What If The Slipper Didn't Fit?

AKA:

Cinderella 3: A Twist in Time

Source:

Sequel to *Cinderella* (1950)

Writers:

Dan Berendsen, Margaret Heidenry, Colleen Millea Ventimilia, Eddie Guzelian (screenplay), Steve Bencich, Ron J. Friedman, Robert Reece, Evan Spiliotopoulos (additional material)

Director:

Frank Nissen

Premiere:

Feb 5, 2007, DVD

Length:

74 min

COLLECTIONS

DVD*/Blu-ray:

2007*, 2012 Special Edition / 2-Movie Collection

Bridge to Terabithia (2007)

DISCOVER A PLACE THAT WILL NEVER LEAVE YOU, AND A FRIENDSHIP THAT WILL CHANGE YOU FOREVER. THE BELOVED NOVEL COMES TO LIFE

Source:

Bridge to Terabithia (1977) Katherine Paterson

Writers:

Jeff Stockwell, David Paterson

Director:

Gabor Csupo

Premiere:

Feb 16, 2007

Length:

96 min

COLLECTIONS

DVD:

2007

Blu-ray:

2007 + Blu-ray 4-Pack: Disney Movies

Digital:

Amazon, iTunes, Vudu

Soundtrack:

2007 *Music From and Inspired By* (CD)

Meet the Robinsons (2007)

If you think your family's different, wait til you meet the family of the future. Have the time travel of your life.

Source:

A Day with Wilbur Robinson (1990) William Joyce

Writers:

Jon Bernstein, Michelle Bochner Spitz, Don Hall, Nathan Greno, Aurian Redson, Joseph Mateo, Stephen J. Anderson

Director:

Stephen J. Anderson

Premiere:

Mar 23, 2007, IMAX

US Release:

Mar 30, 2007 + 3D

Length:

95 min

CONNECTIONS

Video Games:

Meet the Robinsons (2007) X360, X360S, PS3, GBA, PSP, PS2, GC, Wii, DS, PC

COLLECTIONS

DVD*/Blu-ray:

2007, 2011 + 3D

Digital:

Amazon, iTunes, Vudu

Soundtrack:

2007 (CD)

Books:

The Art of Meet the Robinsons (2007) Tracey Miller-Zarneke

Pirates of the Caribbean: At World's End (2007)

Source:

Second sequel to *Pirates of the Caribbean: The Curse of the Black Pearl* (2003)

Writers:

Ted Elliott, Terry Rossio

Director:

Gore Verbinski

Stars:

Johnny Depp, Orlando Bloom, Keira Knightley, Chow Yun-Fat, Geoffrey Rush

Premiere:

May 19, 2007, Anaheim, California

Length:

168 min

CONNECTIONS

Video Games:

Pirates of the Caribbean: At World's End (2007) PSP, Wii, X360, PS3, PC, PS2, DS

COLLECTIONS

DVD/Blu-ray:

2007 + Limited Edition, 2008 Trilogy, 2011 + Ultimate Trilogy Collection + 4-Movie Collection

Digital:

Amazon, iTunes, Vudu

Soundtrack:

2007 + Soundtrack Treasures Collection (CD)

Books:

- *Bring Me That Horizon: The Making of Pirates of the Caribbean* (2007) Michael Singer
- *The Art of Pirates of the Caribbean* (2007) Timothy Shaner and Christopher Meason

Ratatouille (2007)

He's dying to become a chef. (rat-a-too-ee)

Writers:

Jan Pinkava, Jim Capobianco (story), Brad Bird (story/screenplay)

Directors:

Brad Bird, Jan Pinkava (co-director)

Premiere:

Jun 22, 2007, Hollywood

Re-releases:

2012 (3D)

Length:

111 min

CONNECTIONS

Shorts:

Your Friend the Rat (DTV 2007)

Theme Parks:

Ratatouille: L'Aventure Totalement Toquée de Rémy (WDS 2014+), (E TBA)

Video Games:

- *Ratatouille* (2007) Xbox, X360, X306S, DS, GBA, GC, Wii, Mac, PC, PS2, PS3, PSP
- *Ratatouille: Food Frenzy* (2007) DS

COLLECTIONS

DVD/Blu-ray:

2007, 2010 Disney/Pixar: The Ultimate Blu-ray Collection, 2011, 2016

Digital:

Amazon, iTunes, Vudu

Soundtrack:

2007 + *What's Cooking?* (CD)

Books:

The Art of Ratatouille (2007) Karen Paik

The Secret of the Magic Gourd (2007)

AKA:

宝葫芦的秘密 / Bao hu lu de bi mi

Source:

The Secret of the Magic Gourd (1958) Zhang Tian Yi

Writers:

John Chu, Lam Kee To

Directors:

John Chu, Frankie Chung

Premiere:

Jun 29, 2007, Beijing, China

US Release:

Jan 27, 2009, DVD

Length:

84 min

COLLECTIONS

DVD:

2009

Digital:

iTunes, Vudu

Earth (2007)

The incredible story of three families and their amazing journey across the planet we call home.

Source:

Spin-off of *Planet Earth* (2006) BBC TV series

Writers:

Leslie Megahey

Directors:

Alastair Fothergill, Mark Linfield

Narrator:

James Earl Jones

Premiere:
Jul 14, 2007, Vaduz Film Festival, Liechtenstein

US Release:
Apr 4, 2009, Phoenix Film Festival

Length:
96 min

CONNECTIONS

Movies:
Earth: One Amazing Day (2017) Sequel

COLLECTIONS

DVD/Blu-ray:
2009

Books:
True-Life Adventures: A History of Walt Disney's Nature Documentaries (2017) Christian Moran

Underdog (2007)
ONE NATION... UNDER DOG. HAVE NO FEAR

Source:
Underdog (1964–1967) NBC TV series

Writers:
Adam Rifkin, Joe Piscatella, Craig A. Williams

Director:
Frederick Du Chau

Premiere:
Aug 3, 2007

Length:
84 min

COLLECTIONS

DVD/Blu-ray:
2007

Digital:
iTunes, Vudu

Soundtrack:

2008 (iTunes)

The Game Plan (2007)

Joe Kingman had the perfect game plan to win the championship...but first, he has to tackle one little problem.

Writers:

Audrey Wells (story), Kathryn Price, Nichole Millard (story/screenplay)

Director:

Andy Fickman

Stars:

Dwayne "The Rock" Johnson

Premiere:

Sep 23, 2007, Hollywood

Length:

110 min

COLLECTIONS

DVD/Blu-ray:

2008, 2011

Digital:

Amazon, iTunes, Vudu

The Pixar Story (2007)

Writers:

Leslie Iwerks

Director:

Leslie Iwerks

Premiere:

Oct 6, 2007, Mill Valley Film Festival, San Rafael, CA

Length:

87 min.

COLLECTIONS
DVD/Blu-ray:
2008 *WALL·E*

Digital:
Amazon, iTunes, Vudu

Books:
To Infinity and Beyond! The Story of Pixar Animation Studios (2007) Karen Paik & Leslie Iwerks

Enchanted (2007)
THE REAL WORLD AND THE ANIMATED WORLD COLLIDE

Writers:
Bill Kelly

Director:
Kevin Lima

Premiere:
Oct 20, 2007, London Film Festival

US Release:
Nov 17, 2007, Hollywood

Length:
107 min

CONNECTIONS
Movies:
Disenchanted (2018) Sequel

Video Games:
- *Enchanted* (2007) DS
- *Enchanted: Once Upon Andalasia* (2007) GBA, DS

COLLECTIONS
DVD/Blu-ray:
2008, 2011, 2012 The Royal Wedding Collection

Digital:
Amazon, iTunes, Vudu

Soundtrack:

2007 (CD)

National Treasure: Book of Secrets (2007)

AKA:

National Treasure 2: Book of Secrets

Source:

Sequel to *National Treasure* (2004)

Writers:

Gregory Poirier, Ted Elliott, Terry Rossio (story), Marinne Wibberley, Cormac Wibberley (story/screenplay)

Director:

Jon Turteltaub

Stars:

Nicolas Cage

Premiere:

Dec 11, 2007, New York

Length:

124 min

COLLECTIONS

DVD/Blu-ray:

2008 + Collector's Edition, 2011

Digital:

Amazon, iTunes, Vudu

Soundtrack:

2007 (Digital)

Disneyland: Secrets, Stories & Magic (2007)

AKA:

Secrets, Stories & Magic of the Happiest Place on Earth

Director:

Bob Garner, Pete Schuermann (co-director)

Premiere:

Dec 11, 2007, DVD

Length:

81 min

COLLECTIONS

DVD:

2007 *WD Treasures: Disneyland: Secrets, Stories and Magic*

Hannah Montana & Miley Cyrus: Best of Both Worlds Concert (2008)

CATCH THE MOST ANTICIPATED MOVIE EVENT EVER CAPTURED IN DISNEY DIGITAL 3-D

Source:

Spin-off of *Hannah Montana* (2006-2011) TV Series

Director:

Bruce Hendricks

Stars:

Miley Cyrus

Premiere:

Feb 1, 2008, 3D

Length:

74 min (original), 82 min (extended)

CONNECTIONS

Movies:

Hannah Montana: The Movie (2009) See entry for *Hannah Montana* connections

COLLECTIONS

DVD/Blu-ray:

2008 3D Extended Edition

Digital:

iTunes, Vudu

Soundtrack:

2008 (CD)

Snow Buddies (2008)

They Talk. They Mush. They're Snow Cool!

Source:

Spin-off of *Aid Buddies* (DTV 2006)

Writers:

Robert Vince, Anna McRoberts (screenplay), Phil Hanley (additional material)

Director:

Robert Vince

Premiere:

Feb 5, 2008, DVD

Length:

87 min

COLLECTIONS

DVD*/Blu-ray:

2008*, 2009 Buddies 4-Movie Collection*, 2012

Digital:

Amazon, iTunes, Vudu

College Road Trip (2008)

They can't get there fast enough.

Writers:

Emi Mochizuki, Carrie Lee Wilson, Cinco Paul, Ken Daurio

Director:

Roger Kumble

Stars:

Martin Lawrence, Raven-Symoné

Premiere:

Mar 3, 2008, Hollywood

Length:

83 min

COLLECTIONS
DVD/Blu-ray:
2008

Digital:
iTunes, Vudu

Walt & El Grupo (2008)
WITH THE WORLD ON THE BRINK OF WAR, AND NAZI INFLUENCE GROWING IN SOUTH AMERICA, THE U.S. GOVERNMENT SOUGHT HELP FROM A BUNCH OF ARTISTS. THE UNTOLD ADVENTURES

Writers:
Theodore Thomas

Director:
Theodore Thomas

Premiere:
Apr 26, 2008, San Francisco International Film Festival

Length:
107 min

CONNECTIONS
Movies:
- *Saludos Amigos* (1942)
- *The Three Caballeros* (1944)

Short:
South of the Border with Disney (1942) Documentary

COLLECTIONS
DVD:
2010

Digital:
iTunes, Vudu

Books:
South of the Border with Disney: Walt Disney and the Good Neighbor Program 1941-1948 (2009) J.B. Kaufman

The Chronicles of Narnia: Prince Caspian (2008)

EVERYTHING YOU KNOW IS ABOUT TO CHANGE FOREVER.

Source:

- *Prince Caspian* (1951) C.S. Lewis
- Sequel to *The Chronicles of Narnia: The Lion, the Witch and the Wardrobe* (2005)

Writers:

Andrew Adamson, Christopher Markus, Stephen McFeely

Director:

Andrew Adamson

Premiere:

May 9, 2008, Festival Internacional de Cine Acapulco, Mexico

US Release:

May 16, 2008

Length:

150 min

CONNECTIONS

Video Games:

The Chronicles of Narnia: Prince Caspian (2008) DS, PC, Wii, PS3, PS2, X360

COLLECTIONS

DVD*/Blu-ray:

2008 + Collector's Edition + Classroom Edition*, 2010

Digital:

Amazon

Soundtrack:

2008 (CD)

WALL·E (2008)

AFTER 700 YEARS OF DOING WHAT HE WAS BUILT FOR, HE'LL DISCOVER WHAT HE WAS MEANT FOR.

Writers:
Pete Docter (story), Andrew Stanton (story/screenplay), Jim Reardon (screenplay)

Director:
Andrew Stanton

Premiere:
Jun 21, 2008, Los Angeles

Length:
98 min

CONNECTIONS

Comic Books:
WALL·E (#0–7, Nov 2009 – Jun 2010) [Collection > *WALL·E: Recharge* (2010) & *WALL·E: Out There* (2010)]

Movies:
Hello, Dolly! (1969) 20th Century Fox production favoured by WALL·E

Shorts:
BURN·E (DTV 2008) Spin-off

Video Games:
WALL·E (2008) PS2, X360, PS3, PSP, DS

COLLECTIONS

DVD*/Blu-ray:
2008 + Special Edition + Classroom Edition*, 2010 Disney/Pixar: The Ultimate Blu-ray Collection, 2011, 2016

Digital:
Amazon, iTunes, Vudu

Soundtrack:
2008 (CD)

Books:
The Art of WALL·E (2008) Tim Hauser

High School Musical: El Desafío (2008)

AKA:

High School Musical: The Challenge, Viva High School Musical

Source:

Remake of *High School Musical* (2006) TV movie

Writers:

Susana Cardozo, Pablo Lago

Director:

Jorge Nisco

Premiere:

Jul 17, 2008, Argentina

Length:

98 min

CONNECTIONS

TV Series:

High School Musical: La Selecci n (2007) Talent show to find movies actors

COLLECTIONS

Soundtrack:

2008 (CD, Argentina)

The Little Mermaid: Ariel's Beginning (2008)

EVERY TALE HAS A BEGINNING, BUT ONLY ONE BEGINS UNDER THE SEA.

Source:

Prequel to *The Little Mermaid* (1989)

Writers:

Jule Selbo, Jenny Wingfield (story), Robert Reece, Evan Spiliotopoulos (screenplay), Steve Bencich, Peggy Holmes, Tom Rogers, Thania St. John, Rich Burns, Ron J. Friedman (additional material)

Director:

Peggy Holmes

Premiere:

Aug 26, 2008, DVD

Length:

77 min

COLLECTIONS

DVD*/Bu-ray:

2008*, 2013 2-Movie Collection

High School Musical: El Desafío (2008)

AKA:

High School Musical: The Challenge, Viva High School Musical

Source:

Remake of *High School Musical* (2006) TV movie

Writers:

Flavio González Mello, Peter Barsocchini (adaptation), Pablo Lago, Susana Cardozo (original screenplay)

Director:

Eduardo Ripari

Premiere:

Sep 5, 2008, Mexico

Length:

103 min

CONNECTIONS

TV Series:

High School Musical: La Selección (2007) Talent show to find movies actors

COLLECTIONS

DVD:

2008 (Mexico)

Soundtrack:

2008 (CD, Mexico)

Tinker Bell (2008)

Enter The World of Fairies.

Source:

Spin-off of *Peter Pan* (1953)

Writers:

Bradley Raymond (story), Jeffrey M. Howard (story/screenplay)

Director:

Bradley Raymond

Premiere:

Sep 11, 2008, Argentina

US Release:

Sep 19, 2008, Hollywood (Limited)

Length:

78 min

CONNECTIONS

Comic Strips:

Disney Fairies (#1–17, Jan 2010 – Jul 2015)

Movies:

- *Tinker Bell and the Lost Treasure* (2009)
- *Tinker Bell and the Great Fairy Rescue* (2010)
- *Secret of the Wings* (2012)
- *The Pirate Fairy* (2014)
- *Tinker Bell and the Legend of the NeverBeast* (2014)

Shorts:

Pixie Hollow Bake Off (2013) [Collection > *The Pirate Fairy* Blu-ray (2014)]

TV Special:

Pixie Hollow Games (2011) Disney Channel [Collection > *Secret of the Wings* DVD (2012), *Pixie Hollow Games* DVD (2013)]

Theme Parks:

Pixie Hollow (DL 2008+), (MK 2008-2011), (HKD 2011+)

Video Games:

Disney Fairies: Tinker Bell (2008) DS

COLLECTIONS

DVD/Blu-ray:

2008, 2010

Digital:

iTunes, Vudu

Soundtrack:

2008 *Songs from and inspired by Disney Fairies*, 2013 Intrada (CD)

Books:

Tinker Bell: An Evolution (2013) Mindy Johnson

Beverly Hills Chihuahua (2008)

50% WARRIOR. 50% LOVER. 100% CHIHUAHUA. THE CHIHUAHUAS WILL RISE

Writers:

Jeffrey Bushell (story/screenplay), Analisa LaBianco (screenplay)

Director:

Raja Gosnell

Premiere:

Sep 18, 2008, Hollywood

Length:

91 min

CONNECTIONS

Movies:

- *Beverly Hills Chihuahua 2* (DTV 2011) sequel
- *Beverly Hills Chihuahua 3: Viva la Fiesta!* (DTV 2012) sequel

COLLECTIONS

DVD/Blu-ray:

2009, 2011

Digital:

Amazon, iTunes, Vudu

Morning Light (2008)

A 2500-mile journey that will change the course of their lives forever

Writers:

Mark Monroe (screenplay), Leslie DeMeuse, Roy Edward Disney (conception), Thomas J. Pollack (original idea)

Director:

Mark Monroe

Premiere:

Oct 17, 2008 (limited)

Length:

97 min

COLLECTIONS

DVD/Blu-ray:

2009

Digital:

iTunes, Vudu

Books:

What the Sea Teaches Us: The Crew of the Morning Light (2008) Jeff Kurtti

High School Musical 3: Senior Year (2008)

Source:

Second sequel to *High School Musical* (2006) TV movie

Writers:

Peter Barsocchini

Director:

Kenny Ortega

Premiere:

Oct 22, 2008, Sweden/Denmark/France/UK/Switzerland/Ireland

US Release:

Oct 24, 2008

Length:

112 min (original), 117 min (extended)

CONNECTIONS

Video Games:

- *High School Musical 3: Senior Year* (2008) DS
- *High School Musical 3: Senior Year Dance!* (2008) Wii, DS, PS2, PC, X360
- *Disney Sing It! – High School Musical 3: Senior Year* (2009) X360, Wii, PS2, PS3

COLLECTIONS

DVD/Blu-ray:

2009 Deluxe Extended Version, 2010

Digital:

Amazon, iTunes, Vudu

Soundtrack:

2008 (CD)

Roadside Romeo (2008)

Writers:

Jugal Hansraj

Director:

Jugal Hansraj

Stars:

Saif Ali Khan, Kareena Kapoor, Jaaved Jaaferi

Premiere:

Oct 23, 2008, Kuwait/Netherlands

US Release:

Oct 24, 2008 (Limited)

Length:

93 min

COLLECTIONS

DVD:

2009 (India)

Soundtrack:

2008 (CD, India)

Bolt (2008)

FULLY AWESOME

Writers:

Dan Fogelman, Chris Williams

Directors:

Byron Howard, Chris Williams

Stars:

John Travolta, Miley Cyrus

Premiere:

Nov 17, 2008, Hollywood + 3D

Length:

96 min

CONNECTIONS

Shorts:

Super Rhino (DTV 2009) Spin-off

Video Games:

Disney's Bolt (2008) X360, DS, Wii, PS2, PS3, PC

COLLECTIONS

DVD/Blu-ray:

2009 + Deluxe Edition, 2010, 2011 3D, 2017

Digital:

Amazon

Soundtrack:

2008 (CD)

Books:

The Art of Bolt (2008) Mark Cotta Vaz

The Crimson Wing: Mystery of the Flamingos (2008)

A LAKE. A MILLION FLAMINGOES. ONE OF NATURE'S MOST INCREDIBLE STORIES.

Writers:

Matthew Aeberhard, Leander Ward

Director:

Melanie Finn

Premiere:

Dec 17, 2008, France

US Release:

Oct 19, 2010, DVD/Blu-ray

Length:

78 min

COLLECTIONS

DVD/Blu-ray:

2010

Digital:

iTunes, Vudu

Soundtrack:

2009 (CD)

Books:

True-Life Adventures: A History of Walt Disney's Nature Documentaries (2017) Christian Moran

Bedtime Stories (2008)

WHAT IF THE STORIES YOU TOLD CAME TO LIFE?

Writers:

Matt Lopez (story/screenplay), Tim Herlihy (screenplay)

Director:

Adam Shankman

Stars:

Adam Sandler

Premiere:

Dec 24, 2008, Belgium/Switzerland/Egypt/France

US Release:

Dec 25, 2008

Length:

99 min

COLLECTIONS

DVD/Blu-ray:

2009 + Deluxe Edition, 2010

Digital:

Amazon, iTunes, Vudu

Space Buddies (2009)

One Small Step For Dog. One Giant Leap For Dogkind.

Source:

Spin-off of *Air Buddies* (DTV 2006)

Writers:

Robert Vince, Anna McRoberts (screenplay), Phil Hanley (additional material)

Director:

Robert Vince

Premiere:

Feb 3, 2009, DVD/Blu-ray

Length:

84 min

COLLECTIONS

DVD:

2009 + Buddies 4-Movie Collection

Blu-ray:

2009

Digital:

iTunes, Vudu

Soundtrack:

2009 with DVD at Target stores (CD)

Hexe Lilli:
Der Drache und das magische Buch (2009)

AKA:

Lilly the Witch: The Dragon and the Magic Book

Source:

Lilly the Witch: The Dragon and the Magic Book (2008) Knister & Birgit Rieger

Writers:

Stefan Ruzowitzky, Ralph Martin, Armin Toerkell, Knister

Director:

Stefan Ruzowitzky

Premiere:

Feb 19, 2009, Germany

Length:

89 min

CONNECTIONS

Movies:

Hexe Lilli: Die Reise nach Mandolan (2011) Sequel

COLLECTIONS

DVD:

2011 (Germany)

Jonas Brothers: The 3D Concert Experience (2009)

Source:

Jonas Brothers 2008 "Burning Up" tour

Director:

Bruce Hendricks

Premiere:

Feb 27, 2009, 3D

Length:

76 min (original), 85 min (extended)

COLLECTIONS

DVD/Blu-ray:

2009 Deluxe Extended Movie

Digital:

iTunes, Vudu

Soundtrack:

2009 (CD)

Race to Witch Mountain (2009)

THE RACE IS ON

Source:

- *Escape to Witch Mountain* (1968) Alexander H. Key
- Remake of *Escape to Witch Mountain* (1975)

Writers:

Matt Lopez (story/screenplay), Mark Bomback (screenplay)

Director:

Andy Fickman

Stars:

Dwayne Johnson

Premiere:

Mar 11, 2009, Egypt

US Release:

Mar 13, 2009

Length:

98 min

COLLECTIONS

DVD/Blu-ray:

2009 + Deluxe Edition, 2010

Digital:

Amazon, iTunes, Vudu

Soundtrack:

2009 (Digital)

Hannah Montana: The Movie (2009)

SHE HAS THE BEST OF BOTH WORLDS... NOW, SHE HAS TO CHOOSE JUST ONE.

Source:

Spin-off of *Hannah Montana* (2006–2011)

Writers:

Dan Berendsen

Director:

Peter Chelsom

Stars:

Miley Cyrus

Premiere:

Apr 8, 2009, Egypt

US Release:

Apr 10, 2009

Length:

102 min

CONNECTIONS

Movies:

Hannah Montana & Miley Cyrus: Best of Both Worlds Concert (2008)

TV Series:

- *Hannah Montana* (2006-2011) Disney Channel, 98 episodes [Collection > *The Complete First Season* DVD (2008)]
- *Hannah Montana Forever: Final Season* DVD (2011)
- *Hannah Montana Vol 1–7* iTunes (2012)

Video Games:

- *Hannah Montana* (2006) DS
- *Hannah Montana: Music Jam* (2007) DS
- *Hannah Montana: Spotlight World Tour* (2007) PS2, Wii
- *Hannah Montana: The Movie* (2009) X360, DS, S3, Wii, PC
- *Hannah Montana: Rock Out the Show* (2009) PSP

COLLECTIONS
DVD/Blu-ray:
2009

Digital:
Amazon, iTunes, Vudu

Soundtrack:
2009 (CD)

The Boys:
The Sherman Brothers' Story (2009)
brothers. partners. strangers.

Directors:
Gregory V. Sherman, Jeff Sherman

Premiere:
Apr 24, 2009, San Francisco International Film Festival

Length:
101 min

COLLECTIONS
DVD:
2010

Digital:
Vudu

Soundtrack:
2009 *Sherman Brothers Songbook* (CD)

Books:
Walt's Time: From Before to Beyond (1998) Robert B. Sherman & Richard M. Sherman

Trail of the Panda (2009)
AKA:
Xiong mao hui jia lu

Writers:
Jean Chalopin, Jennifer L. Liu

Director:
Zhong Yu

Premiere:
Apr 27, 2009, Chengdu, China

US Release:
Sep 6, 2011, DVD

Length:
87 min

COLLECTIONS

DVD:
2011 Disney World Cinema

Digital:
Amazon, iTunes, Vudu

Up (2009)

Writers:
Pete Docter, Bob Peterson (story/screenplay), Tom McCarthy (story)

Director:
Pete Docter, Bob Peterson (co-director)

Premiere:
May 13, 2009, Cannes Film Festival

US Release:
May 16, 2009, Hollywood, + 3D

Length:
96 min

CONNECTIONS

Shorts:
- *Dug's Special Mission* (DTV 2009) spin-off
- *George & AJ* (DTV 2009) spin-off

Video Games:
Up (2009) DS, Wii, Mac, PSP, PS3, PC, PS2, X360

COLLECTIONS

DVD/Blu-ray:

2009 + Deluxe Edition + Limited Edition Luxo Jr. Collectible Desk Lamp Pack, 2011, 2012 3D, 2016 + 3D

Digital:

Amazon

Soundtrack:

2009 (Digital), 2010 *Songs and Story*, 2011 Intrada (CD)

Books:

The Art of Up (2009) Tim Hauser

G-Force (2009)

THE WORLD NEEDS BIGGER HEROES. GADGETS, GIZMOS, GUINEA PIGS, IN 3-D

Writers:

Hoyt Yeatman, David P.I. James (story), Cormac Wibberley, Marianne Wibberley (screenplay)

Director:

Hoyt Yeatman

Premiere:

Jul 19, 2009, Hollywood, + 3D

Length:

88 min

CONNECTIONS

Video Games:

G-Force (2009) PS3, PSP, PS2, X360, Wii, DS, PC

COLLECTIONS

DVD/Blu-ray:

2009, 2010, 2011 3D

Digital:

Amazon, iTunes, Vudu

X Games 3D: The Movie (2009)

AKA:

X Games: The Movie

Source:

2008 X Games

Writers:

Greg Jennings, Steven Lawrence

Director:

Steven Lawrence

Stars:

Bob Burnquist, Ricky Carmichael, Kyle Loza, Travis Pastrana, Danny Way, Shaun White, Emile Hirsh (narration)

Premiere:

Aug 21, 2009 (Limited) 3D

Length:

92 min

COLLECTIONS

DVD:

2010

Digital:

iTunes, Vudu

Tinker Bell and the Lost Treasure (2009)

Adventure Beyond Pixie Hollow.

Source:

Sequel to *Tinker Bell* (2008)

Writers:

Klay Hall (story), Evan Spiliotopoulos (story/screenplay)

Director:

Klay Hall

Premiere:

Sep 3, 2009, Argentina/Chile

US Release:

Oct 16, 2009, Los Angeles (limited)

Length:

81 min

CONNECTIONS

Comic Strips:

Tinker Bell and the Lost Treasure (Disney Fairies, Apr 2013)

Video Games:

Disney Fairies: Tinker Bell and the Lost Treasure (2009) DS

COLLECTIONS

DVD/Blu-ray:

2009

Digital:

Amazon, iTunes, Vudu

Soundtrack:

2009, 2015 Intrada (CD)

Waking Sleeping Beauty (2009)

From 1984 to 1994 a perfect storm of people and circumstances changed the face of animation forever.

Writers:

Patrick Pacheco

Director:

Don Hahn

Premiere:

Sep 5, 2009, Telluride Film Festival

Length:

86 min

COLLECTIONS

DVD:

2010

Digital:

iTunes, Vudu

Oceans (2009)

Explore the depths of our planet's oceans. Experience the stories that connect their world to ours.

Writers:

Christophe Cheysson, Jacques Cluzaud, Laurent Debas, Stéphane Durand, Laurent Gaudé, Jacques Perrin, Françs Sarano

Directors:

Jacques Perrin, Jacques Cluzaud (co-director)

Premiere:

Oct 13, 2009, Middle East International Film Festival, UAE

US Release:

Apr 21, 2010, RiverRun International Film Festival, Winston-Salem, NC

Length:

84 min

COLLECTIONS

DVD/Blu-ray:

2010

Digital:

iTunes, Vudu

Soundtrack:

2010 France (CD)

Books:

True-Life Adventures: A History of Walt Disney's Nature Documentaries (2017) Christian Moran

Santa Buddies (2009)

The Buddies Are Coming To Town!

AKA:

Santa Buddies: The Legend of Santa Paws

Source:

Spin-off of *Air Buddies* (DTV 2006)

Writers:

Robert Vince, Anna McRoberts

Director:

Robert Vince

Premiere:

Oct 22, 2009, UK, DVD

US Release:

Nov 24, 2009, DVD/Blu-ray

Length:

88 min

CONNECTIONS

Movies:

The Search for Santa Paws (DTV 2010) Prequel

COLLECTIONS

DVD:

2009 + Buddies 4-Movie Collection

Blu-ray:

2009

Digital:

iTunes, Vudu

Soundtrack:

2009 with DVD at Target Stores (CD)

Kniga Masterov (2009)

AKA:

Книга Мастеров, *The Book of Masters*

Source:

Russian folk tales

Writers:

Vadim Sokolovsky, Anna Starobinets

Director:

Vadim Sokolovsky

Premiere:

Oct 29, 2009, Russia/Kazakhstan

Length:

101 min

COLLECTIONS

Blu-ray:

2009 (Russia)

A Christmas Carol (2009)

SEASON'S GREEDINGS

AKA:

Disney's A Christmas Carol

Source:

A Christmas Carol (1843) Charles Dickens

Writers:

Robert Zemeckis

Director:

Robert Zemeckis

Stars:

Jim Carrey

Premiere:

Nov 3, 2009, London

US Release:

Nov 6, 2009 + 3D + IMAX 3D

Length:

96 min

CONNECTIONS

Video Games:
A Christmas Carol (2009) DS

COLLECTIONS

DVD/Blu-ray:

2010 + 3D + 3D Premium Collector's Edition

Digital:

Amazon, Vudu

Soundtrack:

2009 (Digital), 2013 Intrada (CD)

Book:

The Art of Disney's A Christmas Carol (2009) Diana Landau

Old Dogs (2009)

SIT. STAY. PLAY DAD.

Writers:

David Diamond, David Weissman

Director:

Walt Becker

Stars:

John Travolta, Robin Williams

Premiere:

Nov 25, 2009

Length:

88 min

COLLECTIONS

DVD/Blu-ray:

2010, 2011

Digital:

Amazon, iTunes, Vudu

Soundtrack:

2009 (Digital)

The Princess and the Frog (2009)

Source:

- *The Frog Princess* (2002) E.D. Baker
- "The Frog Prince" (1857) Brothers Grimm

Writers:

Jason Oremland, Greg Erb (story), John Musker, Ron Clements (story/screenplay), Rob Edwards (screenplay)

Directors:

Ron Clements, John Musker

Premiere:

Nov 25, 2009, Los Angeles/New York

Length:

97 min

CONNECTIONS

Comic Strips:

The Princess and the Frog (Unknown providence) [Collection > *Disney Princess Comics Treasury* (2015)]

Video Games:

The Princess and the Frog (2009) Wii, DS, PC

COLLECTIONS

DVD/Blu-ray:

2010, 2011, 2012 The Royal Wedding Collection, 2017

Digital:

Amazon, iTunes, Vudu

Soundtrack:

2009 + *Tiana and her Princess Friends*, 2010 *Bayou Boogie: Toe Tappin' Tunes Inspired by...*, 2011 *Songs and Story* (CD)

Books:

The Art of The Princess and the Frog (2009) Jeff Kurtti

PART TEN

Movies: 2010–2014

High School Musical: O Desafio (2010)

MAIS SONHOS PARA CONQUISTAR

AKA:

High School Musical: The Challenge

Source:

Remake of *High School Musical* (2006) TV movie

Writers:

Carolina Castro (adaptation), Susana Cardozo, Pablo Lago (original screenplay)

Director:

César Rodrigues

Premiere:

Feb 5, 2010, Brazil

Length:

90 min

CONNECTIONS

TV Series:

High School Musical: A Seleção (2008) Disney Channel Brazil, 15 episodes, talent show to find movie actors

Alice in Wonderland (2010)

Source:

- *Alice's Adventures in Wonderland* (1865) Lewis Carroll
- Remake of *Alice in Wonderland* (1951)

Writers:

Linda Woolverson

Director:

Tim Burton

Stars:

Johnny Depp

Premiere:

Feb 25, 2010, London

US Release:

Mar 5, 2010 + 3D + IMAX

Length:

108 min

CONNECTIONS

Movies:

Alice Through the Looking Glass (2016) Sequel

Video Games:

Alice in Wonderland (2010) Wii, DS, PC

COLLECTIONS

DVD/Blu-ray:

2010 + 3D, 2011, 2016 + 3D

Digital:

Amazon, iTunes, Vudu

Soundtrack:

2010 + *Almost Alice* (CD)

Books:

- *Alice in Wonderland: A Visual Companion* (2010) Mark Salisbury
- *Walt Disney's Alice in Wonderland: An Illustrated Journey Through Time* (2016) Mark Salisbury

Prince of Persia:
The Sands of Time (2010)

FROM THE PRODUCER OF "PIRATES OF THE CARIBBEAN"

Source:

Prince of Persia (1989+) video game franchise

Writers:

Jordan Mechner (story), Boaz Yakin, Doug Miro, Carlo Bernard (screenplay)

Director:

Mike Newell

Premiere:

May 9, 2010, London

US Release:

May 28, 2010

Length:

116 min

CONNECTIONS

Comic Books:

Prince of Persia: Before the Sandstorm (2010)

COLLECTIONS

DVD/Blu-ray:

2010

Digital:

iTunes, Vudu

Soundtrack:

2010 (CD)

Books:

We Make Our Own Destiny: Behind the Scenes of Prince of Persia: The Sands of Time (2010) Michael Singer

Toy Story 3 (2010)
THE BREAKOUT COMEDY OF THE SUMMER

Source:

Second sequel to *Toy Story* (1995)

Writers:

John Lasseter, Andrew Stanton, Lee Unkrich (story), Michael Arndt (screenplay)

Director:

Lee Unkrich

Premiere:

Jun 12, 2010, Taormina Film Festival, Italy

Re-releases:

Jun 17, 2010, Nantucket Film Festival + 3D + IMAX

Length:

103 min

CONNECTIONS

Comic Strips:

Toy Story 3 Official Movie Magazine (Summer 2010)

Shorts:

- *Toy Story Toons: Hawaiian Vacation* (2011)
- *Toy Story Toons: Small Fry* (2011)
- *Toy Story Toons: Partysaurus Rex* (2012)

TV Specials:

- *Toy Story of Terror* (2013)
- *Toy Story That Time Forgot* (2014)

Video Games:

Toy Story 3: The Video Game (2010) X360, X360S, PC, Wii, DS, PSP, Mac, PS3, PS2

COLLECTIONS

DVD/Blu-ray:

2010, 2011 + 3D, 2015

Digital:

Amazon, iTunes, Vudu

Soundtrack:

2010 (Digital), 2010 *Songs and Story*, 2012 Intrada (CD)

Books:

- *The Art of Toy Story 3* (2010) Charles Solomon
- *The Toy Story Films: An Animated Journey* (2012) Charles Solomon

The Sorcerer's Apprentice (2010)

IT'S THE COOLEST JOB EVER.

Source:

Inspired by "The Sorcerer's Apprentice" from *Fantasia* (1940)

Writers:

Lawrence Konner, Mark Rosenthal (story), Matt Lopez (story/screenplay), Carlo Bernard, Doug Miro (screenplay)

Director:

Jon Turteltaub

Stars:

Nicolas Cage, Jay Baruchel

Premiere:

Jul 6, 2010, New York

Length:

109 min

CONNECTIONS

Video Games:

The Sorcerer's Apprentice (2010) DS

COLLECTIONS

DVD/Blu-ray:

2010, 2011

Digital:

iTunes, Vudu

Soundtrack:

2010 (Digital)

Books:

The Answer is Yes: The Art and Making of The Sorcerer's Apprentice (2010) Michael Singer

Tinker Bell and the Great Fairy Rescue (2010)

What would you do if you met a fairy?

Source:

Second sequel to *Tinker Bell* (2008)

Writers:

Bradley Raymond, Jeffrey M. Howard (story), Bob Hilgenberg, Rob Muir, Joe Ansolabehere, Paul Germain

Director:

Bradley Raymond

Premiere:

Jul 23, 2010, Poland

US Release:

Sep 3, 2010, Los Angeles (Limited)

Length:

76 min

CONNECTIONS

Comic Strips:

Tinker Bell and the Great Fairy Rescue (Disney Fairies, Jul 2010)

Video Game:

Disney Fairies: Tinker Bell and the Great Fairy Rescue (2010) DS

COLLECTIONS

DVD/Blu-ray:

2010

Digital:

Amazon, iTunes, Vudu

Soundtrack:

2015 Intrada (CD)

High School Musical China (2010)

AKA:

Ge wu qing chun, High School Musical China: College Dreams

Source:

Remake of *High School Musical* (2006) TV Movie

Writers:

Li Lin

Director:

Shi-Zheng Chen

Premiere:

Aug 19, 2010, China

US Release:

Sep 6, 2011, DVD

Length:

94 min

COLLECTIONS

DVD:

2011 Disney World Cinema

Digital:

Amazon, iTunes, Vudu

Secretariat (2010)

THE IMPOSSIBLE TRUE STORY

Source:

Secretariat: The Making of a Champion (1975) William Nack

Writers:

Mike Rich

Director:

Randall Wallace

Stars:

Diane Lane, John Malkovich

Premiere:

Sep 30, 2010, Hollywood

Length:

123 min

COLLECTIONS

DVD/Blu-ray:

2011

Digital:

Tunes, Vudu

Do Dooni Chaar (2010)

AKA:

Two Times Two Equals Four

Writers:

Habib Faisal, Rahil Qazi

Director:

Habib Faisal

Stars:

Rishi Kapoor, Neetu Singh

Premiere:

Oct 8, 2010, India

US Release:

Jul 26, 2011, DVD

Length:

112 min

COLLECTIONS

DVD:

2011 Disney World Cinema

Digital:

iTunes, Vudu

The Search for Santa Paws (2010)

FROM THE CREATORS OF THE BUDDIES

Source:

Prequel to *Santa Buddies* (DTV 2009)

Writers:

Robert Vince, Anna McRoberts

Director:

Robert Vince

Premiere:

Nov 9, 2010, Denmark, DVD/Blu-ray

US Release:

Nov 23, 2010, DVD/Blu-ray

Length:

96 min

CONNECTIONS

Movies:

Santa Paws 2: The Santa Pups (DTV 2012) Sequel

COLLECTIONS

DVD/Blu-ray:

2010

Digital:

Amazon, iTunes, Vudu

Tangled (2010)

They're taking adventure to new lengths.

Source:

"Rapunzel" (1812) Brothers Grimm

Writers:

Dan Fogelman

Directors:

Nathan Greno, Byron Howard

Premiere:

Nov 24, 2010 + 3D

Length:

100 min

CONNECTIONS

Comic Strips:

Tangled (2010) [Collection > *Disney Princess Comics Treasury* (2015)]

Shorts:

Tangled Ever After (2012) Sequel

Stage Musical:

Tangled: The Musical (2015+) Disney Magic cruise ship

TV Movie:

Tangled: Before Ever After (2017) Disney Channel, pilot for TV series

TV Series:

Tangled: The Series (2017+) Disney Channel

Video Games:

Disney Tangles: The Video Game (2010) DS, Wii, PC

COLLECTIONS

DVD/Blu-ray:

2011 + 3D, 2016 3D

Digital:

iTunes, Vudu

Soundtrack:

2010, *Songs and Story* (CD), 2015 (LP)

Books:

The Art of Tangled (2010) Jeff Kurtti

Tron: Legacy (2010)

AKA:

TRON: Legacy

Source:

Sequel to *Tron* (1982)

Writers:

Brian Klugman, Lee Strenthal (story), Edward Kitsis, Adam Horowitz (screenplay)

Director:

Joseph Kosinski

Premiere:

Nov 30, 2010, Tokyo, Japan

US Release:

Dec 17, 2010 + 3D + IMAX

Length:

125 min

CONNECTIONS

Comic Strips:

Tron: Betrayal (#1–2, Nov – Dec 2010) [Collection > *Tron: Betrayal* (2010)]

Shorts:

Tron: The Next Day (DTV, 2011) [Collection > Blu-ray (2011)]

TV Series:

Tron: Uprising (2012–2013) Disney XD, 19 episodes

Theme Parks:

- ElecTRONica (DCA 2010–2012)
- *Tron Lightcycle Power Run* (SDL 2016+)

Video Games:

- *Tron: Evolution* (2010) PC, PS3, PSP, X360
- *Tron Evolution: Battle Grids* (2010) Wii, DS

COLLECTIONS

DVD/Blu-ray:

2011 + Limited Edition + 3D, 2016 3D

Digital:

Amazon, iTunes, Vudu

Soundtrack:

2010 + Special Edition, 2011 *Tron: Legacy Reconfigured* (CD), 2015 (LP)

Books:

The Art of Tron: Legacy (2010) Justin Springer

Once Upon a Warrior (2011)

AKA:

Anaganaga O Dheerudu

Writers:
Prakash Kovelamudi, Rahul Koda, Rajasimha, R. Samala

Director:
Prakash Kovelamudi

Premiere:
Jan 14, 2011, India

US Release:
Jan 21, 2011

Length:
133 min

COLLECTIONS

DVD:
2011 Disney World Cinema

Digital:
Amazon, iTunes, Vudu

Beverly Hills Chihuahua 2 (2011)

THE FAMILY JUST GOT BIGGER

Source:
First sequel to *Beverly Hills Chihuahua* (2008)

Writers:
Dannah Feinglass Phirman, Danielle Schneider

Director:
Alex Zamm

Premiere:
Feb 1, 2011, DVD/Blu-ray

Length:
85 min

COLLECTIONS

DVD/Blu-ray:
2011

Digital:
iTunes, Vudu

Hexe Lilli:
Die Reise nach Mandolan (2011)

AKA:

Lilly the Witch: The Journey to Mandolan

Source:

Sequel to *Hexe Lilli: Der Drache und das magische Buch* (2009)

Writers:

Bettine von Borries, Achim von Borries, Knister

Director:

Harald Sicheritz

Premiere:

Feb 17, 2011, Germany

Length:

90 min

COLLECTIONS

DVD:

2011 (Germany)

Soundtrack:

2011 (CD, Germany)

Mars Needs Moms (2011)

MOM NEEDS A LITTLE SPACE.

Source:

Mars Needs Moms (2007) Berkeley Breathed

Writers:

Simon Wells, Wendy Wells

Director:

Simon Wells

Premiere:

Mar 9, 2011, Egypt

US Release:

Mar 11, 2011 + 3D +IMAX

Length:

88 min

COLLECTIONS

DVD/Blu-ray:

2011 + 3D

Digital:

Amazon, iTunes, Vudu

Soundtrack:

2011 (Digital)

Wings of Life (2011)

AKA:

Pollen (France), *Hidden Beauty* (UK), *Disneynature: Wings of Life*

Writers:

Louie Schwartzberg

Director:

Louie Schwartzberg

Narrator:

Meryl Streep

Premiere:

Mar 16, 2011, France

US Release:

Apr 16, 2013

Length:

81 min

COLLECTIONS

DVD/Blu-ray:

2013

Digital:

Amazon, iTunes, Vudu

Books:

True-Life Adventures: A History of Walt Disney's Nature Documentaries (2017) Christian Moran

Winnie the Pooh (2011)

Source:

Winnie the Pooh (1926) A.A. Milne

Writers:

Stephen J. Anderson, Clio Chiang, Don Doughtery, Don Hall, Kendelle Hoyer, Brian Kesinger, Nicole Mitchell, Jeremy Spears

Directors:

Stephen J. Anderson, Don Hall

Premiere:

Apr 6, 2011, Belgium

US Release:

Jul 10, 2011, Hollywood

Length:

63 min

CONNECTIONS

Stage Musical:

Winnie the Pooh KIDS (?) Disney Theatrical Licensing

COLLECTIONS

DVD/Blu-ray:

2011

Digital:

Amazon, iTunes, Vudu

Soundtrack:

2011 (CD)

Zokkomon (2011)

BETRAYAL. FRIENDSHIP. BRAVERY.

AKA:

जॉक्कोमॉन

Writers:

Satyajit Bhatkal, Svati Chakravarty Bhatkal, Lancy Fernandes, Divy Nidhi Sharma

Director:

Satyajit Bhatkal

Premiere:

Apr 17, 2011, Indian Film Festival of Los Angeles

Length:

109 min

COLLECTIONS

DVD:

2011 Disney World Cinema

Digital:

Amazon, iTunes, Vudu

Soundtrack:

2011 (CD, India)

Sharpay's Fabulous Adventure (2011)

FROM THE PRODUCERS OF HIGH SCHOOL MUSICAL

Source:

Spin-off of *High School Musical* (2006) TV movie

Writers:

Peter Barsocchini

Director:

Michael Lembeck

Stars:

Ashley Tisdale

Premiere:

Apr 19, 2011, DVD/Blu-ray

Length:

90 min

COLLECTIONS

DVD/Blu-ray:

2011

Digital:

Amazon, Vudu

Soundtrack:

2011 (CD)

African Cats (2011)

Writers:

Owen Newman (story), Keith Scholey (story/narration), John Truby (narration)

Directors:

Keith Scholey, Alastair Fothergill (co-director)

Premiere:

Apr 21, 2011, Hong Kong/Peru

US Release:

Apr 22, 2011

Length:

89 min

COLLECTIONS

DVD/Blu-ray:

2011

Digital:

iTunes, Vudu

Books:

- *DisneyNature African Cats: The Story Behind the Film* (2011) Amanda Barrett & Keith Scholey
- *True-Life Adventures: A History of Walt Disney's Nature Documentaries* (2017) Christian Moran

Prom (2011)

WHO ARE YOU GOING WITH?

Writers:

Katie Wech

Director:

Joe Nussbaum

Premiere:

Apr 29, 2011

Length:

104 min

CONNECTIONS

Shorts:

Last Chance Lloyd (DTV 2011)

COLLECTIONS

DVD/Blu-ray:

2011

Digital:

Amazon, iTunes, Vudu

Soundtrack:

2011 (CD)

Pirates of the Caribbean: On Stranger Tides (2011)

Source:

- Third sequel to *Pirates of the Caribbean: The Curse of the Black Pearl* (2003)
- *On Stranger Tides* (1987) Tim Powers

Writers:

Ted Elliott, Terry Rossio

Director:

Rob Marshall

Stars:

Johnny Depp, Penélope Cruz, Ian McShane, Geoffrey Rush

Premiere:

May 7, 2011, Anaheim, CA + 3D + IMAX

Length:

136 min

COLLECTIONS

DVD/Blu-ray:

2011 + 3D + Four-Movie Collection, 2017 5-Movie Collection

Digital:

Amazon, iTunes, Vudu

Soundtrack:

2011 (CD)

Books:

The Art of Pirates of the Caribbean: On Stranger Tides (2011) Michael Singer

Cars 2 (2011)

Source:

First sequel to *Cars* (2006)

Writers:

John Lasseter, Brad Lewis, Dan Fogelman (story), Ben Queen (screenplay)

Directors:

John Lasseter, Brad Lewis (co-director)

Premiere:

Jun 18, 2011, Hollywood + 3D + IMAX

Length:

106 min

CONNECTIONS

Comic Books:

Cars 2: The Graphic Novel (Aug 2011)

Video Games:

Cars 2: The Video Game (2011) Wii, PS3, DS, X360, PS3, X360S, Mac, PC

COLLECTIONS

DVD/Blu-ray:

2011 + 3D

Digital:

Amazon, iTunes, Vudu

Soundtrack:

2011 (CD)

Books:

- *The Art of Cars 2* (2011) Ben Queen & Karen Paik
- *Poster Art of Cars* (2017) Victoria Saxon

Spooky Buddies (2011)

Source:
Spin-off of *Air Buddies* (DTV 2006)

Writers:
Robert Vince, Anna McRoberts

Director:
Robert Vince

Premiere:
Sep 20, 2011, DVD/Blu-ray

Length:
88 min

COLLECTIONS

DVD/Blu-ray:
2011

Digital:
Amazon, iTunes, Vudu

The Muppets (2011)
MUPPET DOMINATION

Writers:
Jason Segel, Nicholas Stoller

Director:
James Bobin

Stars:
Jason Segel, Amy Adams, Chris Cooper

Premiere:
Nov 4, 2011, Savannah Film and Video Festival

Length:
103 min

CONNECTIONS

Movies:
Muppets Most Wanted (2014) Sequel

COLLECTIONS

DVD/Blu-ray:

2012 + The Wocka Wocka Value Pack, 2016

Digital:

Amazon, iTunes, Vudu

Soundtrack:

2011, 2014 Intrada *Muppets Most Wanted* (CD)

Treasure Buddies (2012)

Source:

Fifth spin-off of *Air Buddies* (DTV 2006)

Writers:

Robert Vince, Anna McRoberts

Director:

Robert Vince

Premiere:

Jan 31, 2012, DVD/Blu-ray

Length:

93 min

COLLECTIONS

DVD/Blu-ray:

2012

Digital:

iTunes, Vudu

John Carter (2012)

LOST IN OUR WORLD, FOUND IN ANOTHER

Source:

A Princess of Mars (1912) Edgar Rice Burroughs

Writers:

Andrew Stanton, Mark Andrews, Michael Chabon

Director:

Andrew Stanton

Premiere:

Feb 22, 2012, Los Angeles + 3D + IMAX

Length:

132 min

CONNECTIONS

Comic Strips:

John Carter: World of Mars (#1–4, Dec 2011 – Mar 2012) prequel [Collection > *John Carter: World of Mars* (2012)]

COLLECTIONS

DVD/Blu-ray:

2012 + 3D

Digital:

Amazon, iTunes, Vudu

Soundtrack:

2012 (CD)

Books:

The Art of John Carter (2012) Josh Kushins

Chimpanzee (2012)

For Oscar, every day is an adventure.

Writers:

Alastair Fothergill, Mark Linfield (concept/narration), Don Hahn (narration)

Directors:

Alastair Fothergill, Mark Linfield

Premiere:

Mar 31, 2012, Phoenix Film Festival

Length:

78 min

COLLECTIONS

DVD/Blu-ray:

2012

Digital:

Amazon, iTunes, Vudu

Books:

- *Chimpanzee: The Making of the Film* (2012) Christopher Boesch & Sanjida O'Connell
- *True-Life Adventures: A History of Walt Disney's Nature Documentaries* (2017) Christian Moran

The Avengers (2012)

AKA:

Marvel's The Avengers, *Marvel Avengers Assemble* (UK)

Source:

The Avengers (1963+) comic book

Writers:

Zak Penn (story), Joss Whedon (story/screenplay)

Director:

Joss Whedon

Stars:

Robert Downey Jr., Chris Evans, Mark Ruffalo, Chris Hemsworth, Scarlett Johansson, Jeremy Renner, Tom Hiddleston, Samuel L. Jackson

Premiere:

Apr 11, 2012, Hollywood + 3D + IMAX

Length:

143 min

CONNECTIONS

Comic Strips:

- *The Avengers Prelude: Fury's Big Week* (#1–4, Apr – Jun 2012) prequel [Collection > *The Avengers Prelude: Fury's Big Week* (2012)]
- *The Avengers: Black Widow Strikes* (#1–3, Jul – Aug 2012) prequel [Collection > *The Avengers: Black Widow Strikes* (2012)]
- *The Avengers* (#1–2, Feb – Mar 2015)

Movies:

- *Iron Man* (2008) Paramount, MCU#1
- *The Incredible Hulk* (2008) Universal, MCU#1

- *Iron Man 2* (2010) Paramount, MCU#1
- *Thor* (2011) Paramount, MCU#1
- *Captain America: The First Avenger* (2011) Paramount, MCU#1
- *Avengers: Age of Ultron* (2015) Sequel, MCU#2
- *Avengers: Infinity War* (2018) Sequel, MCU#3
- *Avengers: Sequel* (2019) Sequel, MCU#3

Shorts:
Marvel One-Shot: Item 47 (DTV 2012)

TV Series:
- *Marvel's Agents of S.H.I.E.L.D.* (2013+) ABC
- *Avengers Assemble* (2013+) Disney XD

Video Games:
- *Lego Marvel Super Heroes* (2013) PSV, WU, PS3, PC, X360, X1, DS, 3DS, PS4
- *Lego Marvel's Avengers* (2016) PC, 3DS, PS3, PS4, PSV, WU, X360, X1, MAc

COLLECTIONS
DVD/Blu-ray:
2012 + 3D, 2016 3D + 2-Movie Collection

Digital:
Amazon, iTunes, Vudu

Soundtrack:
2012 *Avengers Assemble* + Intrada (CD)

Books:
The Art of Marvel's The Avengers (2012) Jason Surrell

Arjun: The Warrior Prince (2012)
THE UNTOLD STORY OF INDIA'S GREATEST WARRIOR

Writers:
Rajesh Devraj, R.D. Tailang (dialogue)

Director:
Arnab Chaudhuri

Premiere:
May 25, 2012, India + US (Limited)

Length:

96 min

COLLECTIONS

DVD:

2012 (India)

Digital:

iTunes

Brave (2012)

CHANGE YOUR FATE.

Writers:

Brenda Chapman (story/screenplay), Mark Andrews, Steve Purcell, Irene Mecchi (screenplay)

Directors:

Mark Andrews, Brenda Chapman, Steve Purcell (co-director)

Premiere:

Jun 10, 2012, Seattle International Film Festival + 3D

Length:

93 min

CONNECTIONS

Comic Book:

Brave (2012) [Collection > *Disney Princess Comics Treasury* (2015)]

Shorts:

The Legend of Mor'du (DTV 2012)

Video Games:

Disney-Pixar: Brave (2012) PC, Mac, DS, Wii, PS3, X360, PS3, X360S

COLLECTIONS

DVD/Blu-ray:

2012 + Collector's Edition + 3D Ultimate Collector's Edition, 2016 3D Ultimate Collector's Edition

Digital:

Amazon, Vudu

Soundtrack:
2012 + *Songs and Story* (CD)

Books:
The Art of Brave (2012) Jenny Lerew

The Odd Life of Timothy Green (2012)
He's a force of nature.

Writers:
Ahmet Zappa (story), Peter Hedges (screenplay)

Director:
Peter Hedges

Stars:
Jennifer Garner, Joel Edgerton

Premiere:
Aug 15, 2012

Length:
105 min

COLLECTIONS

DVD/Blu-ray:
2012

Digital:
Amazon, iTunes, Vudu

Soundtrack:
2012 Amazon (CD) Manufactured on demand

Secret of the Wings (2012)
Two Worlds. One Magical Secret.

AKA:
Tinker Bell and the Secret of the Wings

Source:
Third sequel to *Tinker Bell* (2008)

Writers:
Roberts Gannaway, Peggy Holmes, Ryan Rowe, Tom Rogers

Directors:

Roberts Gannaway, Peggy Holmes

Premiere:

Aug 17, 2012, Turkey

US Release:

Aug 31, 2012, Hollywood (Limited)

Length:

75 min

CONNECTIONS

Comic Strips:

Tinker Bell and the Secret of the Wings (Disney Fairies, Jul 2014)

COLLECTIONS

DVD/Blu-ray:

2012 + 3D Flitterrific Fairies Double Pack

Digital:

Amazon, iTunes, Vudu

Soundtrack:

2012 *Disney Fairies: Faith, Trust and Pixie Dust* (CD)

Beverly Hills Chihuahua 3: Viva la Fiesta! (2012)

Family Always Matters.

Source:

Second sequel to *Beverly Hills Chihuahua* (2008)

Writers:

Dana Starfield

Director:

Lev L. Spiro

Premiere:

Sep 3, 2012, UK, DVD

Re-releases:

Sep 18, 2012, DVD/Blu-ray

Length:

89 min

COLLECTIONS

DVD/Blu-ray:

2012

Digital:

iTunes, Vudu

Barfi! (2012)

Writers:

Anurag Basu, Tani Basu (story/screenplay), Sanjeev Dutta (dialogue)

Director:

Anurag Basu

Premiere:

Sep 13, 2012, Australia/New Zealand/Kuwait

US Release:

Sep 14, 2012 (Limited)

Length:

151 min

COLLECTIONS

DVD/Blu-ray:

2012 (India)

Digital:

iTunes

Soundtrack:

2012 (CD, India)

Frankenweenie (2012)

FROM THE DIRECTOR OF ALICE IN WONDERLAND

Source:

Remake of *Frankenweenie* (1984) short

Writers:

John August

Director:

Tim Burton

Premiere:

Sep 20, 2012, Fantastic Fest, Austin, TX + 3D + IMAX

Length:

87 min

CONNECTIONS

Comic Books:

Frankenweenie (2014)

Shorts:

Captain Sparky vs the Flying Saucers (DTV 2013)

COLLECTIONS

DVD/Blu-ray:

2013 + 3D

Digital:

Amazon, iTunes, Vudu

Soundtrack:

2012 + *Frankenweenie Unleashed!* (CD)

Books:

Frankenweenie: The Visual Companion (2013) Mark Salisbury

Santa Paws 2: The Santa Pups (2012)

One Magical Wish Can Change Everything!

Source:

Sequel to *The Search for Santa Paws* (DTV 2010)

Writers:

Philip Fracassi, Anna McRoberts, Robert Vince

Director:

Robert Vince

Premiere:

Oct 2, 2012, UK, DVD

US Release:

Nov 20, 2012, DVD/Blu-ray

Length:

88 min

COLLECTIONS

DVD/Blu-ray:

2012

Digital:

Amazon, iTunes, Vudu

Wreck-It Ralph (2012)

Writers:

Rich Moore, Jim Reardon (story), Phil Johnston (story/screenplay), Jennifer Lee (screenplay), John C. Reilly, Sam Levine, Jared Stern (additional material)

Director:

Rich Moore

Stars:

John C. Reilly, Sarah Silverman, Jack McBrayer, Jane Lynch

Premiere:

Nov 1, 2012, UAE/Hungary/Kuwait/Lebanon/Philippines/Russia/ Ukraine

US Release:

Nov 2, 2012 + 3D

Length:

101 min

CONNECTIONS

Movies:

Ralph Breaks the Internet: Wreck-It Ralph 2 (2018) Sequel

Video Games:

Wreck-It Ralph (2012) Wii, DS, 3DS

COLLECTIONS

DVD/Blu-ray:

2013 + Collector's Edition + 3D Ultimate Collector's Edition, 2016 3D Ultimate Collector's Edition

Digital:

Amazon, iTunes, Vudu

Soundtrack:

2012, 2013 *Songs and Story* (CD)

Books:

The Art of Wreck-It Ralph (2012) Maggie Malone & Jennifer Lee

Oz the Great and Powerful (2013)

Source:

Prequel to *The Wonderful Wizard of Oz* (1900) L. Frank Baum and *The Wizard of Oz* (1939) MGM production

Writers:

Mitchell Kapner (story/screenplay), David Lindsay-Abaire (screenplay)

Director:

Sam Raimi

Premiere:

Feb 14, 2013, Hollywood + 3D

Length:

130 min

COLLECTIONS

DVD/Blu-ray:

2013 + 3D

Digital:

Amazon, iTunes, Vudu

Soundtrack:

2013 Intrada (CD)

Books:

The Art of Oz the Great and Powerful (2013) Grant Curtis

Iron Man 3 (2013)

AKA:

Iron Man Three

Source:

- Second sequel to *Iron Man* (2008) Paramount production
- *Iron Man* (Vol 4) #1-6 'Extremis' (2005-2006) Warren Ellis, Adi Granov

Writers:

Drew Pearce, Shane Black

Director:

Shane Black

Stars:

Robert Downey Jr., Gwyneth Paltrow, Don Cheadle, Guy Pearce, Ben Kingsley

Premiere:

Apr 12, 2013, Munich, Germany

US Release:

May 3, 2013

Length:

130 min

CONNECTIONS

Comic Strips:

Marvel's Iron Man 3 Prelude (#1–2, Jan – Feb 2013) [Collection > *Marvel's Iron Man 3 Prelude* (2013)]

Shorts:

Marvel One-Shot: All Hail the King (DTV 2014)

Video Games:

Iron Man 3: The Official Game (2013) Android, iPhone, iPad

COLLECTIONS

DVD/Blu-ray:

2013 + 3D, 2015 Marvel Cinematic Universe: Phase Two Collection

Digital:

iTunes, Vudu

Soundtrack:

2013 + *Heroes Fall: Music Inspired by the Motion Picture* (CD)

Books:

Marvel's Iron Man 3: The Art of the Movie (2013) Ryan Meinerding, Marie Javins & Stuart Moore

Monsters University (2013)

Source:

Prequel to *Monsters, Inc.* (2001)

Writers:

Dan Scanlon, Daniel Gerson, Robert L. Baird

Director:

Dan Scanlon

Premiere:

Jun 5, 2013, London, UK + 3D

US Release:

Jun 8, 2013, Seattle International Film Festival + 3D

Length:

104 min

CONNECTIONS

Shorts:

Party Central (2014) Sequel

COLLECTIONS

DVD/Blu-ray:

2013 + Collector's Edition + 3D Ultimate Collector's Edition, 2017

Digital:

Amazon, Vudu

Soundtrack:

2013 (CD)

Books:

The Art of Monsters University (2013) Karen Paik

The Lone Ranger (2013)

Source:

Lone Ranger character (1933) created by Fran Striker/George W. Trendle

Writers:

Justin Haythe, Ted Elliott, Terry Rossio

Director:

Gore Verbinski

Stars:

Johnny Depp, Armie Hammer

Premiere:

Jun 22, 2013, Anaheim

Length:

150 min

COLLECTIONS

DVD/Blu-ray:

2013

Digital:

Amazon, iTunes, Vudu

Soundtrack:

2013 Intrada + *Wanted: Music Inspired by the Film* (CD)

Books:

The Lone Ranger: Behind the Mask: On the Trail of an Outlaw Epic (2013) Michael SInger

Planes (2013)

FROM ABOVE THE WORLD OF CARS

Source:

Spin-off of *Cars* (2006)

Writers:

John Lasseter, Klay Hall (story), Jeffrey M. Howard (story/screenplay)

Director:

Klay Hall

Premiere:

Aug 5, 2013 + 3D

Length:

91 min

CONNECTIONS

Movies:

Planes: Fire & Rescue (2014) Sequel

Video Games:

Planes (2013) 3DS, Wii, DS, WU, PC

COLLECTIONS

DVD/Blu-ray:

2013 + 3D

Digital:

Amazon, iTunes, Vudu

Soundtrack:

2013 (CD)

Books:

The Art of Planes (2014) Tracey Miller-Zarneke

Super Buddies (2013)

You Don't Need Super Powers To Be A Super Hero

Source:

Sixth spin-off of *Air Buddies* (DTV 2006)

Writers:

Anna McRoberts, Robert Vince

Director:

Robert Vince

Premiere:

Aug 8, 2013, DVD

US Release:

Aug 27, 2013, DVD/Blu-ray

Length:

81 min

COLLECTIONS

DVD/Blu-ray:

2013

Digital:

Amazon, iTunes, Vudu

Saving Mr. Banks (2013)

WHERE HER BOOK ENDED, THEIR STORY BEGAN.

Source:

Making of *Mary Poppins* (1964)

Writers:

Kelly Marcel, Sue Smith

Director:

John Lee Hancock

Stars:

Emma Thompson, Tom Hanks, Paul Giamatti, Jason Schwartzman, Colin Farrell

Premiere:

Oct 20, 2013, BFI London Film Festival

US Release:

Nov 7, 2013, AFI Fest

Length:

125 min

COLLECTIONS

DVD/Blu-ray:

2014

Digital:

iTunes, Vudu

Soundtrack:

2013 + Deluxe Edition (CD)

Books:

- *Mary Poppins, She Wrote: The Life of P.L. Travers* (2013) Valerie Lawson
- *The Vault of Walt: Volume 3* (2014) Jim Korkis

Thor: The Dark World (2013)

Source:

Sequel to *Thor* (2011) Paramount production

Writers:

Don Payne, Robert Rodat (story), Christopher Yost, Christopher Markus, Stephen McFeely (screenplay)

Director:

Alan Taylor

Stars:

Chris Hemsworth, Natalie Portman, Tom Hiddleston, Anthony Hopkins

Premiere:

Oct 22, 2013, London

US Release:

Nov 8, 2013

Length:

112 min

CONNECTIONS

Comic Strips:

Marvel's Thor: The Dark World Prelude (#1-2, Aug – Sep 2013) [Collection > *Marvel's Thor: The Dark World Prelude* (2013)]

Movies:

Thor: Ragnorak (2017) Sequel

Video Games:

Thor: The Dark World – The Official Game (2013) Android, iPhone, iPad

COLLECTIONS

DVD/Blu-ray:

2014 + 3D, 2015 Marvel Cinematic Universe: Phase Two Collection

Digital:

Amazon, Vudu

Soundtrack:

2013 Intrada (CD)

Books:

Marvel's Thor: The Dark World—The Art of the Movie (2013) Marie Javins & Stuart Moore

Frozen (2013)

FROM THE CREATORS OF "TANGLED" AND "WRECK-IT RALPH"

Source:

"The Snow Queen" (1844) Hans Christian Andersen

Writers:

Chris Buck, Shane Morris (story), Jennifer Lee (story/screenplay)

Directors:

Chris Buck, Jennifer Lee

Premiere:

Nov 10, 2013, New York International Children's Film Festival + 3D

Re-releases:

Jan 31, 2014, sing-along version

Length:

102 min

CONNECTIONS

Comic Books:

- *Frozen* (Feb 2015)
- *Disney Frozen* (Jul 2016+)

Movies:

Frozen 2 (2019) sequel

Shorts:

- *Frozen Fever* (2015) sequel
- *Olaf's Frozen Adventure* (2017) sequel

Stage Musical:

Frozen (2018+)

Theme Parks:

- Frozen Sing-Along Celebration (HS 2014+), (DCA 2015-2016), (DP 2015-2017), (HKD 2015), (SD 2016+)
- Frozen: Live at the Hyperion (DCA 2016+)
- Frozen Ever After (E 2016+)

TV Special:

Lego Frozen Northern Lights (2016) Disney Channel

Video Games:

- *Frozen Free Fall* (2013) iPhone, X1, PC, PS3, PS4, X360S, iPad, Android
- *Frozen: Olaf's Quest* (2013) DS, 3DS

COLLECTIONS

DVD/Blu-ray:

2014 Collector's Edition + 3D + Sing-Along Edition

Digital:

Amazon, iTunes, Vudu

Soundtrack:

2013 + Deluxe Edition, 2014 *Frozen: The Songs* (CD), 2014 (LP)

Books:

The Art of Frozen (2013) Charles Solomon

The Pirate Fairy (2014)

The Expedition Begins in 2014

AKA:

Tinker Bell and the Pirate Fairy

Source:

Fourth sequel to *Tinker Bell* (2008)

Writers:

John Lasseter, Peggy Holmes, Roberts Gannaway, Lorna Cook, Craig Gerber (story), Jeffrey M. Howard (story/screenplay), Kate Kondell (screenplay)

Director:

Peggy Holmes

Premiere:

Feb 13, 2014, Denmark, DVD

US Release:

Feb 28, 2014 (Limited)

Length:

78 min

CONNECTIONS

Comic Books:

Tinker Bell and the Pirate Fairy (Disney Fairies, Mar 2015)

COLLECTIONS

DVD/Blu-ray:

2014

Digital:

Amazon, iTunes, Vudu

Soundtrack:

2014 (Digital)

Muppets Most Wanted (2014)

TAKING THE WORLD BY FARCE

Source:

Sequel to *The Muppets* (2011)

Writers:

James Bobin, Nicholas Stoller

Director:

James Bobin

Stars:

Ricky Gervais, Ty Burrell, Tina Fey

Premiere:

Mar 11, 2014, Hollywood

Length:

107 min (Original), 119 min (Extended)

COLLECTIONS

DVD/Blu-ray:

2014 The Unnecessarily Extended Edition (+Original)

Digital:

iTunes, Vudu

Soundtrack:

2014 + Intrada (CD)

Captain America: The Winter Soldier (2014)

Source:

Sequel to *Captain America: The First Avenger* (2011) Paramount production

Writers:

Christopher Markus, Stephen McFeely

Directors:

Anthony Russo, Joe Russo

Stars:

Chris Evans, Scarlett Johansson, Robert Redford, Samuel L. Jackson

Premiere:

Mar 13, 2014, Hollywood + 3D + IMAX

Length:

136 min

CONNECTIONS

Comic Book:

Captain America: The Winter Soldier Prelude (2014)

Movies:

Captain America: Civil War (2016) Sequel

Video Games:

Captain America: The Winter Soldier – The Official Game (2014) iPhone, iPad, Android

COLLECTIONS

DVD/Blu-ray:

2014 + 3D, 2015 Marvel Cinematic Universe: Phase Two Collection

Digital:

iTunes, Vudu

Soundtrack:

2014 Intrada (CD)

Books:

Captain America: The Winter Soldier: The Art of the Movie (2014) Marie Javins

Bears (2014)

Writers:

Alastair Fothergill, Adam Chapman

Directors:

Alastair Fothergill, Keith Scholey, Adam Chapman (co-director)

Premiere:

Apr 5, 2014, Phoenix Film Festival

Length:

78 min

COLLECTIONS

DVD/Blu-ray:

2014

Digital:

Amazon, iTunes

Books:

True-Life Adventures: A History of Walt Disney's Nature Documentaries (2017) Christian Moran

Million Dollar Arm (2014)

SOMETIMES TO WIN, YOU HAVE TO CHANGE THE GAME.

Source:

Based on a true story

Writers:

Tom McCarthy

Director:

Craig Gillespie

Stars:

Jon Hamm

Premiere:

May 9, 2014, India

US Release:

May 16, 2014

Length:

124 min

COLLECTIONS

DVD/Blu-ray:

2014

Digital:

iTunes, Vudu

Soundtrack:

2014 (CD)

Maleficent (2014)

Source:

- Remake of *Sleeping Beauty* (1959)
- "The Sleeping Beauty" in *Histoires ou contes du temps passé* (1697) Charles Perrault

Writers:

Linda Woolverton

Director:

Robert Stromberg

Stars:

Angelina Jolie

Premiere:

May 28, 2014 + 3D + IMAX

Length:

97 min

CONNECTIONS

Video Games:

Maleficent Free Fall (2014) PC, iPhone, iPad, Android

COLLECTIONS

DVD/Blu-ray:

2014 + 3D (UK)

Digital:

Amazon, iTunes, Vudu

Soundtrack:

2014 (CD)

Books:

Once Upon a Dream: From Perrault's Sleeping Beauty to Disney's Maleficent
(2014) Charles Solomon

Planes: Fire & Rescue (2014)

WHEN OTHERS FLY OUT, HEROES FLY IN.

Source:

Sequel to *Planes* (2013)

Writers:

Roberts Gannaway, Jeffrey M. Howard

Director:

Roberts Gannaway

Premiere:

Jul 15, 2014, Hollywood

Length:

83 min

CONNECTIONS

Short:

Vitaminamulch: Air Spectacular (DTV 2014)

Video Games:

Planes: Fire & Rescue (2014) DS, Wii, 3DS, WU

COLLECTIONS

DVD/Blu-ray:

2014

Digital:

Amazon, iTunes, Vudu

Soundtrack:

2014 (CD)

Books:

The Art of Planes (2014) Tracey Miller-Zarneke

Guardians of the Galaxy (2014)

FROM THE STUDIO THAT BROUGHT YOU THE AVENGERS

Source:

Guardians of the Galaxy characters (2008+) created by Dan Abnett and Andy Lanning

Writers:

James Gunn, Nicole Perlman

Director:

James Gunn

Stars:

Chris Pratt, Zoe Saldana, Dave Bautista, Vin Diesel, Bradley Cooper

Premiere:

Jul 21, 2014, Los Angeles + 3D + IMAX

Length:

121 min

CONNECTIONS

Comic Strips:

Guardians of the Galaxy Prelude (2014)

Movies:

Guardians of the Galaxy Vol. 2 (2017) Sequel

TV Series:

Guardians of the Galaxy (2015+) Disney XD

Theme Parks:

Guardians of the Galaxy – Mission: BREAKOUT! (DCA 2017+)

Video Games:

Guardians of the Galaxy: The Universal Weapon (2014) PC, iPhone, iPad, Android

COLLECTIONS

DVD/Blu-ray:

2014 + 3D, 2015 Marvel Cinematic Universe: Phase Two Collection

Digital:

Amazon, iTunes, Vudu

Soundtrack:

2014 *Awesome Mix Vol. 1* + Deluxe Edition (CD), 2014 (LP/Cassette)

Books:

Marvel's Guardians of the Galaxy: The Art of the Movie (2014)

Khoobsurat (2014)

THE ROYAL MISFIT

Source:

Remake of *Khoobsurat* (India, 1980)

Writers:

D.N. Mukherjee (story), Indira Bisht (screenplay), Juhi Chaturvedi (dialogue)

Director:

Shashanka Ghosh

Stars:

Sonam Kapoor, Fawad Khan

Premiere:

Sep 19, 2014

Length:

130 min

COLLECTIONS

DVD:

2014 (India)

Digital:

iTunes

Soundtrack:

2014 (CD, India)

Alexander and the Terrible, Horrible, No Good, Very Bad Day (2014)

So then that happened...

Source:

Alexander and the Terrible, Horrible, No Good, Very Bad Day (1972) Judith Viorst

Writers:

Rob Lieber

Director:

Miguel Arteta

Stars:

Steve Carell, Jennifer Garner

Premiere:

Oct 9, 2014, Argentina, etc.

US Release:

Oct 10, 2014

Length:

81 min

COLLECTIONS

DVD/Blu-ray:

2015

Digital:

Amazon, iTunes, Vudu

Soundtrack:

2014 (Digital)

Big Hero 6 (2014)

FROM THE CREATORS OF WRECK-IT RALPH AND FROZEN

Source:

Big Hero 6 characters (1998+) created by Steven T. Seagle & Duncan Rouleau

Writers:

Jordan Roberts, Robert L. Baird, Daniel Gerson

Directors:

Don Hall, Chris Williams

Premiere:

Oct 23, 2014, Tokyo International Film Festival, Japan

US Release:

Oct 25, 2014, Philadelphia International Film Festival + 3D

Length:

102 min

CONNECTIONS

Comic Books:

Big Hero 6, Vol 1-2 (2015) Manga

TV Series:

Big Hero 6: The Series (2017+) Disney XD

Video Games:

- *Big Hero 6 Bot Fight* (2014) iPhone, iPad, Android, Windows Phone
- *Big Hero 6: Battle in the Bay* (2014) 3DS, DS

COLLECTIONS

DVD/Blu-ray:

2015 + Collector's Edition + 3D (UK)

Digital:

Amazon, iTunes, Vudu

Soundtrack:

2014 Limited Edition (CD)

Books:

The Art of Big Hero 6 (2014) Jessica Julius

Into the Woods (2014)

BE CAREFUL WHAT YOU WISH FOR

Source:

Into the Woods (1986) musical by Stephen Sondheim & James Lapine

Writers:

James Lapine

Director:

Rob Marshall

Stars:

Meryl Streep, Emily Blunt, James Corden, Anna Kendrick, Chris Pine, Johnny Depp

Premiere:

Dec 8, 2014, New York

Length:

125 min

COLLECTIONS

DVD/Blu-ray:

2015

Digital:

Amazon, iTunes, Vudu

Soundtrack:

2014 + Deluxe Edition (CD)

Tinker Bell and the Legend of the NeverBeast (2014)

Source:

Fifth sequel to *Tinker Bell* (DTV 2008)

Writers:

Steve Loter (story), Tom Rogers (story/screenplay), Robert Schooley, Mark McCorkle, Kate Kondell (screenplay)

Director:

Steve Loter

Premiere:

Dec 12, 2014, UK/Ireland

US Release:

Jan 30, 2015, Hollywood (Limited)

Length:

76 min

CONNECTIONS

Comic Books:

Tinker Bell and the Legend of the NeverBeast (Disney Fairies, Jul 2015)

COLLECTIONS

DVD/Blu-ray:

2015

Digital:

Amazon, iTunes, Vudu

Soundtrack:

2015 (Digital)

PART ELEVEN

Movies: 2015–2019

McFarland, USA (2015)

CHAMPIONS CAN COME FROM ANYWHERE

AKA:

McFarland

Source:

Based on a true story

Writers:

Christopher Cleveland, Bettina Gilois (story/screenplay), Grant Thompson (screenplay)

Director:

Niki Caro

Stars:

Kevin Costner

Premiere:

Feb 9, 2015, Hollywood

Length:

129 min

COLLECTIONS

DVD/Blu-ray:

2015

Digital:

iTunes, Vudu

Soundtrack:

2015 (CD)

Cinderella (2015)

Source:

- Remake of *Cinderella* (1950)
- "Cinderella" in *Histoires ou contes du temps passé* (1697) Charles Perrault

Writers:

Chris Weitz

Director:

Kenneth Branagh

Premiere:

Feb 13, 2015, Berlin International Film Festival, Germany

US Release:

Mar 13, 2015

Length:

105 min

COLLECTIONS

DVD/Blu-ray:

2015

Digital:

Amazon, iTunes, Vudu

Soundtrack:

2015 (CD)

Books:

A Wish Your Heart Makes: From the Grimm Brothers' Aschenputtel to Disney's Cinderella (2015) Charles Solomon

Monkey Kingdom (2015)

ADVENTURE IS IN FULL SWING.

Director:

Mark Linfield, Alastair Fothergill (co-director)

Premiere:

Mar 24, 2015, Phoenix Film Festival

Length:

81 min

COLLECTIONS

DVD/Blu-ray:

2015

Digital:

iTunes, Vudu

Soundtrack:

2015 (Digital)

Books:

True-Life Adventures: A History of Walt Disney's Nature Documentaries (2017) Christian Moran

Avengers: Age of Ultron (2015)

Source:

Sequel to *The Avengers* (2012)

Writers:

Joss Whedon

Director:

Joss Whedon

Stars:

Robert Downey Jr., Chris Hemsworth, Mark Ruffalo, Chris Evans, Scarlett Johansson, Jeremy Renner, James Spader, Samuel L. Jackson

Premiere:

Apr 13, 2015, Los Angeles + 3D + IMAX

Length:

141 min

CONNECTIONS

Comic Strips:

Marvel's Avengers: Age of Ultron Prelude (2015)

COLLECTIONS

DVD/Blu-ray:

2015 + 3D Collector's Edition + Marvel Cinematic Universe: Phase Two Collection, 2016 2-Movie Collection

Digital:

Amazon, iTunes, Vudu

Soundtrack:

2015 (CD)

Books:

- *The Road to Marvel's Avenger: Age of Ultron: The Art of the Marvel Cinematic Universe* (2015)
- *Marvel's Avengers: Age of Ulton: The Art of the Movie* (2015)

Tomorrowland (2015)

FROM THE DIRECTOR OF THE INCREDIBLES & MISSION: IMPOSSIBLE – GHOST PROTOCOL

AKA:

Tomorrowland: A World Beyond

Source:

Inspired by Tomorrowland area of Disney theme parks

Writers:

Jeff Jensen (story), Brad Bird, Damon Lindelof (story/screenplay)

Director:

Brad Bird

Stars:

George Clooney

Premiere:

May 9, 2015, Anaheim, CA + IMAX

Length:

130 min

CONNECTIONS

Theme Parks:

- Tomorrowland (DL 1955+), (MK 1971+), (TD 1983+), (HKD 2005+), (SD 2016+)

- Discoveryland (DP 1992+)

COLLECTIONS
DVD/Blu-ray:
2015

Digital:
Amazon, iTunes, Vudu

Soundtrack:
2015 (CD)

Books:
Before Tomorrowland (2015) Jeff Jensen & Jonathan Case, novel

Inside Out (2015)
MEET THE LITTLE VOICE INSIDE YOUR HEAD.

Writers:
Ronnie Del Carmen (story), Pete Docter (story/screenplay), Meg LeFauve, Josh Cooley (screenplay), Michael Arndt, Simon Rich, Bill Hader, Amy Poehler (additional material)

Directors:
Pete Docter, Ronnie Del Carmen (co-director)

Premiere:
May 18, 2015, Cannes Film Festival, France

US Release:
Jun 4, 2015, Seattle International Film Festival +3D + IMAX

Length:
95 min

CONNECTIONS
Shorts:
Riley's First Date? (DTV 2015) Sequel

Video Games:
Inside Out: Thought Bubbles (2015) iPhone, iPad, Android

COLLECTIONS
DVD/Blu-ray:
2015 + 3D Ultimate Collector's Edition, 2016

Digital:
Amazon, iTunes, Vudu

Soundtrack:
2015 (CD), 2015 (LP)

Books:
The Art of Inside Out (2015)

ABCD 2 (2015)

AKA:
Any Body Can Dance 2

Source:
Sequel to *ABCD: Any Body Can Dance* (2013) non-Disney release

Writers:
Remo, Tushar Hiranandani, Mayur Puri (dialogue)

Director:
Remo

Stars:
Varun Dhawan, Prabhu Deva, Shraddha Kapoor

Premiere:
Jun 19, 2015 + 3D

Length:
154 min

COLLECTIONS

DVD/Blu-ray:
2015 (India)

Digital:
iTunes

Soundtrack:
2015 (CD, India)

Ant-Man (2015)

HEROES DON'T GET ANY BIGGER

Source:

Ant-Man character (1962+) created by Stan Lee, Larry Leiber, & Jack Kirby

Writers:

Edgar Wright, Joe Cornish (story/screenplay), Adam McKay, Paul Rudd (screenplay)

Director:

Peyton Reed

Stars:

Paul Rudd, Evangeline Lilly, Corey Stoll, Bobby Cannavale, Michael Peña, Michael Douglas

Premiere:

Jun 29, 2015, Los Angeles + 3D + IMAX

Length:

117 min

CONNECTIONS

Comic Books:

Marvel's Ant-Man Prelude (2015)

Movies:

Ant-Man and the Wasp (2018) Sequel

COLLECTIONS

DVD/Blu-ray:

2015 + 3D + Marvel Cinematic Universe: Phase Two Collection

Digital:

iTunes, Vudu

Soundtrack:

2015 (CD)

Books:

Marvel's Ant-Man: The Art of the Movie (2015)

The Good Dinosaur (2015)

FROM THE CREATORS OF INSIDE OUT

Writers:

Bob Peterson, Peter Sohn, Kelsey Mann, Erik Benson (story), Meg LeFauve (screenplay), Peter Hedges, Adrian Molina (additional material)

Director:

Peter Sohn

Premiere:

Nov 10, 2015, Paris, France

US Release:

Nov 17, 2015, Los Angeles + 3D

Length:

93 min

COLLECTIONS

DVD/Blu-ray:

2016 + 3D Ultimate Collector's Edition

Digital:

Amazon, iTunes, Vudu

Soundtrack:

2015 (CD)

Books:

The Art of the Good Dinosaur (2015) Karen Paik

Star Wars: The Force Awakens (2015)

AKA:

Star Wars: Episode VII – The Force Awakens

Source:

Episode VII of the Star Wars saga (1977+)

Writers:

Lawrence Kasdan, J.J. Abrams, Michael Arndt

Director:

J.J. Abrams

Premiere:

Dec 14, 2015, Los Angeles + 3D + IMAX

Length:

136 min

CONNECTIONS

Comic Books:

- *Journey to Star Wars: The Force Awakens – Shattered Empire* (2015)
- *Star Wars: The Force Awakens* (#1–6, Aug 2016 – Jan 2017) [Collection > *Star Wars: The Force Awakens Adaptation* (2016)]

Movies:

- *Star Wars: Episode IV – A New Hope* (1977) 20th Century Fox original
- *Star Wars: Episode V – The Empire Strikes Back* (1980) 20th Century Fox sequel
- *Star Wars: Episode VI – Return of the Jedi* (1983) 20th Century Fox sequel
- *Star Wars: Episode I – The Phantom Menace* (1999) 20th Century Fox prequel
- *Star Wars: Episode II – Attack of the Clones* (2002) 20th Century Fox prequel
- *Star Wars: Episode III – Revenge of the Sith* (2005) 20th Century Fox prequel
- *Star Wars: The Last Jedi* (2017) sequel
- *Star Wars: Episode IX* (2019) sequel

Theme Parks:

- Star Tours (DL 1986-2010), (TDL 1989-2012), (HS 1989-2010), (DP 1992-2016)
- Jedi Training: Trials of the Temple (HS 2007+), (DL 2006+), (DP 2015+), (HKD 2016+)
- Star Tours: The Adventures Continue (HS 2011+), (DL 2011+), (TDL 2013+)
- Star Wars Launch Bay (DL 2015+), (HS 2015+), (SD 2016+)
- Star Wars: A Galactic Spectacular (HS 2016+)
- Star Tours: L'Aventure Continue (DP 2017+)
- Star Wars: Galaxy's Edge (DL 2019+), (HS 2019)

Video Games:
Lego Star Wars: The Force Awakens (2016) PS3, PS4, X360, X1, PSV, WU, 3DS, X360S, PC, Android

COLLECTIONS
DVD/Blu-ray:
2016 + 3D Collector's Edition

Digital:
Amazon, Vudu

Soundtrack:
2015 (CD), 2016 (LP/Cassette)

Books:
The Art of Star Wars: The Force Awakens (2015) Phil Szotak

The Finest Hours (2016)
WE ALL LIVE OR WE ALL DIE. BASED ON THE INCREDIBLE TRUE STORY

Source:
The Finest Hours (2009) Michael J. Touglas & Casey Sherman

Writers:
Scott Silver, Paul Tamasy, Eric Johnson

Director:
Craig Gillespie

Stars:
Chris Pine, Casey Affleck, Ben Foster, Eric Bana

Premiere:
Jan 27, 2016, Belgium

US Release:
Jan 29, 2016 + 3D + IMAX

COLLECTIONS
DVD/Blu-ray:
2016

Digital:
Amazon, iTunes, Vudu

Soundtrack:

2016 (Digital)

Zootopia (2016)

FROM THE CREATORS OF FROZEN *AND* BIG HERO 6

AKA:

Zootropolis, *Zoomania*

Writers:

Byron Howard, Rich Moore, Jim Reardon, Josie Trinidad, Jennifer Lee (story), Jared Bush, Phil Johnston (story/screenplay)

Directors:

Byron Howard, Rich Moore, Jared Bush (co-director)

Premiere:

Feb 11, 2016, Denmark

US Release:

Feb 17, 2016, Hollywood + 3D + IMAX

Length:

108 min

CONNECTIONS

Comic Books:

Zootopia Comics Collection (2016)

Video Games:

Zootopia Crime Files (2016) iPhone

COLLECTIONS

DVD/Blu-ray:

2016 + 3D Ultimate Collector's Edition

Digital:

Amazon, iTunes, Vudu

Soundtrack:

2016 (CD)

Books:

The Art of Zootropolis (2016) Jessica Julius

The Jungle Book (2016)

Source:

- *The Jungle Book* (1894) and *The Second Jungle Book* (1895) Rudyard Kipling
- Remake of *The Jungle Book* (1967)

Writers:

Justin Marks

Director:

Jon Favreau

Stars:

Bill Murray, Ben Kingsley, Idris Elba, Lupita Nyong'o, Giancarlo Esposito, Christopher Walken, Neel Sethi

Premiere:

Apr 4, 2016, Los Angeles + 3D + IMAX

Length:

106 min

CONNECTIONS

Movies:

The Jungle Book 2 (TBC) Sequel

Video Games:

The Jungle Book: Mowgli's Run (2016) iPhone, iPad, Android

COLLECTIONS

DVD/Blu-ray:

2016 + 3D Collector's Edition

Digital:

Amazon, iTunes, Vudu

Soundtrack:

2016 (CD)

Books:

The Art of The Jungle Book (2016) Ellen Wolff

Captain America: Civil War (2016)

UNITED WE STAND. DIVIDED WE FALL.

Source:

Sequel to *Captain America: The Winter Soldier* (2014)

Writers:

Christopher Markus, Stephen McFeely

Directors:

Anthony Russo, Joe Russo

Stars:

Chris Evans, Robert Downey Jr., Scarlett Johansson, Sebastian Stan, Jeremy Renner, Don Cheadle, Anthony Mackie, Paul Bettany, Elizabeth Olsen, Daniel Brühl

Premiere:

Apr 12, 2016, Los Angeles + 3D + IMAX

Length:

147 min

CONNECTIONS

Comic Strips:

Captain America: Civil War Prelude (#1-4, Feb – Mar 2016) [Collection > *Captain America: Civil War Prelude* (2016)]

COLLECTIONS

DVD/Blu-ray:

2016 + 3D Collector's Edition

Digital:

iTunes, Vudu

Soundtrack:

2016 (CD)

Books:

Marvel's Captain America: Civil War: The Art of the Movie (2016)

Alice Through the Looking Glass (2016)

IT'S TIME FOR A LITTLE MADNESS

Source:

Sequel to *Alice in Wonderland* (2010)

Writers:

Linda Woolverton

Director:

James Bobin

Stars:

Johnny Depp, Anne Hathaway, Mia Wasikowska, Helena Bonham Carter, Sacha Baron Cohen

Premiere:

May 10, 2016, London

US Release:

May 27, 2016 + 3D + IMAX

Length:

113 min

COLLECTIONS

DVD/Blu-ray:

2016 + 3D (UK)

Digital:

Amazon, iTunes, Vudu

Soundtrack:

2016 (CD)

Books:

Walt Disney's Alice in Wonderland: An Illustrated Journey Through Time (2016) Mark Salisbury

The BFG (2016)

From the human beans that created "E.T." and the author of "Charlie and the Chocolate Factory" and "Matilda" The World Is More Giant Than You Can Imagine

Source:

The BFG (1982) Roald Dahl

Writers:

Melissa Mathison

Director:

Steven Spielberg

Premiere:

May 14, 2016, Cannes Film Festival, France

US Release:

Jun 21, 2016, Los Angeles + 3D

Length:

117 min

CONNECTIONS

Video Games:

The BFG Game (2016) iPhone, iPad, Android

COLLECTIONS

DVD/Blu-ray:

2016 + 3D (UK)

Digital:

iTunes, Vudu

Soundtrack:

2016 (CD)

Finding Dory (2016)

An unforgettable journey she probably won't remember.

Source:

Sequel to *Finding Nemo* (2003)

Writers:

Andrew Stanton (story/screenplay), Victoria Strouse (screenplay), Bob Petersen, Angus MacLane (additional material)

Directors:

Andrew Stanton, Angus MacLane (co-director)

Premiere:

Jun 8, 2016, Los Angeles + 3D + IMAX

Length:
97 min

CONNECTIONS
Comic Books:
Disney Pixar Finding Dory (Jul 2016)

COLLECTIONS
DVD/Blu-ray:
2016 + 3D Ultimate Collector's Edition

Digital:
Amazon, iTunes, Vudu

Soundtrack:
2016 (CD)

Books:
The Art of Finding Dory (2016)

Pete's Dragon (2016)
Some Secrets Are Too Big To Keep.

Source:
Remake of *Pete's Dragon* (1977)

Writers:
David Lowery, Toby Halbrooks

Director:
David Lowery

Stars:
Bryce Dallas Howard, Oakes Fegley, Wes Bentley, Karl Urban, Robert Redford

Premiere:
Jul 31, 2016, London, UK

US Release:
Aug 8, 2016, Los Angeles + 3D

Length:
102 min

COLLECTIONS
DVD/Blu-ray:
2016

Digital:
Amazon, iTunes, Vudu

Soundtrack:
2016 (CD)

Books:
The Art of Disney's Dragons (2016) Tom Bancroft

Born in China (2016)
AKA:
Wo men dan sheng zai zhong guo (China)

Writers:
David Fowler, Brian Leith, Phil Chapman, Chuan Lu

Director:
Chuan Lu

Premiere:
Aug 5, 2016, China

US Release:
Apr 9, 2017, San Francisco International Film Festival

Length:
79 min

CONNECTIONS
Movies:
Ghosts in the Mountains (2017) Behind the scenes documentary

COLLECTIONS
DVD/Blu-ray:
2017

Digital:
tbc

Soundtrack:
2017 (Digital)

Books:
True-Life Adventures: A History of Walt Disney's Nature Documentaries (2017) Christian Moran

Mohenjo Daro (2016)

Writers:
Ashutosh Gowariker (story/screenplay), Preeti Mamgain (dialogue)

Director:
Ashutosh Gowariker

Premiere:
Aug 12, 2016

Length:
155 min

COLLECTIONS

DVD/Blu-ray:
2016 (India)

Soundtrack:
2016 (CD, India)

Queen of Katwe (2016)

Source:
The Queen of Katwe (2012) Tim Crothers

Writers:
William Wheeler

Director:
Mira Nair

Stars:
David Oylowo, Luita Nyong'o, Madina Nalwanga

Premiere:
Sep 10, 2016, Toronto International Film Festival, Canada

US Release:
Sep 23, 2016

Length:
124 min

COLLECTIONS

DVD/Blu-ray:
2017

Digital:
Amazon, Vudu

Soundtrack:
2016 (CD) Deluxe Edition (Digital)

Doctor Strange (2016)

THE IMPOSSIBILITIES ARE ENDLESS

Source:
Doctor Strange character (1963+) created by Steve Ditko & Stan Lee

Writers:
Jon Spaihts, Scott Derrickson, C. Robert Cargill

Director:
Scott Derrickson

Stars:
Benedict Cumberbatch, Chiwetel Ejiofor, Rachel McAdams, Benedict Wong, Mads Mikkelsen, Tilda Swinton

Premiere:
Oct 13, 2016, Hong Kong

US Release:
Oct 20, 2016, Los Angeles + 3D + IMAX

Length:
115 min

CONNECTIONS

Comic Strips:
Doctor Strange Prelude (Oct 2016)

COLLECTIONS

DVD/Blu-ray:
2017 + 3D Cinematic Universe Edition

Digital:
Amazon, iTunes, Vudu

Soundtrack:

2016 (CD)

Books:

Marvel's Doctor Strange: The Art of the Movie (2016) Jacob Johnston

Moana (2016)

From the creators of ZOOTOPIA & FROZEN

Writers:

Jared Bush (screenplay), Ron Clements, John Musker, Chris Williams, Don Hall, Pamela Ribon, Aaron Kandell, Jordan Kandell

Directors:

Ron Clements, John Musker, Don Hall (co-director), Chris Williams (co-director)

Stars:

Dwayne Johnson, Auli'I Cravalho

Premiere:

Nov 14, 2016, AFI Fest + 3D

Re-releases:

2017 Sing-along version (limited)

Length:

107 min

CONNECTIONS

Shorts:

Gone Fishing (DTV 2017)

COLLECTIONS

DVD/Blu-ray:

2017 + 3D Ultimate Collector's Edition

Digital:

Amazon, iTunes, Vudu

Soundtrack:

2016 + Deluxe Edition (CD), 2016 (LP)

Books:

The Art of Moana (2016) Jessica Julius & Maggie Malone

Growing Up Wild (2016)

Source:

Compilation edited from *African Cats* (2011), *Chimpanzee* (2012), *Bears* (2014) and *Monkey Kingdom* (2015)

Directors:

Mark Linfield, Keith Scholey

Premiere:

Dec 8, 2016, Netflix

Length:

77 min

COLLECTIONS

Digital:

iTunes, Vudu

Rogue One: A Star Wars Story (2016)

AKA:

Rogue One, Star Wars: Rogue One

Source:

Spin-off of *Star Wars: Episode IV – A New Hope* (1977)

Writers:

John Knoll, Gary Whitta (story), Chris Weitz, Tony Gilroy (screenplay)

Director:

Gareth Edwards

Premiere:

Dec 10, 2016, California + 3D + IMAX

Length:

133 min

CONNECTIONS

Comic Strips:

Star Wars: Rogue One (#1-4, Jun – Sep 2017)

COLLECTIONS
DVD/Blu-ray:
2017 + 3D

Digital:
Amazon, iTunes, Vudu

Soundtrack:
2016 (CD/LP)

Books:
The Art of Rogue One: A Star Wars Story (2016) Josh Kushins

Dangal (2016)
Writers:
Piyush Gupta, Shreyas Jain, Nikhil Mehrota, Nitesh Tiwari

Director:
Nitesh Tiwari

Premiere:
Dec 21, 2016

Length:
161 min

COLLECTIONS
DVD/Blu-ray:
2017 (India)

Digital:
Netflix

Soundtrack:
2016 (CD, India)

Beauty and the Beast (2017)
Source:
Remake of *Beauty and the Beast* (1991)

Writers:
Stephen Chbosky, Evan Spiliotopoulos

Director:

Bill Condon

Stars:

Emma Watson, Dan Stevens, Luke Evans, Kevin Kline, Josh Gad, Ewan McGregor, Stanley Tucci, Audra McDonald, Gugu Mbatha-Raw, Ian McKellen, Emma Thompson

Premiere:

Feb 23, 2017, London

US Release:

Mar 17, 2017 + 3D + IMAX + Sing-along version

Length:

129 min

COLLECTIONS

DVD/Blu-ray:

2017

Digital:

Amazon, iTunes, Vudu

Soundtrack:

2017 + Deluxe Edition (CD), 2017 (LP)

Books:

Tale As Old As Time: The Art and Making of Beauty and the Beast (2nd Edition, 2017) Charles Solomon

Guardians of the Galaxy Vol. 2 (2017)

Source:

Sequel to *Guardians of the Galaxy* (2014)

Writers:

James Gunn

Director:

James Gunn

Stars:

Chris Pratt, Zoe Saldana, Dave Bautista, Vin Diesel, Bradley Cooper, Kurt Russell

Premiere:

Apr 19, 2017, Los Angeles + 3D + IMAX

Length:

136 min

CONNECTIONS

Comic Strips:

Guardians of the Galaxy Vol 2. Prelude (2017)

COLLECTIONS

DVD/Blu-ray:

2017 + 4K Cinematic Universe Edition

Soundtrack:

2017 *Awesome Mix Vol. 2* (CD), 2017 Score (Digital)

Books:

Marvel's Guardians of the Galaxy Vol. 2: The Art of the Movie (2017) Jacob Johnston

Pirates of the Caribbean: Dead Men Tell No Tales (2017)

AKA:

Pirates of the Caribbean: Salazar's Revenge

Source:

Fourth sequel to *Pirates of the Caribban: The Curse of the Black Pearl* (2003)

Writers:

Terry Rossio (story), Jeff Nathanson (story/screenplay)

Directors:

Joachim Rønning, Espen Sandberg

Stars:

Johnny Depp, Javier Bardem, Geoffrey Rush

Premiere:

May 11, 2017, Shangai, China

US Release:

May 26, 2017 + 3D + IMAX

Length:
129 min

COLLECTIONS

DVD/Blu-ray:
2017 + 4K

Soundtrack:
2017 (CD/LP/Cassette)

Ghost of the Mountains (2017)

Source:
Behind the scenes of *Born in China* (2016)

Director:
Ben Wallis

Premiere:
Sep 14, 2017, Disney Movies Anywhere

Length:
78 min

COLLECTIONS

Digital:
Amazon, iTunes, Vudu

Cars 3 (2017)

FROM THIS MOMENT, EVERYTHING WILL CHANGE.

Source:
Second sequel to *Cars* (2006)

Writers:
Brian Fee, Ben Queen, Eyal Podell, Jonathon E. Stewart (story), Kiel Murray, Bob Peterson, Mike Rich (screenplay)

Director:
Brian Fee

Premiere:
Jun 10, 2017, Los Angeles + 3D + IMAX

Length:

102 min

CONNECTIONS

Shorts:

Miss Fritter's Racing Skoool (Digital, 2017)

Video Games:

Cars 3: Driven to Win (2017) PS4, PS3, NS, X1, X360, WU

COLLECTIONS

DVD:

2017

Blu-ray:

2017 + 3D Ultimate Collector's Edition + 4K

Digital:

Amazon, iTunes, Vudu

Soundtrack:

2017 *Original Motion Picture Soundtrack* (CD), 2017 *Original Score* (CD)

Books:

- *The Art of Cars 3* (2017)
- *Poster Art of Cars* (2017) Victoria Saxon

Jagga Jasoos (2017)

Writers:

Anurag BasU, Samrat Chakraborty

Director:

Anurag Basu

Premiere:

Jul 13, 2017, UAE/Kuwait

US Release:

Jul 14, 2017

Length:

161 min

COLLECTIONS
DVD/Blu-ray:
2017 (India)

Thor: Ragnarok (2017)

Source:
Sequel to *Thor: The Dark World* (2013)

Writers:
Eric Pearson, Craig Kyle, Christopher Yost

Director:
Taika Waititi

Stars:
Chris Hemsworth, Tom Hiddleston, Cate Blanchett, Idris Elba, Jeff Goldblum, Tessa Thompson, Karl Urban, Mark Ruffalo, Anthony Hopkins

Premiere:
Oct 10, 2017, Los Angeles + 3D + IMAX

Length:
130 min

CONNECTIONS
Comic Strips:
Marvel's Thor Ragnarok Prelude (2017)

COLLECTIONS
DVD/Blu-ray:
2018 + 3D + 4K

Digital:
Amazon, iTunes, Vudu

Soundtrack:
2017 (CD)

Books:
Marvel's Thor: Ragnarok: The Art of the Movie (2017)

Coco (2017)

THE CELEBRATION OF A LIFETIME

Source:

Mexican "Day of the Dead" holiday

Writers:

Adrian Molina, Matthew Aldrich (story/screenplay), Lee Unkrich, Jason Katz (story)

Director:

Lee Unkrich

Premiere:

Oct 20, 2017, Festival Internacional de Cine de Morelia, Mexico

US Release:

Nov 21, 2017 + 3D

Length:

105 min

CONNECTIONS

Shorts:

Dante's Lunch (2017) Teaser for forthcoming film

COLLECTIONS

DVD/Blu-ray:

2018

Digital:

Amazon, iTunes, Vudu

Soundtrack:

2017 (CD)

Books:

The Art of Coco (2017)

Star Wars: The Last Jedi (2017)

AKA:

Star Wars: Episode VIII – The Last Jedi

Source:

Sequel to *Star Wars: The Force Awakens* (2015)

Writers:

Rian Johnson

Director:

Rian Johnson

Premiere:

Dec 9, 2017, Los Angeles + 3D + IMAX

Length:

152 min

CONNECTIONS

Comic Strips:

Journey to Star Wars: The Last Jedi – Captain Phasma (#1-4, Nov – Dec 2017)

COLLECTIONS

DVD/Blu-ray:

2018

Digital:

Amazon, iTunes, Vudu

Soundtrack:

2017 (CD)

Books:

The Art of Star Wars: The Last Jedi (2017) Phil Szostak

Black Panther (2018)

Source:

- *Black Panther* character (1966+) created by Stan Lee & Jack Kirby
- Character introduced in *Captain America: Civil War* (2016)

Writers:

Ryan Coogler, Joe Robert Cole

Director:

Ryan Coogler

Stars:

Chadwick Boseman, Michael B. Jordan, Lupita Nyong'o, Danai Gurira, Martin Freeman, Angela Bassett, Forest Whitaker, Andy Serkis

Premiere:

Jan 29, 2018, Los Angeles + IMAX +3D

Length:

134 min

CONNECTIONS

Comic Strips:

Marvel's Black Panther Prelude (#1-2, 2018)

COLLECTIONS

DVD/Blu-ray:

2018 + 4K

Digital:

Amazon, iTunes, Vudu

Soundtrack:

2018 *Black Panther: The Album* (CD), Score (digital)

Books:

Marvel's Black Panther: The Art of the Movie (2018)

A Wrinkle in Time (2018)

Source:

- *A Wrinkle in Time* (1962) Madeleine L'Engle
- Remake of *A Wrinkle in Time* (2003) TV Movie

Writers:

Jennifer Lee

Director:

Ava DuVernay

Stars:

Oprah Winfrey, Reese Witherspoon, Mindy Kaling, Storm Reid, Zach Galifianakis, Chris Pine

Premiere:

Feb 26, 2018, Hollywood + 3D + IMAX

Length:

109 min

COLLECTIONS
DVD/Blu-ray:

2018 + 4K

Digital:

Amazon, iTunes, Vudu

Soundtrack:

2018 (CD)

Books:

The World of a Wrinkle in Time: The Making of the Movie (2018) Kate Egan

Disneynature: Blue (2018)

AKA:

Dolphins

Directors:

Alastair Fothergill, Kevin Scholey

Release:

May 2, 2018, Netherlands

US Release:

TBC

Length:

78 min

Avengers: Infinity War (2018)

Source:

Sequel to *Avengers: Age of Ultron* (2015) and other MCU movies

Writers:

Christopher Markus, Stephen McFeely

Directors:

Anthony Russo, Joe Russo

Stars:

Robert Downey Jr., Chris Hemsworth, Mark Ruffalo, Chris Evans, Scarlett Johansson, Don Cheadle, Benedict Cumberbatch, Tom Holland, Chadwick Boseman, Zoe Saldana, Paul Bettany, Elizabeth Olsen, Anthony Mackie, Sebastian Stan, Danai Gurira, Letitia Wright, Dave Bautista, John Brolin, Chris Pratt

Premiere:
Apr 23, 2018, Los Angeles + IMAX + 3D

Length:
149 min

CONNECTIONS
Comic Strips:
Marvels' Avengers: Infinity War Prelude (#1-2, 2018)

COLLECTIONS
DVD/Blu-ray:
2018 + 4K + 3D

Digital:
Amazon, iTunes, Vudu

Soundtrack:
2018 (CD)

Books:
- *The Road to Marvel's Avengers: Infinity War* (2018)
- *The Art of Marvel's Avengers: Infinity War* (2018)

Solo: A Star Wars Story (2018)
Source:
Prequel to *Star Wars: A New Hope* (1977)

Writers:
Jon Kasdan, Lawrence Kasdan

Director:
Ron Howard

Stars:
Alden Ehrenreich, Woody Harrelson, Emilia Clarke, Donald Glover, Thandie Newton, Paul Bettany

Premiere:
May 10, 2018, Los Angeles + IMAX + 3D

Length:
135 min

CONNECTIONS
Comic Strips:

Solo: A Star Wars Story (2018)

COLLECTIONS
DVD/Blu-ray:

2018 + 4K + 3D

Soundtrack:

2018 (CD)

Books:

The Art of Solo: A Star Wars Story (2018) Phil Szostak

Incredibles 2 (2018)

Source:

Sequel to *The Incredibles* (2004)

Writers:

Brad Bird

Director:

Brad Bird

Premiere:

Jun 5, 2018, Los Angeles + IMAX +3D

Length:

118 min

CONNECTIONS
Comic Strips:

- *Incredibles 2: Heroes at Home* (2018)
- *Incredibles 2: Crisis in Mid-Life! & Other Stories* (#1-3, 2018)

COLLECTIONS
DVD/Blu-ray:

2018 + 4K + 3D

Soundtrack:

2018 (CD)

Books:

The Art of Incredibles 2 (2018) Karen Paik

The following movies had not been released at the time of writing, so this information is liable to change. The movie-making business is difficult to predict, and it remains to be seen whether Disney's acquisition of 21st Century Fox will go ahead and how it might affect future releases. Any new movies would of course be addressed in a future edition of *Disney Connections & Collections: Movies*!

Ant-Man and the Wasp (2018)

Source:

Sequel to *Ant-Man* (2015)

Writers:

Chris McKenna, Erik Sommers, Andrew Barrer, Gabriel Ferrari, Paul Rudd

Director:

Peyton Reed

Stars:

Paul Rudd, Evangeline Lilly, Michael Peña, Walton Goggins, Hannah John-Kamen, Michelle Pfeiffer, Laurence Fishburne, Michael Douglas

US Release:

Jul 4, 2018

Christopher Robin (2018)

Sooner or later, your past catches up to you

Source:

Inspired by *Winnie the Pooh* (1966) & *The House at Pooh Corner* (1928) A.A. Milne

Writers:

Alex Ross Perry, Allison Schroeder, Tom McCarthy

Director:

Marc Foster

Stars:

Ewan McGregor

US Release:
Aug 3, 2018

The Nutcracker and the Four Realms (2018)

Source:
The Nutcracker and the Mouse King (1816) E.T.A. Hoffman

Writers:
Simon Beaufoy, Ashleigh Powell

Directors:
Lasse Hallström, Joe Johnston

US Release:
Nov 2, 2018

Ralph Breaks the Internet: Wreck-It Ralph 2 (2018)

Source:
Sequel to *Wreck-It Ralph* (2012)

Writers:
Pamela Ribon, Phil Johnston, Rich Moore

Directors:
Phil Johnston, Rich Moore

US Release:
Nov 21, 2018

Mary Poppins Returns (2018)

Source:
- *Mary Poppins* series (1934–1988) P.L. Travers
- Sequel to *Mary Poppins* (1964)

Writers:
David Magee

Director:
Rob Marshall

US Release:

Dec 25, 2018

Captain Marvel (2019)

Source:

Captain Marvel/Carol Danvers character (1968+) created by Roy Thomas, Gene Colan

Writers:

Geneva Robertson-Dworet, Meg LeFauve, Nicole Perlman

Directors:

Anna Boden, Ryan Fleck

US Release:

Mar 8, 2019

Penguins (2019)

Note:

Disneynature documentary

US Release:

Apr 19, 2019

Dumbo (2019)

Source:

Remake of *Dumbo* (1941)

Writers:

Ehren Kruger

Director:

Tim Burton

US Release:

Mar 29, 2019

Avengers: Endgame (2019)

Source:

Sequel to *Avengers: Infinity War* (2018)

Writers:

Christopher Markus, Stephen McFeely

Directors:

Anthony Russo, Joe Russo

US Release:

May 3, 2019

Aladdin (2019)

Source:

Remake of *Aladdin* (1992)

Writers:

John August, Guy Ritchie, Vanessa Taylor

Director:

Guy Ritchie

US Release:

May 24, 2019

Toy Story 4 (2019)

Source:

Third sequel to *Toy Story* (1995)

Writers:

Stephany Folsom, Rashida Jones, Will McCormack, John Lasseter, Andrew Stanton, Pete Docter, Lee Unkrich

Director:

Josh Cooley

US Release:

Jun 21, 2019

The Lion King (2019)

Source:

Remake of *The Lion King* (1994)

Writers:

Jeff Nathanson

Director:
Jon Favreau

US Release:
Jul 19, 2019

Artemis Fowl (2019)

Source:
Artemis Fowl (2001) Eoin Colfer

Writers:
Michael Goldenberg, Adam Kline, Conor McPherson

Director:
Kenneth Branagh

US Release:
Aug 9, 2019

Frozen 2 (2019)

Source:
Sequel to *Frozen* (2013)

Writers:
Jennifer Lee

Director:
Chris Buck, Jennifer Lee

US Release:
Nov 27, 2019

Star Wars: Episode IX (2019)

Source:
Sequel to *Star Wars: The Last Jedi* (2017)

Writers:
J.J. Abrams, Derek Connolly, Chris Terrio, Colin Trevorrow

Director:
J.J. Abrams

US Release:
Dec 20, 2019

Mulan (2020)

Source:

Remake of *Mulan* (1998)

Writers:

Lauren Hynek, Rick Jaffa, Elizabeth Martin, Amanda Silver

Director:

Niki Caro

US Release:

Mar 27, 2020

Disney Movie Checklist

The following checklist of Disney movies released between 1937 and mid-2018 serves as an index of sorts to help you locate movies within the book when you don't know what year they were released. It also doubles as a checklist to keep track of the movies you've seen or own. Those entries marked with an asterisk (*) were released directly to video, DVD or digital.

A

- ☐ ABCD 2 (2015)
- ☐ The Absent-Minded Professor (1961)
- ☐ Academy Award Review of Walt Disney Cartoons (1937)
- ☐ The Adventures of Bullwhip Griffin (1967)
- ☐ The Adventures of Huck Finn (1993)
- ☐ The Adventures of Ichabod and Mr. Toad (1949)
- ☐ The Adventures of Tom Thumb & Thumbelina (2002)*
- ☐ African Cats (2011)
- ☐ The African Lion (1955)
- ☐ Air Bud (1997)
- ☐ Air Bud 3: World Pup (2000)*
- ☐ Air Buddies (2006)*
- ☐ Air Bud: Golden Receiver (1998)
- ☐ Air Bud: Seventh Inning Fetch (2002)*
- ☐ Air Bud: Spike's Back (2003)*
- ☐ Aladdin (1992)
- ☐ Aladdin and the King of Thieves (1996)*
- ☐ Alexander and the Terrible, Horrible, No Good, Very Bad Day (2014)
- ☐ Alice in Wonderland (1951)
- ☐ Alice in Wonderland (2010)
- ☐ Alice Through the Looking Glass (2016)
- ☐ Aliens of the Deep (2005)
- ☐ Almost Angels (1962)
- ☐ America's Heart & Soul (2004)
- ☐ Amy (1981)
- ☐ Angels in the Outfield (1994)

- ❑ Ant-Man (2015)
- ❑ The Apple Dumpling Gang (1975)
- ❑ The Apple Dumpling Gang Rides Again (1979)
- ❑ The Aristocats (1970)
- ❑ Arjun: The Warrior Prince (2012)
- ❑ Around the World in 80 Days (2004)
- ❑ Atlantis: Milo's Return (2003)*
- ❑ Atlantis: The Lost Empire (2001)
- ❑ The Avengers (2012)
- ❑ Avengers: Age of Ultron (2015)
- ❑ Avengers: Infinity War (2018)

B

- ❑ Babes in Toyland (1961)
- ❑ Bambi (1942)
- ❑ Bambi II (2006)
- ❑ The Barefoot Executive (1971)
- ❑ Barfi! (2012)
- ❑ Bears (2014)
- ❑ The Bears and I (1974)
- ❑ Beauty and the Beast (1991)
- ❑ Beauty and the Beast (2017)
- ❑ Beauty and the Beast: The Enchanted Christmas (1997)*
- ❑ Bedknobs and Broomsticks (1971)
- ❑ Bedtime Stories (2008)
- ❑ Belle's Magical World (1998)*
- ❑ Belle's Tales of Friendship (1999)*
- ❑ Benji the Hunted (1987)
- ❑ The Best of Walt Disney's True-Life Adventures (1975)
- ❑ Beverly Hills Chihuahua (2008)
- ❑ Beverly Hills Chihuahua 2 (2011)*
- ❑ Beverly Hills Chihuahua 3: Viva la Fiesta! (2012)*
- ❑ The BFG (2016)
- ❑ The Big Green (1995)
- ❑ Big Hero 6 (2014)
- ❑ Big Red (1962)
- ❑ The Biscuit Eater (1972)
- ❑ Blackbeard's Ghost (1968)
- ❑ The Black Cauldron (1985)
- ❑ The Black Hole (1979)
- ❑ Black Panther (2018)
- ❑ Blank Check (1994)
- ❑ The Boatniks (1970)

- ❑   Bolt (2008)
- ❑   Bon Voyage! (1962)
- ❑   The Book of Pooh: Stories from the Heart (2001)*
- ❑   Born in China (2016)
- ❑   The Boys: The Sherman Brothers' Story (2009)
- ❑   Brave (2012)
- ❑   The Brave Little Toaster (1987)
- ❑   The Brave Little Toaster Goes to Mars (1998)*
- ❑   The Brave Little Toaster to the Rescue (1997)*
- ❑   Breakin' Through (1985)*
- ❑   Bridge to Terabithia (2007)
- ❑   Brother Bear (2003)
- ❑   Brother Bear 2 (2006)*
- ❑   A Bug's Life (1998)
- ❑   Buzz Lightyear of Star Command: The Adventure Begins (2000)*

C

- ❑   Candleshoe (1977)
- ❑   Captain America: Civil War (2016)
- ❑   Captain America: The Winter Soldier (2014)
- ❑   Cars (2006)
- ❑   Cars 2 (2011)
- ❑   Cars 3 (2017)
- ❑   The Castaway Cowboy (1974)
- ❑   The Cat from Outer Space (1978)
- ❑   Charley and the Angel (1973)
- ❑   Charlie, the Lonesome Cougar (1967)
- ❑   Cheetah (1989)
- ❑   Chicken Little (2005)
- ❑   Chimpanzee (2012)
- ❑   A Christmas Carol (2009)
- ❑   The Chronicles of Narnia: Prince Caspian (2008)
- ❑   The Chronicles of Narnia: The Lion, the Witch and the Wardrobe (2005)
- ❑   Cinderella (1950)
- ❑   Cinderella (2015)
- ❑   Cinderella II: Dreams Come True (2002)*
- ❑   Cinderella III: A Twist in Time (2007)*
- ❑   Coco (2017)
- ❑   College Road Trip (2008)
- ❑   The Computer Wore Tennis Shoes (1969)
- ❑   Condorman (1981)
- ❑   Confessions of a Teenage Drama Queen (2004)
- ❑   Cool Runnings (1993)

- ❏ The Country Bears (2002)
- ❏ The Crimson Wing: Mystery of the Flamingos (2008)*

D

- ❏ D2: The Mighty Ducks (1994)
- ❏ D3: The Mighty Ducks (1996)
- ❏ Dangal (2016)
- ❏ Darby O'Gill and the Little People (1959)
- ❏ Davy Crockett and the River Pirates (1956)
- ❏ Davy Crockett: King of the Wild Frontier (1955)
- ❏ The Devil and Max Devlin (1981)
- ❏ Dinosaur (2000)
- ❏ Disneyland: Secrets, Stories & Magic (2007)*
- ❏ Disneynature: Blue (2018)
- ❏ Disney's The Kid (2000)
- ❏ Doctor Strange (2016)
- ❏ Dr. Syn, Alias the Scarecrow (1963)
- ❏ Do Dooni Chaar (2010)*
- ❏ Doug's 1st Movie (1999)
- ❏ Dragonslayer (1981)
- ❏ DuckTales the Movie: Treasure of the Lost Lamp (1990)
- ❏ The Duke (1999)*
- ❏ Dumbo (1941)

E

- ❏ Earth (2007)
- ❏ Eight Below (2006)
- ❏ Emil and the Detectives (1964)
- ❏ The Emperor's New Groove (2000)
- ❏ Enchanted (2007)
- ❏ Endurance (1999)
- ❏ Escape to Witch Mountain (1975)
- ❏ An Extremely Goofy Movie (2000)*

F

- ❏ Fantasia (1940)
- ❏ Fantasia/2000 (1999)
- ❏ A Far Off Place (1993)
- ❏ The Fighting Prince of Donegal (1966)
- ❏ Finding Dory (2016)
- ❏ Finding Nemo (2003)
- ❏ The Finest Hours (2016)

- ❑ First Kid (1996)
- ❑ Flight of the Navigator (1986)
- ❑ Flubber (1997)
- ❑ Follow Me, Boys! (1966)
- ❑ The Fox and the Hound (1981)
- ❑ The Fox and the Hound 2 (2006)*
- ❑ Frank and Ollie (1995)
- ❑ Frankenweenie (2012)
- ❑ Freaky Friday (1976)
- ❑ Freaky Friday (2003)
- ❑ Frozen (2013)
- ❑ Fun and Fancy Free (1947)

G

- ❑ The Game Plan (2007)
- ❑ Gargoyles the Movie: The Heroes Awaken (1995)*
- ❑ George of the Jungle (1997)
- ❑ George of the Jungle 2 (2003)*
- ❑ G-Force (2009)
- ❑ Ghost of the Mountains (2017)*
- ❑ Ghosts of the Abyss (2003)
- ❑ Glory Road (2006)
- ❑ The Gnome-Mobile (1967)
- ❑ The Good Dinosaur (2015)
- ❑ A Goofy Movie (1995)
- ❑ The Greatest Game Ever Played (2005)
- ❑ The Great Locomotive Chase (1956)
- ❑ The Great Mouse Detective (1986)
- ❑ Greyfriars Bobby (1961)
- ❑ Growing Up Wild (2016)*
- ❑ Guardians of the Galaxy (2014)
- ❑ Guardians of the Galaxy Vol.2 (2017)
- ❑ Gus (1976)

H

- ❑ Hannah Montana & Miley Cyrus: Best of Both Worlds Concert (2008)
- ❑ Hannah Montana: The Movie (2009)
- ❑ The Happiest Millionaire (1967)
- ❑ The Haunted Mansion (2003)
- ❑ Heavyweights (1995)
- ❑ Herbie Fully Loaded (2005)
- ❑ Herbie Goes Bananas (1980)

- ❑ Herbie Goes to Monte Carlo (1977)
- ❑ Herbie Rides Again (1974)
- ❑ Hercules (1997)
- ❑ Hercules: Zero to Hero (1999)*
- ❑ Hexe Lilli: Der Drache und das Magische Buch (2009)
- ❑ Hexe Lilli: Die Reise nach Mandolan (2011)
- ❑ High School Musical 3: Senior Year (2008)
- ❑ High School Musical China (2010)*
- ❑ High School Musical: El Desafío (2008) *Argentina*
- ❑ High School Musical: El Desafío (2008) *Mexico*
- ❑ High School Musical: O Desafio (2010)
- ❑ Hocus Pocus (1993)
- ❑ Holes (2003)
- ❑ Home on the Range (2004)
- ❑ Homeward Bound: The Incredible Journey (1993)
- ❑ Homeward Bound II: Lost in San Francisco (1996)
- ❑ Honey, I Blew Up the Kid (1992)
- ❑ Honey, I Shrunk the Kids (1989)
- ❑ Honey, We Shrunk Ourselves (1997)*
- ❑ The Horse in the Gray Flannel Suit (1968)
- ❑ Hot Lead and Cold Feet (1978)
- ❑ The Hunchback of Notre Dame (1996)
- ❑ The Hunchback of Notre Dame II (2002)*

I

- ❑ I'll Be Home For Christmas (1998)
- ❑ The Incredible Journey (1963)
- ❑ The Incredibles (2004)
- ❑ Incredibles 2 (2018)
- ❑ In Search of the Castaways (1962)
- ❑ Inside Out (2015)
- ❑ Inspector Gadget (1999)
- ❑ Inspector Gadget 2 (2003)*
- ❑ Into the Woods (2014)
- ❑ Invincible (2006)
- ❑ Iron Man 3 (2013)
- ❑ Iron Will (1994)
- ❑ The Island at the Top of the World (1974)

J

- ❑ Jagga Jasoos (2017)
- ❑ James and the Giant Peach (1996)

- ❑ John Carter (2012)
- ❑ Johnny Tremain (1957)
- ❑ Jonas Brothers: The 3D Concert Experience (2009)
- ❑ The Journey of Natty Gann (1985)
- ❑ The Jungle Book (1967)
- ❑ The Jungle Book (1994)
- ❑ The Jungle Book (2016)
- ❑ The Jungle Book 2 (2003)
- ❑ The Jungle Book: Mowgli's Story (1998)*
- ❑ Jungle 2 Jungle (1997)
- ❑ Jungle Cat (1959)

K

- ❑ Khoobsurat (2014)
- ❑ A Kid in King Arthur's Court (1995)
- ❑ Kidnapped (1960)
- ❑ King of the Grizzlies (1970)
- ❑ Kniga Masterov (2009)
- ❑ Kronk's New Groove (2005)*

L

- ❑ Lady and the Tramp (1955)
- ❑ Lady and the Tramp II: Scamp's Adventure (2001)*
- ❑ The Last Flight of Noah's Ark (1980)
- ❑ The Legend of Lobo (1962)
- ❑ Leroy & Stitch (2006)*
- ❑ Lt. Robin Crusoe, U.S.N. (1966)
- ❑ The Light in the Forest (1958)
- ❑ Lilo & Stitch (2002)
- ❑ Lilo & Stitch 2: Stitch Has a Glitch (2005)*
- ❑ The Lion King (1994)
- ❑ The Lion King 1½ (2004)*
- ❑ The Lion King II: Simba's Pride (1998)*
- ❑ The Little Mermaid (1989)
- ❑ The Little Mermaid: Ariel's Beginning (2008)*
- ❑ The Little Mermaid II: Return to the Sea (2000)*
- ❑ The Littlest Horse Thieves (1976)
- ❑ The Littlest Outlaw (1955)
- ❑ The Living Desert (1953)
- ❑ The Lizzie McGuire Movie (2003)
- ❑ The Lone Ranger (2013)
- ❑ The Love Bug (1968)

M

- ❑ Madeline: Lost in Paris (1999)*
- ❑ Make Mine Music (1946)
- ❑ Maleficent (2014)
- ❑ The Man Behind the Mouse: The Ub Iwerks Story (1999)
- ❑ Man of the House (1995)
- ❑ The Many Adventures of Winnie the Pooh (1977)
- ❑ Mars Needs Moms (2011)
- ❑ Mary Poppins (1964)
- ❑ Max Keeble's Big Move (2001)
- ❑ McFarland, USA (2015)
- ❑ Meet the Deedles (1998)
- ❑ Meet the Robinsons (2007)
- ❑ Melody Time (1948)
- ❑ Mickey, Donald, Goofy: The Three Musketeers (2004)*
- ❑ Mickey's House of Villains (2002)*
- ❑ Mickey's Magical Christmas: Snowed in at the House of Mouse (2001)*
- ❑ Mickey's Once Upon a Christmas (1999)*
- ❑ Mickey's Twice Upon a Christmas (2004)*
- ❑ Midnight Madness (1980)
- ❑ The Mighty Ducks (1992)
- ❑ Mighty Ducks the Movie: The First Face-Off (1997)*
- ❑ Mighty Joe Young (1998)
- ❑ Million Dollar Arm (2014)
- ❑ The Million Dollar Duck (1971)
- ❑ Miracle (2004)
- ❑ Miracle of the White Stallions (1963)
- ❑ The Misadventures of Merlin Jones (1964)
- ❑ Mr. Magoo (1997)
- ❑ Mr. Toad's Wild Ride (1996)
- ❑ Moana (2016)
- ❑ Mohenjo Daro (2016)
- ❑ The Monkey's Uncle (1965)
- ❑ Monsters, Inc. (2001)
- ❑ Monsters University (2013)
- ❑ Moon Pilot (1962)
- ❑ The Moon-Spinners (1964)
- ❑ Monkey Kingdom (2015)
- ❑ Morning Light (2008)
- ❑ Mulan (1998)
- ❑ Mulan II (2004)*
- ❑ The Muppet Christmas Carol (1992)

- ❑ The Muppets (2011)
- ❑ Muppets Most Wanted (2014)
- ❑ Muppet Treasure Island (1996)
- ❑ Music Land (1955)
- ❑ My Favorite Martian (1999)

N

- ❑ Napoleon and Samantha (1972)
- ❑ National Treasure (2004)
- ❑ National Treasure: Book of Secrets (2007)
- ❑ Never a Dull Moment (1968)
- ❑ Never Cry Wolf (1983)
- ❑ Newsies (1992)
- ❑ Night Crossing (1982)
- ❑ The Nightmare Before Christmas (1993)
- ❑ Nikki, Wild Dog of the North (1961)
- ❑ No Deposit, No Return (1976)
- ❑ The North Avenue Irregulars (1979)
- ❑ Now You See Him, Now You Don't (1972)

O

- ❑ Oceans (2009)
- ❑ The Odd Life of Timothy Green (2012)
- ❑ Old Dogs (2009)
- ❑ Old Yeller (1957)
- ❑ Oliver & Company (1988)
- ❑ Once Upon a Warrior (2011)
- ❑ The One and Only, Genuine, Original Family Band (1968)
- ❑ One Hundred and One Dalmatians (1961)
- ❑ 101 Dalmatians (1996)
- ❑ 101 Dalmatians II: Patch's London Adventure (2003)*
- ❑ 102 Dalmatians (2000)
- ❑ One Little Indian (1973)
- ❑ One Magic Christmas (1985)
- ❑ One of Our Dinosaurs is Missing (1975)
- ❑ Operation Dumbo Drop (1995)
- ❑ The Other Side of Heaven (2001)*
- ❑ Oz the Great and Powerful (2013)

P

- ❑ The Pacifier (2005)
- ❑ The Parent Trap (1961)

- ❑ The Parent Trap (1998)
- ❑ Perfect Game (2000)*
- ❑ Perri (1957)
- ❑ Peter Pan (1953)
- ❑ Pete's Dragon (1977)
- ❑ Pete's Dragon (2016)
- ❑ Piglet's Big Movie (2003)
- ❑ Pinocchio (1940)
- ❑ The Pirate Fairy (2014)
- ❑ Pirates of the Caribbean: At World's End (2007)
- ❑ Pirates of the Caribbean: Dead Man's Chest (2006)
- ❑ Pirates of the Caribbean: Dead Men Tell No Tales (2017)
- ❑ Pirates of the Caribbean: On Stranger Tides (2011)
- ❑ Pirates of the Caribbean: The Curse of the Black Pearl (2003)
- ❑ The Pixar Story (2007)
- ❑ Planes (2013)
- ❑ Planes: Fire & Rescue (2014)
- ❑ Pocahontas (1995)
- ❑ Pocahontas II: Journey to a New World (1998)*
- ❑ Pollyanna (1960)
- ❑ Pooh's Grand Adventure: The Search for Christopher Robin (1997)*
- ❑ Pooh's Heffalump Halloween Movie (2005)*
- ❑ Pooh's Heffalump Movie (2005)
- ❑ Popeye (1980)
- ❑ Prince of Persia: The Sands of Time (2010)
- ❑ The Princess and the Frog (2009)
- ❑ The Princess Diaries (2001)
- ❑ The Princess Diaries 2: Royal Engagement (2004)
- ❑ Prom (2011)

Q

- ❑ Queen of Katwe (2016)

R

- ❑ Race to Witch Mountain (2009)
- ❑ Rascal (1969)
- ❑ Ratatouille (2007)
- ❑ Recess: All Growed Down (2003)*
- ❑ Recess Christmas: Miracle on Third Street (2001)*
- ❑ Recess: School's Out (2001)
- ❑ Recess: Taking the Fifth (2003)*
- ❑ The Reluctant Dragon (1941)

- ❑ Remember the Titans (2000)
- ❑ The Rescuers (1977)
- ❑ The Rescuers Down Under (1990)
- ❑ Return from Witch Mountain (1978)
- ❑ The Return of Jafar (1994)*
- ❑ Return to Never Land (2002)
- ❑ Return to Oz (1985)
- ❑ Return to Snowy River (1988)
- ❑ Ride a Wild Pony (1975)
- ❑ Roadside Romeo (2008)
- ❑ Robin Hood (1973)
- ❑ Rob Roy: The Highland Rogue (1953)
- ❑ The Rocketeer (1991)
- ❑ RocketMan (1997)
- ❑ Rogue One: A Star Wars Story (2016)
- ❑ The Rookie (2002)
- ❑ Roving Mars (2006)
- ❑ Run, Cougar, Run (1972)

S

- ❑ Sacred Planet (2004)
- ❑ Saludos Amigos (1942)
- ❑ Santa Buddies (2009)*
- ❑ The Santa Clause (1994)
- ❑ The Santa Clause 2 (2002)
- ❑ The Santa Clause 3: The Escape Clause (2006)
- ❑ Santa Paws 2: The Santa Pups (2012)*
- ❑ Savage Sam (1963)
- ❑ Saving Mr. Banks (2013)
- ❑ Scandalous John (1971)
- ❑ The Search for Santa Paws (2010)*
- ❑ Secretariat (2010)
- ❑ Secrets of Life (1956)
- ❑ The Secret of the Magic Gourd (2007)*
- ❑ Secret of the Wings (2012)
- ❑ The Shaggy D.A. (1976)
- ❑ The Shaggy Dog (1959)
- ❑ The Shaggy Dog (2006)
- ❑ Sharpay's Fabulous Adventure (2011)*
- ❑ Shipwrecked (1990)
- ❑ The Sign of Zorro (1958)
- ❑ Sky High (2005)
- ❑ Sleeping Beauty (1959)

- ❏ Smith! (1969)
- ❏ Snowball Express (1972)
- ❏ Snow Buddies (2008)*
- ❏ Snow Dogs (2002)
- ❏ Snow White and the Seven Dwarfs (1937)
- ❏ So Dear to My Heart (1949)
- ❏ Solo: A Star Wars Story (2018)
- ❏ Something Wicked This Way Comes (1983)
- ❏ Son of Flubber (1963)
- ❏ Song of the South (1946)
- ❏ The Sorcerer's Apprentice (2010)
- ❏ Space Buddies (2009)*
- ❏ Spooky Buddies (2011)*
- ❏ Squanto: A Warrior's Tale (1994)
- ❏ Star Wars: The Force Awakens (2015)
- ❏ Star Wars: The Last Jedi (2017)
- ❏ Stitch! The Movie (2003)*
- ❏ The Story of Robin Hood and His Merrie Men (1952)
- ❏ The Straight Story (1999)
- ❏ The Strongest Man in the World (1975)
- ❏ Summer Magic (1963)
- ❏ Summer of the Monkeys (1998)*
- ❏ Super Buddies (2013)*
- ❏ Superdad (1973)
- ❏ Swiss Family Robinson (1960)
- ❏ The Sword and the Rose (1953)
- ❏ The Sword in the Stone (1963)

T

- ❏ Tall Tale (1995)
- ❏ Tangled (2010)
- ❏ Tarzan (1999)
- ❏ Tarzan & Jane (2002)*
- ❏ Tarzan II (2005)*
- ❏ Ten Who Dared (1960)
- ❏ Tex (1982)
- ❏ That Darn Cat! (1965)
- ❏ That Darn Cat (1997)
- ❏ Third Man on the Mountain (1959)
- ❏ Thor: Ragnarok (2017)
- ❏ Thor: The Dark World (2013)
- ❏ Those Calloways (1965)
- ❏ The Three Caballeros (1944)

- ❏ The Three Lives of Thomasina (1963)
- ❏ The Three Musketeers (1993)
- ❏ A Tiger Walks (1964)
- ❏ The Tigger Movie (2000)
- ❏ Tinker Bell (2008)
- ❏ Tinker Bell and the Great Fairy Rescue (2010)
- ❏ Tinker Bell and the Legend of the NeverBeast (2014)
- ❏ Tinker Bell and the Lost Treasure (2009)
- ❏ Toby Tyler, or Ten Weeks with a Circus (1960)
- ❏ Tom and Huck (1995)
- ❏ Tomorrowland (2015)
- ❏ Tonka (1958)
- ❏ Toy Story (1995)
- ❏ Toy Story 2 (1999)
- ❏ Toy Story 3 (2010)
- ❏ Trail of the Panda (2009)*
- ❏ Treasure Buddies (2012)*
- ❏ Treasure Island (1950)
- ❏ Treasure of Matecumbe (1976)
- ❏ Treasure Planet (2002)
- ❏ Trenchcoat (1983)
- ❏ Tron (1982)
- ❏ Tron: Legacy (2010)
- ❏ Tuck Everlasting (2002)
- ❏ 20,000 Leagues Under the Sea (1954)

U

- ❏ The Ugly Dachshund (1966)
- ❏ Underdog (2007)
- ❏ Unidentified Flying Oddball (1979)
- ❏ Up (2009)

V

- ❏ Valiant (2005)
- ❏ The Vanishing Prairie (1954)
- ❏ Victory Through Air Power (1943)

W

- ❏ Waking Sleeping Beauty (2009)
- ❏ WALL·E (2008)
- ❏ Walt & El Grupo (2008)
- ❏ The Watcher in the Woods (1980)

- ❑ Westward Ho, the Wagons! (1956)
- ❑ Where the Red Fern Grows (2003)
- ❑ Where the Toys Come From (1984)*
- ❑ Whispers: An Elephant's Tale (2000)
- ❑ White Fang (1991)
- ❑ White Fang 2: Myth of the White Wolf (1994)
- ❑ White Wilderness (1958)
- ❑ Who Framed Roger Rabbit (1988)
- ❑ The Wild (2006)
- ❑ The Wild Country (1970)
- ❑ Wild Hearts Can't Be Broken (1991)
- ❑ Wings of Life (2011)
- ❑ Winnie the Pooh (2011)
- ❑ Winnie the Pooh: A Very Merry Pooh Year (2002)*
- ❑ Winnie the Pooh: Seasons of Giving (1999)*
- ❑ Winnie the Pooh: Springtime with Roo (2004)*
- ❑ The World's Greatest Athlete (1973)
- ❑ Wreck-It Ralph (2012)
- ❑ A Wrinkle in Time (2018)

X

- ❑ X Games 3D: The Movie (2009)

Y

- ❑ The Young Black Stallion (2003)

Z

- ❑ Zokkomon (2011)
- ❑ Zootopia (2016)
- ❑ Zorro the Avenger (1959)

Further Reading

In researching this book I consulted and cross-checked many different websites and books to try and source the most accurate information. Below is a list of useful websites to help you find out more about some of the media mentioned in this book:

- **Blu-ray** [blu-ray.com]. Information relating to DVD and Blu-ray releases in the US and beyond. With reviews, cover artwork and region details.
- **Grand Comics Database** [comics.org]. Stories, cover images, biographical information and more.
- **D23: The Official Disney Fan Club** [d23.com]. The website of D23 includes an online, searchable version of Dave Smith's essential Disney A-Z: The Official Encyclopedia.
- **Disney Wiki** [disney.wikia.com]. A wiki dedicated to many, many aspects of the world of Disney, similar to Wikipedia.
- **DVDizzy.** [dvdizzy.com]. An excellent DVD/Blu-ray review site, with dedicated Disney listings, featuring detailed reviews of movie releases and their content.
- **Giant Bomb** [giantbomb.com]. A curiously named database of computer games.
- **Internet Movie Database** [imdb.com]. For a whole host of information about individual movies. More accurate than Wikipedia, although not infallible.
- **JustWatch** [justwatch.com]. Find out where you can legally stream movies and TV shows in the US and beyond.
- **Laserdisc Database** [lddb.com]. If you like an old format release, check out this database!
- **Soundtrack Collector** [soundtrackcollector.com]. Track listings and alternative versions of soundtracks on CD, LP and more.
- **The Ultimate Disney Books Network** [didierghez.com]. Updated regularly by Disney author Didier Ghez, this is the place

to find out about Disney books already published and those yet to come, including those from Theme Park Press.

- **VHS Collector** [vhscollector.com]. A helpful though incomplete archive of VHS video releases.

In addition to the books mentioned throughout Disney Connections & Collections, the following volumes are invaluable sources of information about Disney movies (and comics):

- Disney A-Z: The Official Encyclopedia (5th edition, 2016). Dave Smith
- Disney Comics: The Whole Story (2016). Alberto Becattini. An essential guide to the whole world of Disney comics.
- The Disney Films (4th edition, 2000). Leonard Maltin. Covers in-depth information on every movie released during Walt Disney's lifetime, with a more generalised overview of those released after 1967.
- The Disney Studio Story (1988). Richard Hollis and Brian Sibley. Half of this history of the Disney studio is dedicated to a comprehensive filmography.

Acknowledgments

This book grew out of my Ph.D research, so I would like to thank my supervisors, Simon Popple and Dr Ian Macdonald who helped me through that process.

During my Ph.D research I got in touch with Theme Park Press' Bob McLain, who was generous enough to agree to be interviewed, and then later enthusiastically backed my proposal for this volume. Thank you for fulfilling my dream of becoming a Disney author!

With me throughout the process and beyond I've been blessed to have my husband, Andrew Oakes, who has been my cheerleader, proofreader, and so much more.

About the Author

Dr James R. Mason has enjoyed watching and collecting Disney movies since his parents bought him Disney Classics on VHS as a child. His personal interest eventually led to an academic interest. While studying for a Masters degree in Film Studies at the University of Bradford he kept returning to Disney for his papers and presentations, eventually writing a dissertation about the overlooked package features of the 1940s. From this came the inspiration for further study at the University of Leeds and the authoring of a Ph.D about Disney movies and their adult audiences.

James' Ph.D research gathered data on 390 Disney movies released to cinemas in the US between 1937 and 2015. He used this data to define a Disney film genre. At the same time he sought the opinions of adult audiences through an online questionnaire and focus groups that reached over 3,500 people. Then he compared audience perceptions of Disney movies with the movies themselves, revealing the biases that exist around animation and their implications for adult audiences and their appreciation of Disney movies.

Having earned his Ph.D in late 2017 through an examination that included animation scholar Professor Paul Wells, James is currently in the early stages of turning his Ph.D thesis into a book. Aside from writing, he also works as a proofreader and copy editor. He continues to collect Disney media and longs to return to the Disney parks one day someday soon.

www.jamesdoes.co.uk

About Theme Park Press

Theme Park Press publishes books primarily about the Disney company, its history, culture, films, animation, and theme parks, as well as theme parks in general.

Our authors include noted historians, animators, Imagineers, and experts in the theme park industry.

We also publish many books by first-time authors, with topics ranging from fiction to theme park guides.

And we're always looking for new talent. If you'd like to write for us, or if you're interested in the many other titles in our catalog, please visit:

www.ThemeParkPress.com

• •

Theme Park Press Newsletter

Subscribe to our free email newsletter and enjoy:

- ◆ Free book downloads and giveaways
- ◆ Access to excerpts from our many books
- ◆ Announcements of forthcoming releases
- ◆ Exclusive additional content and chapters
- ◆ And more good stuff available nowhere else

To subscribe, visit www.ThemeParkPress.com, or send email to newsletter@themeparkpress.com.

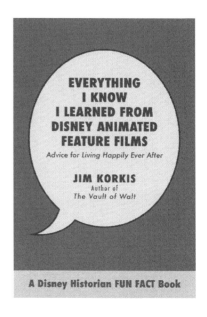

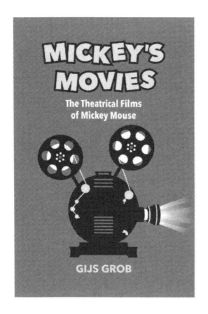

Read more about these books
and our many other titles at:

www.ThemeParkPress.com

Printed in Great Britain
by Amazon